SECOND PERSON SINGULAR

Victorian Literature and Culture Series

JEROME J. MCGANN AND
HERBERT F. TUCKER,
EDITORS

Second Person Singular

LATE VICTORIAN WOMEN POETS
AND THE BONDS OF VERSE

Emily Harrington

University of Virginia Press
Charlottesville and London

University of Virginia Press
© 2014 by the Rector and Visitors of the University of Virginia
All rights reserved
Printed in the United States of America on acid-free paper

First published 2014

9 8 7 6 5 4 3 2 1

LIBRARY OF CONGRESS CATALOGING-IN-PUBLICATION DATA
Harrington, Emily, 1975–
  Second Person Singular : late Victorian women poets and the bonds of verse /
Emily Harrington.
    pages   cm.—(Victorian Literature and Culture Series)
    Includes bibliographical references and index.
    ISBN 978-0-8139-3612-3 (cloth : acid-free paper)—ISBN 978-0-8139-3613-0 (e-book)
    1. English poetry—19th century—History and criticism. 2. English poetry—Women
authors—History and criticism. 3. Lyric poetry—History and criticism—Theory, etc.
I. Title.
    PR595.W6H37 2014
    821'.8099287—dc23

                                                              2013044115

For my parents,
John and Karen Harrington

Contents

Acknowledgments

A book about poetic intimacy must first and foremost acknowledge the dialogues, exchanges, and relationships that went into its writing. This book began at the University of Michigan, where wonderful teachers, colleagues, and friends made it ideal ground for cultivating the study of nineteenth-century poetry. Martha Vicinus, Yopie Prins, and Adela Pinch fostered my research in its earliest stages. I am deeply grateful for their continued support over the years. Ross Chambers, Marjorie Levinson, and Rei Terada also taught me a great deal about how to read poetry. I am indebted to the keen insights of a wonderful group of fellow scholars of nineteenth-century poetry at Michigan in those years: Julia Carlson, Jacqueline George, Mary-Catherine Harrison, Charles LaPorte, Meredith Martin, and Jessica Roberts. Mary-Catherine Harrison's critical eye and sage advice have been invaluable to the writing process in the ensuing years. Colleagues from Penn State have generously read portions of this work: Eric Hayot, Marcy North, and Lisa Sternlieb. I thank them for their detailed comments and their encouragement. Lisa Sternlieb also provided material and moral support at crucial times. I am also grateful to Claire Colebrook and Susan Squier for their mentorship. During their brief time at Penn State, Jeannie Britton and Danielle Coriale were the best of writing partners. Special thanks to the Nineteenth-Century Reading Group at Penn State for a lively conversation about an early version of chapter 5. My research assistant, Timothy Bober, provided essential help with checking sources and preparing the final manuscript.

Several grants have supported my research. A grant from the Rackham Graduate School at the University of Michigan enabled archival research for chapter 3 at the Bibliothèque Nationale de France. A course release was made possible by an Individual Faculty Grant from the Institute for the Arts and Humanities at Penn State. The English Department at Penn State gave me a semester of research leave, which allowed me to complete the manuscript. I am also extremely grateful for funding from the National Endowment for the Humanities to attend a summer seminar at the William Andrews Clark Memorial Library at UCLA, where I discovered the work of Dollie Radford. Many thanks to my fellow "Clarkies" for our invigorating discussions of all things fin de siècle, especially Kasey Bass Baker, Kristin Mahoney, Diana Maltz, Beth Newman, and Julie Wise. I am grateful to Joseph Bristow not only for his leadership of that seminar but also for his incisive comments on this work at both early and late stages.

I am indebted to the staff at the University of Virginia Press for supporting this project. Warm thanks in particular to Cathie Brettschneider and Ellen Satrom for shepherding the book through the editorial process and to Colleen Romick Clark for her careful copyediting. The insightful comments of the series editors, Jerome McGann and Herbert Tucker, as well as of an anonymous reader, helped me to improve the book considerably.

This work has profited from responses and conversations at a number of conferences where I presented nascent drafts: the 2012 Modern Language Association, the 2010 and 2004–2006 conferences of the North American Victorian Studies Association, the Women Writers of the Fin de Siècle conference at the Institute of English Studies in 2010, the Victorians Institute conference in 2006, the British Women Writers Association conference in 2006, and "Victorian Soundings," the Dickens Project conference in 2003. Many thanks to the organizers of these conferences and to my fellow panelists and audience members for their astute comments.

Part of chapter 2 appeared as "'Appraise Love and Divide': Measuring Love in Augusta Webster's *Mother and Daughter*" in *Victorian Poetry* 50, no. 3 (2012): 259–78. It is reprinted here in revised and expanded form with permission from West Virginia University Press. Part of chapter 3 previously appeared as "The Strain of Sympathy: A. Mary F. Robinson, The New Arcadia, and Vernon Lee" in *Nineteenth-Century Literature* 61, no. 1 (June 2006): 66–98, © 2006 by the Regents of the University of California. Thanks to the University of California Press for permission to reprint it in a longer form here. Thanks also to the William Andrews Clark Memorial Library, University of California, Los Angeles, for permission to publish from the Dollie Radford Papers.

Words cannot begin to account for my debt to my parents, John and Karen Harrington, whose love and patience know no bounds. My father's love of words and my mother's love of music are united here in the study of poetry; this book is dedicated to them. Thanks to my brother, David, for his good humor and for his inspiring tenacity. I have the most supportive in-laws a person can hope for in Malay and Dola Ghosh, ever mindful of the importance of "kaj." Special gratitude goes to my mother and mother-in-law, who have traveled great distances to care for my children while I worked. I know all too well the feeling that Dollie Radford expresses, "But I can sing, these evening times, / Only the children's songs and rhymes." I am grateful to the unparalleled teachers and staff at the Bennett Family Center, whose loving care of my children gave me the time and peace of mind to write about all kinds of late Victorian women's "songs." Debashis Ghosh has been with me since this project began and has given encouragement and support beyond measure. And finally, I am grateful for Mira and Leena, who teach me about intimacy every day.

SECOND PERSON SINGULAR

Introduction

With the 1898 publication of her essay "Second Person Singular," Alice Meynell put "thou" instead of "I" at the center of poetic diction. Meynell's essay pays homage to this antiquated pronoun, comparing the "literary Genius" to a gardener that keeps "for us a plot of language apart for the phrase of piety and poetry." Familiar from biblical diction and poetic tradition, "thou" calls only to a specific, individual "you," and in doing so establishes a bond between a singular voice and its distinct addressee. For Meynell, then, this pronoun marks poetry as an explicitly relational genre, one that enacts a dynamic between "I" and "thou." The intimacy inherent in the use of the second person singular emerges in everyday language; Meynell notes that in French the ordinary use of the second person singular has "two keen significances — the first use in love and the disuse in the reproof of children." In French, an initial use of this pronoun contains a frisson of intimacy, a sign of love. Withdrawing this pronoun suggests a withdrawal of love: a parent's address of a child with the formal "vous" instead of the familiar, singular "tu" contains a formidable, unalterable reproach, because this pronoun "touches the personality, and alters the relations of life."[1] This severe linguistic punishment, Meynell suggests, might damage the attachment between parent and child. Even the term "second person singular" indicates the most basic elements of a relationship: it points to the simultaneous existence of an individual and of more than one. "Second person" tells us that there are necessarily two or more people, "singular" points to the individuality of each. Rapprochement, yes; but also distance.

The second part of my title also gestures toward the convergence of poetic form and intimacy. It alludes to "the bonds of verse," a phrase that appears most prominently in Coventry Patmore's mid-century treatise on meter, "An Essay on English Metrical Law." A close friend and admirer of Alice Meynell, Patmore asserts that in poetry "the language should always seem to *feel,* though not to *suffer from,* the bonds of verse."[2] He uses the word "bonds" here to characterize the metrical rules that constrain the poet and his language. Arguing that poetic language should not read like prose or ordinary speech, that the laws of verse should result in "beautiful" "deformities," Patmore articulates rules for a "fancy prosody" that constitutes one of the most important trends in meter in the last half of the century. Of all of the prosodic concepts introduced in Patmore's essay, Meynell was perhaps most drawn to the idea of the "bonds of verse." For Meynell, the structures of verse are akin to the structures of love; the space created by foot divisions and pauses enacts the distance she views as necessary for true intimacy. My title thus refers to two definitions of "bonds": one that signifies a restraint and another that connotes a connection. For all of the poets in this book, those restraints circumscribe poetic relationships. These poets' compressed lyrical styles exemplify the boundaries of relationships, both painful and liberating. For fin de siècle women poets, unifying bonds are often enabled by the restraints of poetic form.

Women poets in this period were particularly drawn to the restraints of short lyrical forms, such as songs and sonnets. Although they wrote in multiple forms long and short, from Mathilde Blind's epic *The Ascent of Man* to Dollie Radford's eight-line trimeters entitled simply "Song," women poets contributed to the fin de siècle's preference in poetry for the short "gem," a resurgence in lyric that Marion Thain identifies as the single unifying trait to fin de siècle poetry.[3] This book focuses primarily on these short poetic forms, which lend themselves to reflections on presence and absence, subject and object, the performance of gender, formal play, musicality, and a poetics of pause. Fin de siècle women poets experiment within these forms, using them to articulate new ways of thinking about intimacy with distance. While these poets conveyed ideas about relationships thematically, their theories about intimacy also emerged in their formal poetic practice, in the call and response of repetition, in prosodic back-and-forth, and in modes of address. They capitalize on a paradox of short lyrical forms like the sonnet: although frequently considered to be the genres of intimacy, chosen for declarations of love, these poems are also strikingly impersonal.[4] Too brief to provide readers the details to imaginatively construct a full and complex human being or her world, songs and sonnets are more about a thought or a feeling than an author or a character.[5] In other words, these short poems can be emotionally resonant without reference to a particular person or situation.

Fin de siècle women poets use these forms to represent modes of interaction that exhibit proximity without identification, where subjects are both separate and connected, where someone can be fully aware of another's feelings without needing to try to feel them herself. The distance implicit in Meynell's essay "Second Person Singular," with its articulation of the distinctness of the "thou," prevents a merger of souls, a feeling of being united "as one," but it allows the "I" and "thou" to comprehend and appreciate each other. This study investigates the numerous types of bonds that women in the late nineteenth century write about: between mother and child, between poet and predecessor, in collaborative partnerships, in friendships, in erotic relationships, even in connection with God. Meynell, Augusta Webster, and Dollie Radford all wrote about maternal love and used poetic and prosodic strategies to convey how separation is as much a part of that relationship as unity. Writing in response to her romantic friend Vernon Lee, A. Mary F. Robinson used discordant meters to try to bridge the gap with the impoverished people she wrote about. Mary E. Coleridge wrote about her friendships with other women. By understanding the range of relationships that women wrote about and the diversity of their poetic strategies for representing them, we can better understand the verse culture of the late nineteenth century.

In writing a poetics of impersonal intimacy, women poets at the end of the nineteenth century took many cues from Christina Rossetti, whose poetry seeks to unmake rather than constitute a "speaking" subject. Unraveling the notion of a self, especially in poems whose utterances come from beyond the grave, Rossetti's poetry epitomizes the impersonal. Rossetti's well-known "Song," central to the canon of Victorian women's poetry, both pulls in its addressee by imagining the signs of his sorrow and pushes him away by refusing those signs:

> When I am dead, my dearest,
>   Sing no sad songs for me;
> Plant thou no roses at my head,
>   Nor shady cypress tree:
> Be the green grass above me
>   With showers and dewdrops wet;
> And if thou wilt, remember,
>   And if thou wilt, forget.[6]

The poem's negations make the graveside tribute simultaneously absent and present, calling it to mind in its very disavowal. "Energized by the presence of opposite meanings," as Constance Hassett notes, this poem and others like it originate the dynamic of rapprochement and distance that I argue is at the heart of late Victorian women's verse.[7] Mathew Rowlinson reads "When I am dead, my dearest" as emblematic of trends in all of Victorian lyric, which, circulating almost entirely in print, reflects on an always already absent voice. The centrality of absence and silence in Victorian lyric, he suggests, illustrates "the gendered allegory that structures the field, the unmediated song of which the print-lyric is the mediated effect or trace [and] is characteristically figured as a woman's."[8] In other words, a mute woman is a figure for lyric itself; Victorians idealized the song that can no longer be heard, the idea of authentic spontaneous song, as feminine. This conceptual link between gender and genre provided an occasion for late Victorian women poets both to exploit and to question the generic conventions of songs and sonnets.

The generation of women poets after Rossetti often adopt and adapt what Hassett calls Rossetti's "patience of style," a phrase she uses to characterize Rossetti's "reticence" and "reserve," her "muteness, understatement, gently restrained rhythm."[9] In my reading, Rossetti's patient stance set the stage for the impersonal intimacy in the short lyrical poems of late nineteenth-century women. As I will show, the "I's" of Rossetti's poems often allow listening and receptivity to whatever or whoever in the poem is posited as "other." Her embrace of silence, distance, and a paradoxically submissive power served later poets as a model. *Second Person Singular* demonstrates that this reserved approach is not only a hallmark of Rossetti's own style but also a trend that other poets develop over the course of Rossetti's lifetime and beyond. Fin de siècle women poets lay claim to presumably feminine and negative qualities such as silence, passivity, and submissiveness to remind readers of the absent presences that are especially complicated in women's "song" in the nineteenth century. Rossetti's impersonal poetics and concomitant embrace of silence also gave poets who came after her license to find poetic power in often devalued concepts such as silence, pause, distance, and waiting. Recent approaches to women's poetry recognize that speech is not necessarily coterminous with activity and power, and that especially in an age of circulation via print, as Rowlinson proposes, silence is a shaping force.[10] By writing a poetic intimacy that relies on silence and distance, women poets at the fin de siècle claim stereotypes of femininity as a source of power in their work. Fin de siècle women poets privilege distance in order to represent the difficult negotiations between self and other and to emphasize the necessity of silence, patience, waiting, and acceptance as a means of accommodating the difference and even discordance of otherness.

With chapters focusing on Christina Rossetti, Augusta Webster, A. Mary F. Robinson, Alice Meynell, and Dollie Radford, and a conclusion that considers Mary E. Coleridge, *Second Person Singular* emphasizes not only short lyric forms but also poets that inherit Rossetti's emphasis on silence, restraint, and reserve. For all of these poets, reserve and distance are essential to their ideas about intimacy and to their poetic practice. Whether they write about erotic desire, as Rossetti, Meynell, and Radford do, or about social, cross-class sympathy, as Robinson and Radford do, or religious devotion, as Rossetti and Meynell do, all of these poets aim to create an I-thou interaction within their poems. In many cases, they aim not so much to describe a relationship that already exists, but to establish one within the poem. For example, in Meynell's sonnet "Renouncement," the speaker refuses to think of "thee," only to give "I" and "thou" full reign in dreams: "I run, I run, I am gathered to thy heart."[11] All of the poets treated here are preoccupied with the power of the poetic voice, or its silent representation on the page, to make interaction happen. Frequently, they figure their poems as singing. In Webster's sonnet sequence *Mother and Daughter,* the daughter tells the mother, "But something in thy tones brings music near; / As though thy song could search me and divine," suggesting that the song enables intimate knowledge of another.[12] Similarly, A. Mary F. Robinson declares, "and so I sing" in order to make rural poverty vivid to her readers and to create sympathy for the poor, suggesting that song conveys special knowledge.[13] Dollie Radford counters the expectations of poems like Webster's and Robinson's by expressing hesitation that the song will not establish intimacy: "I am wanting to send you a song, love."[14] In invoking song explicitly in their printed poems, these poets call attention to distance as the very condition of their work. I present this set of poets because they represent a wide range of relationships, they all investigate how a poem itself can embody a relational dynamic, and they all draw on strategies of distance and reserve.

Of course, not all women poets of the late Victorian period rely on distance to shape their concept of intimacy. In a book about intimacy and British women poets at the end of the nineteenth century, the absence of Michael Field (Katharine Bradley and Edith Cooper) may seem like a significant omission. Yet in many ways their lesbian coauthorship and their celebration of it make them a unique case, a case that does not fit the embrace of distance and silence characteristic of the poets in this study. Although there are instances in their poetry of a more detached approach to relationality, as in the poems on death in *Underneath the Bough* and in *Sight and Song,* their lyrics are dominated by abundant and famous instances of an idealized intimacy in which two subjects are closely identified with each other, mutually absorbed, or "as one." In their ambivalent tribute poem to Christina Rossetti, Michael Field understood her to be "fleeing from love" rather than redefining its terms. Whereas Michael Field critiques her reticence as a lack of engagement, other poets take it up as a mode of engagement and interaction. Michael Field is on the margins of the genre of "women poets," not wanting to be read as "women poets" and not considered as such until 1907, when Alfred H. Miles included them in the volume of women poets in his *Poets and Poems of the Century.*

Their expressed wish not to be read as women poets demonstrates that the genre was not determined only by the gender of the writer.

Second Person Singular aims to identify how women poets themselves were defining the genre they wrote in, in terms both of gender and of poetic form. But as the necessary omission of Michael Field from this study attests, as does the omission of other poets such as Rosamund Mariott Watson and Amy Levy, women's poetry at the fin de siècle was a wide and varied field. In many ways, these decades were a heyday for women's poetry. Oscar Wilde observed, "No country has ever had so many poetesses at once. . . . The work done by women in the sphere of poetry is really of a very high standard of excellence."[15] Richard Le Gallienne, poet, tastemaker, and literary gatekeeper of the '90s, considered the "woman poet" to be "practically an invention of the present century" and asserted "the onward movement of the world to be embodied in women."[16] Virtually ignored for nearly a century, women's poetry from the late nineteenth century has received scholarly attention in recent decades that has broadened our understanding of the culture of aestheticism and the fin de siècle.[17] Women participated in London's vigorous salon culture at the fin de siècle and they published with John Lane and Elkin Mathews at the Bodley Head, the central venue for aestheticist verse. Recent scholars of fin de siècle women's poetry have documented the deep engagement of this cohort with male writers, as well as with the literary and social world. Ana Parejo Vadillo asserts that these women were engaged in the lives and literary communities of their neighborhoods and in London. She argues that for them, poetry serves as a "mode of transportation between the 'I' and the urban social" and is thereby a vehicle of mobility and connection.[18] According to the special issue of *Victorian Literature and Culture* devoted to late nineteenth-century women's poetry, these social connections signal women poets' engagement with modernity, with its attendant economic, scientific, and political developments, and their investment in their own time as a moment of "renewal."[19]

Despite the demonstrable centrality of women to literary culture and the esteem in which women's poetry was held, this body of work was typically read specifically as "women's poetry." The routine segregation of women's poetry from men's, in anthologies such as in Elizabeth Sharp's *Women Poets of the Victorian Era* (1890) and in a separate volume of Alfred Miles's *The Poets and Poetry of the Century* (1907), suggests that fin de siècle readers placed women's verse in a separate category with different expectations.[20] The members of the Rhymers' Club (Arthur Symons, Ernest Dowson, Lionel Johnson, W. B. Yeats, to name a few), who until recently were the only well-known poets of the fin de siècle, anthologized themselves into two all-male volumes when they published the first and second *Book of the Rhymers' Club.* Not only were women's works grouped together, but the women themselves often gathered in single-sex salons. Dollie Radford's diary records an evening when she returns from an "at home" where she met many who had been at the Women Writers dinner. As she arrives, her poet husband, Ernest, departs for a meeting of the all-male Rhymers' Club.[21] Book reviews of women poets almost always took the poets' gender into account. This review of a reprint of Elizabeth Barrett Browning's poems, for instance, provides a glimpse into some prevalent assumptions about women poets: "The reason why no woman has ever, except in lyric, yet produced a work of art even approximately perfect is, that owing to the ethical basis of her nature her imagination is stifled before it can reach the selfish domain of pure art."[22] This review, on the cusp of the fin de siècle and its reputation for elevating the principal of art for art's sake, dissociates aesthetic value from ethical value, dismissing in the process the grounds on which much women's poetry was valued in the nineteenth century. Because nineteenth-century culture continued to differentiate between women's poetry and men's poetry, it remains important to consider women's poetry as its own generic category, even as that category began to shift at the end of the century. I claim that women poets at the end of the century presented their work as valuable on the very grounds on which this reviewer dismisses it; their work argues for the importance of the lyrical and the relational.

In the nineteenth century, women poets were often referred to as "poetesses," a term that, as Yopie Prins has argued, refers to a figure rather than to a person and is a placeholder for expectations about gender and genre.[23] In the 1820s and 1830s Felicia Hemans and L.E.L. exemplified the expectations that women write about what Isobel Armstrong calls "the affective moment and its relation to moral convention and religious and cultural constraint."[24] Hemans produced poems that, on the surface, promote domestic and national piety, while L.E.L.'s "Improvisatrice," for instance, contributed to the idea that women's poetry was the spontaneous performance of sincere feeling. Tracing the evolution of the poetess figure over the course of the nineteenth century, Susan Brown has argued that the publication of Elizabeth Barrett Browning's *Aurora Leigh* aimed to shift the view of the woman poet from the spontaneously expressive "poetess" to the professional writer. Brown also notes that by the 1870s, the "project of keeping poets and poetesses in separate literary spheres is breaking down."[25] Arguing in 1894 that "the masculine and feminine are ingredients alike of man and woman," Richard Le Gallienne contends that poetry should not be categorized into gendered types. He dispenses with the term "poetess," calling it "barbarous," the suffix a vestige of a more conservative mode of thought.[26] The end of the century saw dramatic changes in conventional views of women poets. By the turn of the century, generic constructions of the figure of the woman poet remained open to debate.

A generation ago, scholars at the forefront of recovering women's poetry seemed most of all concerned with defining women's subjectivity and with establishing that their political discourse moved beyond the apparent sentimentality of much of mid-Victorian women's poetry. Armstrong's concept of the Victorian "double poem" shows how women's poems with a "simple moral and emotional surface" in fact questioned the very assumptions they might initially seem to support. They complicated the "expressive theory" in which poetic language attempts to represent secret, hidden emotion, thought to be at the core of women's poetry.[27] Angela Leighton's *Victorian Women Poets: Writing Against the Heart* examines how these poets variously struggle with expectations that they represent a sincere sensibility that accords with stringent social and sexual moral standards. According to Dorothy Mermin, Victorian women poets sought to escape the conundrum wherein the woman poet struggles to be both the desiring, writing subject and the object of desire, both "the damsel and the knight."[28] Mermin reminds us that the "feminine" qualities of lyric function quite well for a male poet's projection of an alternate self, but the "privacy" of lyric made it difficult for women to write because the perceived passivity and silence of femininity and lyric were not productive, creative qualities. These scholars all consider how the woman poet can establish a poetic subjectivity that provides authorial agency.

Scholars whose work followed in the footsteps of these earlier critics sought to change the terms of the debate, demonstrating that far from being primarily concerned with a male-female erotic dynamic, women poets were engaged in literary, political, economic, and urban communities. Talia Schaffer, Kathy Psomiades, Marion Thain, and Ana Vadillo have demonstrated the place of women poets in cultures of aestheticism. Linda Peterson and Paula Feldman have considered how poets from Felicia Hemans to Alice Meynell entered the literary marketplace.[29] Cynthia Scheinberg and F. Elizabeth Gray, among others, have indicated how women poets were embedded in religion. All of this work places women's poetry at the center rather than at the margins of dominant cultures. Scholarship on women poets in the last two decades represents women poets, and their poetry, as deeply engaged in the public sphere. In light of this work, *Second Person Singular* returns to the question of the I-thou dynamic, no longer just a poet and a muse, or sister poets, but positions that can be reconceived in a variety of relationships.[30] Work of the scholars listed above has made apparent the many contexts in which women wrote: familial, religious, social, and political. By returning to the pronouns that constitute primary components of songs and sonnets, I and thou, *Second Person Singular* demonstrates that late Victorian women poets addressed relationality in these cultural milieus with astonishingly varied, creative, formal poetic strategies.

Because Rossetti was so central to the achievements of fin de siècle women poets, my book begins with a chapter on her work. Chapter 1 argues that Rossetti develops a poetics that relies on a dynamic of self-dissolution in order to establish intimacy, especially with God. Rossetti's poems struggle to balance a desire for equality with the necessity of a hierarchy. In order to solve this problem, Rossetti embraces submissiveness as a position that affords an openness to the other and abasement of self essential for mutual responsiveness. I explore poems in which Rossetti triangulates relationships between a lyric "I," a beloved, and God: "Twice" (1866) and "Monna Innominata" (1881). These poems show the inadequacy for Rossetti of a love tied to two selves, which her lyrics renounce in order to embrace an all-encompassing and completely mutual love shared with God, one that ultimately erases the triangulation. This destabilization of the self allows her to participate in a depersonalized, and thereby fully lyric, love. To understand Rossetti's concept of the lyric voice as unlinked from a self, I turn to some of Rossetti's most famous early poems of the 1860s that are voiced from beyond the grave. I read these in conjunction with an entry from her devotional prose diary, *Time Flies* (1884), in which Rossetti attempts to understand the voice by comparing the voice in heaven to the voice heard on a mechanical recording. Both voices can exist in some manner after the death of the person who originated the voice, but, as I show, the recorded voice functions more strongly as a metaphor for Rossetti's understanding of the lyric voice. Both are defined by repetition and mechanical or metrical functioning and a disembodied state. Rossetti's "beyond the grave" poems imagine intimacy not from a state of subjectivity, but from this impersonal, disembodied lyric voice. Only death brings about an intimate exchange with God, where the "I" preserves a sense of identity that is aligned precisely with giving herself to God, and the collective song she will sing in heaven.

Although the other poets I study do not embrace an impersonal intimacy on religious grounds, they incorporate these ideas into their own approaches to lyric to test the bounds of relational dynamics within the genre. Chapter 2 investigates how Augusta Webster's sonnet sequence *Mother and Daughter* (1894) uses poetic devices to reveal the inevitability of measuring maternal love. Particularly in a sonnet addressed to mothers of siblings, and implied throughout, Webster's sequence articulates the startling proposition that love is a limited resource that can be divided, meted out. I argue that Webster writes lyric intimacy in the very performance of such a measurement, in the counting of lines, syllables, and accents. Webster uses the typically erotic form of the sonnet sequence, transposing onto a parent-child relationship concerns about how much love is possible, how long love lasts, and how deep it is. Webster emphasizes that a mother's love cannot escape measurement because she must track the growth of her daughter, their increasing distance, and a gap between the experiences of mother and daughter that is both pedagogical and nostalgic. As the sonnets both wish for love's infinitude and doubt it, the meter reinforces this tension, rushing during tropes of stillness, halting with extra stress to slow the passage of time, and interrupting with caesuras; poetic forms themselves "appraise and divide" a mother's love as they express her anxiety. While meter counts the poetic voice of the poems, the poems also address the fleeting quality of the mother's own voice, noting how the human voice measures the passage of time as it ages.

Whereas chapter 1 considers erotic and divine relationships and chapter 2 addresses a familial relationship, chapter 3 examines the debate between the poet A. Mary F. Robinson and the art critic Vernon Lee, her intimate friend, about the potential for cross-class identification in poetry. Their friendship nurtured writing that emerged from a private dialogue about ethical aesthetics and appeared publicly as works dedicated to each other. Together, they envisioned aesthetic experience as responsive and interactive rather than solitary. Ever dubious of her era's efforts at aesthetic philanthropy, in her collection of poems about the rural poor, *The New Arcadia* (1884), Robinson asked whether and how poetry can sympathize with and generate sympathy for the poor. Vernon Lee, for her part, encouraged Robinson in her "Dialogue on Poetic Morality" (1880) to believe that aesthetic creation fulfilled, rather than detracted from, ethical obligation. Jointly, Lee and Robinson aimed to establish an alternative to the sort of Paterian aestheticism that was often accused of solipsism. I argue that Robinson offers another way for art to confront poverty, one in which those who want to help must try to understand the perspective of the other, however futile the attempt. Her poems attempt to fulfill an ethical responsibility and imaginatively identify with the poor by cultivating jarring discordant prosodic and lyric techniques to jolt readers out of their complacency. Robinson wrote *The New Arcadia* not only to expose the difficulty of rural poverty but also to question how poetry might engender that sympathy in a way that avoids the paternalistic, controlling attitudes that underwrote much aesthetic philanthropy. Together with Lee, she debated to what extent practical moral action and activism was a necessary product of feelings of cross-class intimate identification. Chapter 3 examines how a collaborative partnership produces poetry and questions what kind of relationship with readers and subjects a poem can establish.

Chapter 4 argues that Alice Meynell paradoxically requires silence and distance, qualities for which she is well known, to establish intimacy. Meynell's writing importantly distinguishes between detachment and distance. Whereas detachment severs bonds, distance makes room for them. Distance allows one subject to see another's difference clearly; it keeps one subject's fantasies of the other from overshadowing the reality of the other, even if that reality is never fully scrutable. Meynell's prosody even maintains boundaries in its insistence on the metrical foot to measure verse, as opposed to simpler accentual meter. While it seems intuitive that speech connects and silence separates, for Meynell, silence creates room in which two subjects establish separate identities. Only with that separation can they form a bond; otherwise, their link would be mere unification or absorption. At the same time, Meynell's emphasis on distance acknowledges that it is never possible to fully know the other and thereby cultivates respect for that unknowability. Here, I explore the different kinds of relationships, the types of self and other, that Meynell addresses in poetry and in prose: poet and reader, mother and child.

The final chapter of *Second Person Singular* argues that Dollie Radford uses many of the same poetic devices used by other poets in the study, whom she admired and imitated, to suggest, unlike them, that lyric poetry cannot establish intimacy. I investigate her turn to the concept of song and musical settings to create a sense of lyric intimacy, and when that proves not to solve the problem of lyric absence for her, Radford instead proposes the patience of waiting as the solution. Instead of conversation, or even soliloquy, Radford presents lyric as simply a space for waiting. Considering Radford's frequent title "song" alongside early musical settings of her poems, I show how even musical performance cannot establish a presence that is always lost or wished for in lyric poetry; indeed, as my previous chapters show, poets can simulate a dual poetic presence that makes a poem more akin to a conversation than to a soliloquy. She seeks musical settings to her poems deliberately to show that they do not create the sense of presence that poetry lacks. The tantalizing presence of singer and accompanist in collaboration does not replace the idealized, unheard music of lyric poems. I go on to show how Radford illuminates the importance of the "smallness" that also caused such anxiety. The position of the minor poet—with a small audience and a presumably limited impact—allowed her the freedom to be boldly unoriginal. While decrying the failures of the "song," she shows how songs that repeat tired tropes can be nonetheless satisfying. Ultimately her novel embrace of the unoriginal establishes her as an important voice of fin de siècle feminine lyric poetics. She shows fin de siècle lyric to be in a holding pattern, but then tells us that welcoming new developments requires the openness and attentiveness of the wait. In Radford's view, patience is as important to progress as action, much of which might, as lyric poetry does, turn in self-consuming circles. She makes no claims of finding or producing what is new or original. Ultimately, what she does defend is the small, the minor, the incomplete. As she elevates waiting to an important ethical and aesthetic status, she also looks not for the replacement of a lost original, but for something that will be truly new, if always still incomplete. To find that new, she suggests, one must have the capacity to reject old fantasies and to remain open and attentive. Waiting constitutes a full availability to the "other" that is not yet known and not yet present, an intimacy with the new of the future. Radford's poetics clarify how fin de siècle women poets helped to pave the way for the modern.

Fin de siècle women poets, working against biographical readings, cultivating an educated, aesthetically minded readership, ever-conscious of their place in literary tradition and culture, were especially invested in a mode of writing and reading songs and sonnets that would open up new ways of reading poetic relationships. Although Mermin argues that women poets remained trapped within a dynamic where they could not be both credible speakers and those who listen and wait, fin de siècle women poets began to escape that trap by presenting the position of listening and silence to be as essential as speaking. Each of the poets in the following chapters presents different kinds of poetic intimacies, but all of them are invested in the bonds of verse.

🐾 1

"I, for Thou Callest Such"

CHRISTINA ROSSETTI'S HEAVENLY INTIMACY

In the first sonnet of "The Thread of Life" (*A Pageant and Other Poems,* 1881), a series of three, Christina Rossetti institutes a poetic reversal whereby inanimate objects talk to the poet. This reverse apostrophe emphasizes the importance of listening for Rossetti, while also leading to a question that haunts her poetry:

> The irresponsive silence of the land,
>> The irresponsive sounding of the sea,
>> Speak both one message of one sense to me:—
> Aloof, aloof, we stand aloof, so stand
> Thou too aloof bound with the flawless band
>> Of inner solitude; we bind not thee;
>> But who from thy self-chain shall set thee free?
> What heart shall touch thy heart? What hand thy hand?—[1]

In the standard understanding of apostrophe, it does not matter that the inanimate or absent object cannot respond; simply imagining an interlocutor constitutes the speaking power of the poet.[2] Yet by reversing the apostrophe, embedding its capital "O" within the proliferating "o" and "oo" sounds in these lines, the opening sonnet of "The Thread of Life" posits the poet as someone who listens and responds rather than as someone who primarily speaks. The very unresponsiveness of the sea and land isolates them, discourages the poet from following their example, and causes her to seek the "touch" of another. By highlighting poetry's capacity to listen as well as to speak and to sing, Rossetti asserts its potential as a medium of intimacy. This chapter gives a new account of Christina Rossetti's poetics that considers how she confronts the problem of how to connect with others.

Many critics tend to think of Rossetti as socially isolated, and they read a fierce autonomy in her work that corresponds to this isolation. Indeed, interpersonal relationships, particularly heterosexual erotic ones, fail more often than not in her poems. Those who would approach her work biographically consider her refusal of two opportunities of marriage and measure the many instances of disappointed love in her poetry against these facts.[3] Others think of her autonomy in terms of her aesthetic practice. Reading as emblematic "Winter, My Secret," which hinges on a taunting refusal to disclose a secret that may not even exist, Jerome McGann insists on Rossetti's "independence" and "integrity," an uncompromising adherence to her individuality.[4] Antony Harrison, attempting to reconcile her aesthetic and devotional impulses, focuses on her "solipsistic withdrawal from active life in the world," while Tricia Lootens calls her a "radically autonomous instead of a relative creature."[5] Constance Hassett has done important work showing how Rossetti engages with her literary forebears, including Dante and Petrarch, Felicia Hemans and L.E.L., and her own brother.[6] Yet none of these models looks to Rossetti as a writer who uses poetry to imagine intimacy. I argue that Rossetti uses her poetry to conceptualize an ideal relational dynamics. Admittedly, human relationships often fail in her poetry, but in those failures and in her vision of a relationship with God, we see an intimacy that depends on mutual exchange and responsiveness.

Despite this emphasis on mutuality, Rossetti's idea of intimacy still hinges on hierarchies of dominance and submissiveness; trying to square these opposing principles forms the cornerstone of the problem of intimacy for her. Especially in relation to God, a position of submission is a position of honor, one that elevates. Submission is a stance of openness to the other, and without it, Rossetti's poems show, any relationship must implode. Rossetti's ideal of intimacy finds a balance of dominance and submissiveness.

This chapter begins with an exploration of where intimacy fails and where it succeeds in two poems that triangulate the relationship of a lover and a beloved with God: "Twice" and "Monna Innominata." These instances of triangulation show how Rossetti models intimacy with God on what should but does not work in heterosexual erotic relationships. Her ideal here is one of openness to such a degree that intimate partners can change places; they do not merge into a single "I" or unified entity, but rather move between distinct positions. These poems show how for Rossetti, intimate partners can never be equal, but they can alternate positions. For Rossetti, submissiveness is essential for intimacy, for it occasions listening and openness to the other and demonstrates devotion.

I go on to consider how Rossetti's ideals of intimacy fit within her concept of poetic voice that escapes the bonds of individual subjectivity. To do so, I look at how subjectivity evaporates in Rossetti's "death lyrics," poems articulated from beyond the grave, while at the same time an intense longing for love persists. In these poems, Rossetti uses repetition as a poetic technique to enact the love formally that can only be desired semantically. I go on to examine her meditation on voice and music in her devotional diary *Time Flies.* Rossetti considers how poetry can be both "written words" and "something not music, yet most musical." This meditation reveals poetry to be a kind of purgatory, its voices neither earthly nor divine. These are not the voices of subjectivities imaginary or real, but rather often multivocal, blurring the boundaries between the interior and exterior of consciousness. Her use of repetition best captures both the lack of the interior subjectivity we might think of as a "speaker" and the intimacy that results from this lack of determinacy. Rossetti's frequent use of repetition often functions as a system of call-and-response, on the model of an echo—the title of one of her most celebrated poems, one I discuss in detail below. Her poetics draws attention to the relationships between words, especially when those words are repeated. At the level of words, phrases, and forms, repetition allows Rossetti to reflect on questions of sameness and difference and to consider whether a repetition is an internal reverberation or recontextualization or whether in fact words respond to each other within single poems. In this way, poems that seem to come from a single voice—an idea that is problematic for Rossetti—can seem dialogic within themselves. For Rossetti, lyric intimacy is impersonal, not emerging from a dramatic subjectivity but from the dissolution of it. An unstable "I" allows the positions of subject and object to alternate. A poem's repetition creates responsiveness within the form that allows indeterminate entities, an interchangeable "I" and "thou," a supplicant and a God, to create a poetic mutuality.

"I Cannot Love You If I Love Not Him": A Triangulated Relationship with God

In *Goblin Market and Other Poems,* two well-known poems, "Cousin Kate" and "Maude Clare," present a triangulated relationship involving the spurned fallen woman and the woman who accepts this duplicitous man, both of whom, in contrast to the fallen woman, are honorable only on the surface of social convention. These poems question the presumed sanctity of marriage and, more important, form a part of Rossetti's supposed elevation of the independent woman who rises above this fray. Yet, for all of the lonely women in her oeuvre, Rossetti also establishes the single woman as a woman whose life is filled with love and expansive intimacy. She alters the concept of the triangle, so filled with bitterness in "Cousin Kate" and "Maude Clare," to query the place of God in an erotic relationship and to explore how intimacy with God functions in the earthly realm and opens imaginatively on

to Heaven. Here, I read "Twice" and the sonnet of sonnets "Monna Innomi-
nata" to argue that while Rossetti turns to erotic relationships as a model
for divine intimacy, ultimately the divine relationship supersedes the erotic,
offering a greater capacity for mutual understanding and sympathy.

In "Twice" (*Prince's Progress*, 1866), a spurned lover reestablishes and
imaginatively repeats her relationship with an earthly beloved with God;
hence the title: the relationship happens twice, but in the second version
Rossetti presents an ideal of how a lyric intimacy can take place. Contrary to
Eric Griffiths's assertion that "the poem does not tell us how to understand
the relation, if there is one (or more than one), between the human beloved
and the divine," Rossetti does give readers important ideas about how a re-
lationship with the divine functions.[7] She depicts an idealized interchange
with God as a combination of the self-empowerment that the first relation-
ship denied, but also a willing self-negation, epitomized by Rossetti's use of
address and personal pronouns. At the heart of Rossetti's vision of intimacy
is the inherent contradiction of empowerment coupled with negation. It is
precisely a logic of indeterminate subjectivity that makes negation an em-
powering position.

"Twice" recontextualizes the actions of a dismissive suitor so that the
submissive-dominant dynamic so painful in the erotic relationship becomes
a loving dynamic that puts the submissive party if not on equal footing, then
in a position of mutuality. Rossetti accomplishes this reversal by means of
some fancy poetic footwork centering on strategic repetitions and uncertain-
ties about the status of "I" and "thou." "Twice" complicates the question of
address in the first stanza. By using parentheses, Rossetti ambiguates both the
addressee and the tense:

> I took my heart in my hand
>   (O my love, O my love),
> I said: Let me fall or stand,
>   Let me live or die,
> But this once hear me speak—
>   (O my love, O my love)—
> Yet a woman's words are weak;
>   You should speak, not I.[8]

Here, the lover, the "I" of the poem, retells her beloved what she told him
in the past while also addressing him in the present, even as she interrupts
herself. The confusing double tense of this stanza establishes her words as
already repeated, refracting the moment of the stanza into a palimpsest of
past and present. This refraction fragments the "I" and "you" into past and

present selves as well. Just as the words "Let me fall" begin as a repetition, the beloved's refusal to hear replays itself as well. The only way she can appear to be heard is to ask him to speak, which he does in order to say of her heart, "It is still unripe, / Better wait awhile."[9] The lover's discouragement from speech signals the failure of intimacy with her beloved, which follows in the subsequent stanzas. He "scans" her heart with a "critical eye," dismissing it as unripe. Her request to be heard signals the importance of hearing the other for intimacy to happen. Her recoil from speech and his harsh criticism suggest that his failure to hear breaks down his capacity for intimacy.

The lover, on the other hand, painfully retains her capacity to hear the other. The disappointment that follows denies the lover her capacity for joy and song, but not for full receptiveness of his words:

> As you set it [heart] down it broke—
>   Broke, but I did not wince;
> I smiled at the speech you spoke,
>   At your judgment that I heard:
> But I have not often smiled
>   Since then, nor questioned since,
> Nor cared for corn-flowers wild,
>   Nor sung with the singing bird.[10]

The redundancy of "speech you spoke" underscores the beloved's capacity for expression, while the lover can only receive words from him rather than exchanging them. Her heartbreak also shuts down her capacity to question, presumably both outwardly and inwardly; it limits not only her powers of expression but her thought as well. When the lover turns to God instead, she repeats the tropes and actions from her relationship with the beloved: she gives God her heart and asks him to judge it. She also asks him to "scan" it, repeating the verb she used to describe the beloved's appraisal and signaling the emotional violence that a reader of poetry can do to a poem. Indeed, she asks God to understand fully her heart's flaws, to improve it, and to continue to hold it, in terms that are reminiscent of Rossetti's own style of editing her own poems: "Refine with fire its gold, / Purge Thou its dross away— / Yea hold it in Thy hold."[11] This refinement does not eschew judgment but rather asks for improvement instead of rejection as a mode of response and engagement. In asking God to repeat the beloved's actions, she also reconsiders them as a form of care rather than of rejection. In other words, God can hear her, accept her flaws, and respond back to her in a way that the beloved could not.

When Rossetti introduces God into the poem, she also repeats the words of the first stanza, changing the past tense to present, replacing "love" with "God" and removing the parentheses:

> I take my heart in my hand,
>   O my God, O my God,
> My broken heart in my hand:
>   Thou hast seen, judge Thou.
> My hope was written on sand,
>   O my God, O my God;
> Now let Thy judgment stand—
>   Yea, judge me now.[12]

These small changes, which render whole the present moment and cast aside the need for two modes of address, suggest that the divine relationship does away with the divisions and changeability inherent in the earthly relationship. This repetition from the first stanza suggests that by turning to God, the lover refines the type of intimacy that she wanted with her beloved, that she tries again and improves on her earlier efforts. The likeness also signals crucial similarities and differences between erotic and divine relationships. Or rather, the divine relationship finally fulfills the ideal of the erotic relationship, which can only end in disappointment. The divine offers sympathy and responsiveness. The lover also modifies her approach, emphasizing God rather than herself. Extending the "-and" rhyme to four lines instead of two, intensifying the repetition, the word "stand" rhymes with "hand" five lines in now, and this time the lover asks not for herself to stand, but for God's judgment to stand. The repeated apostrophes, prompting reflection on similarities and differences between the relationships, are also accompanied here by the power of an imperative that expects a response. That response comes in the final stanza when God "calls" back to her: "I for Thou callest such."

The final stanza of "Twice" puts the "I" and "Thou" face-to-face, seeming to keep them distinct, but then abruptly confuses the issue:

> I take my heart in my hand—
>   I shall not die, but live—
> Before Thy face I stand;
>   I, for Thou callest such:
> All that I have I bring,
>   All that I am I give,
> Smile Thou and I shall sing,
>   But shall not question much.[13]

What does that "such" stand for? For a "Thou" to call "I" an "I" seems to signal at once that God gives her her identity by authorizing her use of the first-person pronoun, but also that He gives her his own identity, or loans her his "I," in which case they are identified with each other. Alternatively, "I, for Thou callest such" might suggest that God calls her "thou" just as she calls him "thou," establishing a kind of mutuality to their relationship. The echo chamber of pronouns in this line renders the face-to-face distinctions in the previous line impossible. Does "such" refer to "I" or "Thou" or to some absent but assumed referent? The difficulty of answering this question suggests that "I" and "Thou" can occupy interchangeable positions, so that they exist in reference to each other. The imperative and the promise of the last two lines suggests an exchange and a return of power to the "I" that God's smile, echoing the smile that she was deprived of earlier, elicits. The promise not to question "much" implies deference without utter submission, while at the same time reserving the right to question, a right that her heartbreak previously had denied her. The "I" has agency to sing and occasionally to question, and the power to relinquish authority to the other (in this case to God) in a way that does not compromise her core individuality. This poem importantly distinguishes speech from song. Although she fails to speak earlier in the poem, her projected capacity to sing in Heaven elevates song as a more intimate medium than speech.

This posture of power within submissiveness in "Twice" echoes excellent recent scholarship situating Rossetti's poetics within Tractarianism. Focusing on the concept of imagination, Dinah Roe emphasizes the relationship with God as an epistemological one, asking to what extent we can know God and how we imagine him. She shows Rossetti to adhere to the tenet of reserve in Tractarianism, according to which we can never fully know God. Yet for her, the Tractarian concept of analogy stimulates the imagination to see the divine in the earthly, and thereby to conceptualize God's love.[14] Through the lens of both "reserve" and "analogy," the devout can acknowledge God's omnipotence and mystery yet still attain a level of mastery in gaining an interpretive glimpse into that mystery. In showing how Rossetti incorporates Tractarian principles in her poetry, Roe argues largely against Lynda Palazzo, who claims that Rossetti rejected the Tractarians' insistence on the subordinate role of women.[15] Diane D'Amico also focuses on the place of God's love in Rossetti's devotional ideals, noting that for Rossetti the love people show one another reflects God's love. D'Amico argues that Rossetti expresses love for other people in the very act of writing poetry, which, by sharing her devotion, fulfills "her duty to others." This explanation posits poetry as a medium of relating to readers but neglects the ways in which poetry both enacts and models relational dynamics in the play of "I" and "thou."[16]

Whereas in "Twice" the triangle turns into a complex mutually constituting dyad, "Monna Innominata" depicts a process of shedding aspirations toward earthly love to embrace love itself as an intransitive and divine action. Opening with a preface that declares the barrier between lovers "sacred" and closing with "Silence of love that cannot sing again," "Monna Innominata" seems to reinforce the solitude of the female lover and female poet. The preface to Rossetti's sequence of fourteen sonnets imagines these poems as the product of an unknown lady of "poetic aptitude," older than the celebrated Beatrice or Laura, muses of the Troubadours who preceded them. In addition to situating herself in a Petrarchan sonnet tradition, with epigraphs from Dante and Petrarch to each poem, the preface announces the sequence as an alternative to Barrett Browning's "Portuguese Sonnets."[17] Had Barrett Browning only been "unhappy instead of happy," she might have written poems like the ones in "Monna Innominata." Although these assertions seem to elevate solitude as the ideal position for a woman poet, "Monna Innominata" explores the problems of intimacy in such a way that overcomes them by focusing on the relationship with God and the act of loving itself. Sonnets 5–8, which center on the triangulated relationship of the lover, the beloved, and God, reinforce the necessity of intimacy. The lover considers how to measure the intensity, even quantity, of her love for her beloved against her love for God, and out of this conflict she concludes that love itself is more significant than its object.

In "Monna Innominata," the lover tries to create a role for God in an erotic relationship and a role for her beloved within her devotion by structuring various types of triangles between them. These efforts ultimately fail, suggesting that the divine relationship must always replace the erotic one. Yet for all that it is about an earthly relationship that can never be consummated, "Monna Innominata" ultimately proposes a mode of love that transcends specific objects and exists as an intransitive activity. Here, to love God is, quite simply, to love. Rossetti presents this love as expansive in a way that the efforts at triangulation aimed to, but could not, be.

The second "quatrain" of her sequence of fourteen sonnets prefigures the failure of the relationship that follows the "turn" of the sequence by interrogating the quantity of love: who loves who more, and how can one continue to love God if one loves another person so much? Behind these concerns are further questions about identification, difference, and separateness. The first sonnet of this macrosonnet "quatrain" presents the lovers both as identifying with each other and as distinct: as mirror images of each other, but also as occupying separate roles, especially in relation to God:

> O my heart's heart, and you who are to me
>> More than myself myself, God be with you,
>> Keep you in strong obedience leal and true
> To Him whose noble service setteth free,
> Give you all good we see or can foresee,
>> Make your joys many and your sorrows few,
>> Bless you in what you bear and what you do,
> Yea, perfect you as He would have you be.
> So much for you; but what for me, dear friend?
>> To love you without stint and all I can
> Today, tomorrow, world without an end;
>> To love you much and yet to love you more,
>> As Jordan at his flood sweeps either shore;
> Since woman is the helpmeet made for man.[18]

The first two lines present the beloved as a more fully realized incarnation of the lover herself, "More than myself myself." This interpretation is an outgrowth of sonnet 4, where she declares, "With separate 'I' and 'thou' free love has done. / For one is both and both are one in love."[19] It seems, then, that as the lover asks for God to make her beloved obedient to Him, to make him achieve perfection in God's eyes, she also requires the same for herself. However, the turn of the sonnet asserts that the octave was only about him, and not him as a substitution for or extension of her. The use of separate pronouns at the turn—"So much for you; but what for me?"—undoes the identification that the octave establishes and prefaces a different set of wishes for the lover, one that mirrors her hopes for him. She puts her beloved in a relationship with God and herself in a parallel relationship with her lover: her devotion to her lover mirrors the devotion she wants him to have to God. In this way, their relationship is based on identification, but also on triangulation. The lover and the beloved are similarly submissive, but to different beings. The lover's relationship with God is mediated by her relationship with her beloved, and similarly, it is at the lover's request, via the indirect address of "God be with you," that the beloved relates to God. Our own contemporary readers might balk at the submissiveness suggested by the word "helpmeet," which seems to undermine the declaration in sonnet 7 that the pair are "happy equals."[20] Yet the term "helpmeet" encapsulates the sonnet's complicated triangulation, one that relies on dutiful obedience that the most submissive party orchestrates. Because she positions herself as his helpmeet, starting the triangulation by asking God to make her lover obedient, she also has the honor and power (as the poem conceives it) of being most submissive, as well as of, paradoxically, dictating the structure of their relationship.

In the following sonnet, however, we learn that her beloved has questioned her schema. It implies that when she says she will "love you much and yet to love you more," she puts the beloved above God. She goes on to try to clarify how her love for him and her love for God are balanced:

> Trust me, I have not earned your dear rebuke,
>   I love, as you would have me, God the most;
>   Would lose not Him, but you, must one be lost,
> Nor with Lot's wife cast back a faithless look
> Unready to forego what I forsook;
>   This say I, having counted up the cost,
>   This, tho' I be the feeblest of God's host,
> The sorriest sheep Christ shepherds with His crook.
> Yet while I love my God the most, I deem
>   That I can never love you overmuch;
>   I love Him more, so let me love you too;
> Yea, as I apprehend it, love is such
> I cannot love you if I love not Him,
>   I cannot love Him if I love not you.[21]

This sonnet aims to assuage the beloved's objections by enclosing "Him" within "you" in a chiasmus, suggesting that God's divine presence is in the beloved, identifying the beloved with God rather than with the lover. However, the poem still accedes that devotion must pay for earthly love, and that devotion comes at a price. The lover declares that she has "counted up the cost" and would without hesitation give up her beloved if God required it. The poem has to convert a cost to a benefit by transforming what seems like a subtraction from the love of God into an addition, in a sense altering the method of "counting up the cost." Love for God must be seen to be enhanced rather than reduced by the lover's erotic attachment. Because the sonnet sequence must make room for the beloved within the lover's spiritual life, she must view her love for him as a variation on her love for God. It is no wonder, then, that her feelings require a careful emotional accounting. This sonnet attempts to configure a continually shifting triangulated hierarchy so that the beloved stands both one notch below God and contains Him, while the lover toggles between being the lowest (or "feeblest") within it and, if not the highest, then the most actively loving. Rossetti explicitly uses sonnet logic—a problem is always seen from more than one angle—to destabilize the subject positions of her triangle, so that "I" and "thou" become fluid terms.[22]

The following sonnet is a paean to the power of love that opens by asking the lovers to repeat the same words to each other, "'Love me, for I love you'—and answer me, / 'Love me, for I love you'—so shall we stand / As happy equals in the flowering land." These lines seem to undo the problems presented in the preceding two sonnets, yet even the invitation to repeat these words indicates an inequality at the level of meter. Most would normally scan the words "Love me" as a spondee, which renders these two lines unequal in the number of stresses from the other lines of the poem. Alternatively, it would be possible to scan "love me" as either an iamb or a trochee, but with this uncertainty the lines are not necessarily equal either; one partner might stress "love" and the other could stress "me." The sestet re-recognizes the problem that the lovers must continually part, but closes with a citation of *The Song of Solomon* that suggests that God himself is love: "Still I find comfort in his Book, who saith, / Tho' jealousy be cruel as the grave, / And death be strong, yet love is strong as death."[23] Jealousy, the hallmark of triangulated relationships, and the element that the previous poems attempt to dissolve with their fluid positions, reasserts itself as untenable; and love itself, with the absence of loving subject or loved object, stands alone as an action, an attitude or a feeling, disconnected from a person.

This quatrain within the sonnet of sonnets concludes with a poem where the lover draws a parallel between herself and Esther, the Jewish queen responsible for saving her people from a genocidal massacre. It is important to recount this story in order to understand the sonnet because, as Scheinberg points out, the tale contains complicated dynamics of submission and autonomy, especially in its female heroine.[24] In the biblical story of Esther, King Ahasuerus banishes his first wife, Vashti, because she refuses to appear unveiled before his guests. After staging a competition of sorts, he chooses Esther, who was orphaned and raised by her cousin Mordecai. Mordecai earns the favor of the king by warning him of a plot against him, but then falls out of favor because he refuses to comply with a new decree ordering all to bow down before Haman, whom the king had chosen to honor in this way. Mordecai refuses to bow down because his Jewish faith forbids bowing before anyone but God. As a result, Haman declares he will take revenge by killing all the Jews in the Persian empire. Mordecai tells Esther that she will also be killed if she does not persuade the king to stop Haman's plan. However, if Esther attempts to appear before the king without being summoned, she can be put to death. Esther gets the courage to flout this rule and appear before the king, and the king accepts her visit. She then succeeds over a period of several days, during which the king decides to honor Mordecai for having previously saved his life. Esther then tells the king that she is Jewish and the king puts a stop to Haman's genocidal plan.

Rossetti's sonnet 8 of "Monna Innominata" begins with Esther's decision to go to the king: "I, if I perish, perish." On the surface, this tautology underscores Esther's willingness to sacrifice herself, but its grammatical structure, dividing subject and verb, suggests not only Esther's internal resolve but also an internal dialogue, a conditional clause interrupting an affirmative statement. The "if" that embeds uncertainty within certainty emphasizes that this tautology does anything but represent a truth; the difference between the two clauses is a matter of life or death. With this act of will in which Esther has to assert her own power by giving herself up to the unknown, Rossetti signals thus that to give up individuality is not to give up authority and autonomy. The isolation of the first "I" might also register aurally as "aye," in a pun that indicates the status of the lyric "I" as free-floating emotion rather than a subjectivity, even as it refers simultaneously to a biblical character. The rest of the octave describes her methods of persuasion as especially seductive, with her "perfumed hair" and "pomp of loveliness" meant to "take / Her husband thro' his eyes at unaware." Several critics have noted the surprisingly sensual nature of Rossetti's Esther, which she embellishes from the Bible if not invents. Importantly, in referring to this story as parallel to the scenario of the sonnets, the poem does not position the king as either the lover or the beloved. The king here is instrumental, and instrumentality within an erotic relationship has already been presented to be a problem: the beloved refuses to allow the lover's love for him to be a conduit in her relationship with God. The marriage between Esther and the king, as it is presented in this sonnet, demonstrates why the rationale of sonnet 6 will not work.

Sonnet 8 concludes with a new triangle, which positions the beloved as "love" and God as "Love," in another attempt to align the beloved with God by using the same word to refer to both:

> She vanquished him by wisdom of her wit,
>   And built her people's house that it should stand:—
>   If I might take my life so in my hand,
> And for my love to Love put up my prayer,
> And for love's sake by Love be granted it![25]

Here, the beloved, "my love," corresponds to the Jewish people and Love corresponds to the King. In this way, the lover identifies her beloved, as well as her feelings for him, both of which "my love" might refer to, with a religious mission. There are three different "loves" here, the beloved, the feeling, and the godlike entity to whom she prays, "Love," producing another instance of triangulated identification. By creating a parallel between this dynamic and the story of Esther, the lover presents her appeal on behalf of her "love" as a form of divine supplication. At the same time, however, given the critique in the octave of marriage as a form of earthly instrumentality, the object of this triangulated identification cannot be marriage, and therefore cannot function as a solution to the problem of the lovers' absence from one another. The content of the "prayer" is deliberately ambiguous here. A reader might imagine that she prays to be united with her beloved, but this prayer could just as easily be "for" him in the sense that it is on his behalf rather than to possess him.

This sonnet appears in a crucial position within the sequence, as Scheinberg notes, between the lover's attempts to merge her spiritual devotion with her erotic desire and her concession in sonnet 9 to "all / That might have been and now can never be." But whereas Scheinberg reads Rossetti's Esther as aligning her sexual and spiritual desire, I read Esther's sensual seduction not as evidence of her own erotic desires, but as a feminine power that she *uses* in order to save her people. By analogy, the lover would use her own power to persuade God to have something for her "love's sake." She thereby presents herself as the seductress of God, signaling the likeness between erotic and divine relationships. However, the triangulation of the preceding sonnets begins to shut down in these lines, as the same word comes to represent the lover, the beloved, and God. We can, and should, read these transitional lines in two ways that reflect Rossetti's use of repetition to signal sameness and difference simultaneously. The repetition of "love" to refer to three entities in the same line indicates how each of these loves functions separately, supplicating, granting, receiving desire. At the same time, these actions can collapse into each other, suggesting that they all are a form of loving. It is by wisdom of Rossetti's wit that she is able to have it both ways, to differentiate the lover from and identify her with her beloved and her God. The conclusion of the sequence disconnects love from its subjects and objects, allowing the lover a measure of divine intimacy in the very act of continuing to love, since, as she makes clear in these final lines of sonnet 8, God is "Love."

The concluding "sestet" of "Monna Innominata," which settles on the permanence of the sacred "barrier between them" in the preface, detaches "love" from its object. In sonnet 9, the lover declares that she is "yet not hopeless quite nor faithless quite / Because not loveless."[26] The idea that someone might be satisfied by love whether or not it is returned and whether or not it is acted upon in a mutual, physically present relationship might seem like the ultimate solipsism. Yet the lover asserts the power and constancy of her feeling and continues to insist upon its spiritual relevance:

> But by my heart of love laid bare to you,
>   My love that you can make not void nor vain,
> Love that foregoes you but to claim anew
>   Beyond this passage of the gate of death,
>   I charge you at the Judgment make it plain
> My love of you was life and not a breath.[27]

Although the shifting triangulation of lover-beloved-God of sonnets 4–8 ultimately did not work, the lover can still transfer her love from the beloved man so that it exists when she enters Heaven; by "foregoing" the beloved, her love can make a claim in the afterlife. Yet her dependence on the beloved has not dissolved; she asks him to vouch for its constancy by asking him to assert that it was "life and not a breath." Here, as in other phrases in the sestet of sonnets, Rossetti reduces and ultimately abandons the use of pronouns. To say "my life" would reinforce a sense of solipsism here, but by leaving out the pronoun, she seems to suggest that the love exists outside of her, a life-form in itself that merits entry to the afterlife, and is not simply extinguished or vanishing like a breath.[28] Rossetti presents this love as expansive, originating in but not limited to a pair of individuals. Indeed, she presents her beloved's marriage to another as an opportunity not for jealousy, but for them finally to be "happy equals." It is precisely their separation that allows her to reassert the sentiment from sonnet 4, "For verily love knows not 'mine' or 'thine'":

> But since the heart is yours that was mine own,
>   Your pleasure is my pleasure, right my right,
>   Your honourable freedom makes me free,
>   And you companioned I am not alone.[29]

This declaration might seem like an ultimately hollow attempt to recover from the loss, a requisite post-breakup "I'm happy for you" that must necessarily give way to the forlornness of the final sonnet. But such a reading results from a dramatic and narrative, rather than a lyric, reading practice. Dramatic and narrative reading practices often invite readers to identify with the emotions represented; here, Rossetti presents us with an ideal of intimacy rather than flawed realism. These lines from sonnet 12 are, of course, the opposite of selfishness, and convincing coming from a lyric voice in a way they would not be if they came from a narrative character. Rossetti teaches us to read not for a self but to hear how the proliferation of "you"s and "I"s, "your"s and "my"s in this poem echoes the repetition of other words—"pleasure, pleasure," "right, right," "freedom, free"—in such a way that the pronouns detach from referents.[30]

The turn in the sonnet of sonnets indicates not merely a divide between the possibility of mutual presence and its impossibility, but a realization that the physical presence of two selves is not the point. As Adela Pinch has persuasively argued of the first sonnet of this sequence, Rossetti presents "thought as practice or action—rather than as a particular content" in such a way that "renders spectral or purely grammatical the 'you of address.'"[31] Not only thinking, but loving, throughout the sequence is something the lover does, and in moving away from the beloved object, Rossetti renders the verb "love" intransitive. Although this might seem like an isolating rather than an intimate move, Rossetti does this so that the loving entities—lover, beloved, God—can merge without having to identify with each other, or declare sameness. It is not a question of one self absorbing another, as in Dante Gabriel's model of erotic love in *The House of Life,* but rather of selves being joined in the same practice of loving.

This mode of reading casts new light on what many readers see as the defeated tone of the final sonnet. For Rossetti, resignation is rarely about defeat; giving up is the necessary posture in order to welcome divine intimacy. Although the final sonnet seems to leave the lover alone, condemning her to solitude, silence, age, and ugliness, there is an embrace of these features that suggests she expects their opposites in the world beyond the poem, in the afterlife. Although her "youth" and "beauty" are gone, most important, this is what "remains":

> The longing of a heart pent up forlorn,
>   A silent heart whose silence loves and longs;
>   The silence of a heart which sang its songs
> While youth and beauty made a summer morn,
> Silence of love that cannot sing again.[32]

The silence here takes us back to the preface, reminding readers that these sonnets "imagine many a lady as sharing her lover's poetic aptitude," and that these poets remain only in the silence of the women's poetry that we do not have. But we should not be tempted to read silence here as absence. This silence is an active silence: it loves and longs. Here there are no more possessive pronouns, and not only are "loves" and "longs" intransitive verbs, they are also verbs without a person or character performing the action. Rossetti leaves readers with emotions without an "I" or a "you," with a pared-down lyric intimacy that consists of only the most essential component: love it-self. As Alison Chapman has argued, by "deleting subjectivity," Rossetti not only flouts expectations that women's poetry be autobiographical, thereby critiquing gender norms, she also opens up a "new process" of subjectivity.[33] This process, I suggest, is precisely what allows for responsiveness, rather than mere expressiveness.

Between Heaven and Earth: Poetic Voice

I have shown how in "Twice" and in "Monna Innominata," the unstable "I" creates room for an intimate "I-thou" exchange, and even for a verb in no need of a subject. By the time she wrote these poems, Rossetti had a long history of experimenting with an "I" that can in no way be called a "speaker." Early in her career, Rossetti wrote a number of poems, frequently antholo-gized, that are now referred to as "death lyrics." Although they are dead, the women in these poems still express awareness of their surroundings, and at times they glimpse the heaven that awaits them. As McGann has shown, these poems reflect the theological view, called Soul Sleep or psychopannychism, that deserving souls must wait in the grave until Judgment Day, when they can ascend into Heaven. McGann describes these poems as using Soul Sleep to imagine a dream vision of Paradise. He argues that Rossetti presents poetry as thrice removed from Paradise itself, as a dream of a dream of Paradise.[34] Questioning what a disembodied voice might be, the "death lyrics" provide a case study in Rossetti's view of the poetic voice. By understanding how Ros-setti places lyric voice in the disembodied space of Soul Sleep, and how she imagines souls meet in this purgatory, we can see how the intimacy she ideal-izes is one that she can know only in poetry.

Of all of the poems that use the "beyond the grave" conceit, "Echo" is the most radically disorienting. As others have noted, Rossetti ruthlessly elimi-nated stanzas from earlier drafts that gave the poem more narrative structure, and this editing establishes the poem's mysteriousness and obscurity.[35] The shorter poem as she published it also creates a sense of pervasive absence, not just of the beloved but also of the loving "speaker" herself. "Echo" explores the idea of the repetition of voices, laying the groundwork for a theory of lyric voice that endured throughout Rossetti's career.

The title's allusion to the myth of Echo and Narcissus alerts readers not only to the echoes to come within the poem, but to the status of its voice as originating not within one subjectivity but reverberating between two enti-ties. This allusion also reminds readers that repetition recontextualizes so that words that sound and look the same in a new context might mean something different. In "Echo," because the voice is disconnected from an idea of a person, repetitions within the poem can speak to each other:

> Come to me in the silence of the night;
>   Come in the speaking silence of a dream;
> Come with soft rounded cheeks and eyes as bright
>   As sunlight on a stream;
>   Come back in tears,
> O memory, hope, love of finished years.[36]

By the end of this first stanza of the poem, it becomes clear that what the poem desires is repetition itself, a return of past experience and feeling. The poem performs the desire for repetition, as well as the desire for intimacy, in its poetic strategies. Each repetition of the word "come" introduces a new idea, which makes the poem seem as much a dialogue as a monologue. Whether that dialogue is internal or external is hardly relevant, for there is hardly a recognizable interiority. The first line, "Come to me in the silence of the night," sounds as though it calls out for the lover to come in secret for a midnight tryst. The second line responds to the first, repeating the words and the idea "come in silence," this time modifying it to introduce the oxymoron "speaking silence." This term refers to the poem itself as well as to a dream, suggesting that both poem and dream are a state of expression without vocalization and that both conjure alternative states. Indeed, silence is written into the poem in the final line of this stanza, where a pause between "hope" and "love," both stressed, must function as an unstressed "syllable," audible as space and visible in the comma, but not signified by a word. The final line of the first stanza is an apostrophe, but to multiple objects: memory, hope, love. These emotions and the "tears" in which they are to return all might exist within an addressed beloved or in a "speaker" herself. The ambiguity of address here reinforces the ambiguity of the voice. There is no "I" in the first two stanzas, only a "me," so that the presumed speaker positions herself as an object, with the beloved as the subject of the imperative "come." This emphasis on the object implies a relation between an object and subject. Although the ambiguity of person and voice might intuitively disallow intimacy, which seems to require two distinct subjects, in fact it admits of structures of responsiveness that allow an intimacy and relationality within the poem itself. Just as words repeat in different combinations, such as "come to me" and "come back to me" or "sweet, too sweet, bitter sweet," meters also change with the repetitions of these words. The poem begins with unusual trochaic descending meter, with the emphasis on the first syllable: "*Come* to me." By the third line, it reverts to the more conventional iambic meter: "Come *back* to me." Rossetti embodies disembodied thoughts and feelings in the poetic body of meter and rhyme.

The apostrophic, vocative "O" at the end of the first stanza shifts to a simple sigh of "Oh" at the beginning of the second:

> Oh dream how sweet, too sweet, too bitter sweet,
>> Whose wakening should have been in Paradise,
> Where souls brimfull of love abide and meet;
>> Where thirsting longing eyes
>>> Watch the slow door
> That opening, letting in, lets out no more.[37]

When she says, "Oh dream," she does not address the dream, but goes on to talk about it. This shift from "O" to "Oh" blurs the distinction between an address and an undirected sound, making the apostrophe into simply a potential sigh, and the "Oh" into only a one-line address if it is one at all. The poem, then, like the dream it longs for, is a "speaking silence," unwilling to act out speech with a bolder apostrophe. The poem creates a *mise en abyme* effect, since this stanza is a dream of the dream of Heaven. This must be a recurring vision, something imagined over and over, since its "wakening should have been in Paradise." The past perfect here implies that there is the dream as she imagines it should be, and the dream as it is, one that is sweet, another version that is too bitter sweet. Her fantasy of Paradise here is one in which people who love one another are reunited for eternity. Envisioning it as a room with an opening door that only allows entrances, never exits, Rossetti likens Paradise with its entering souls to a stanza, the Italian word for room, thereby characterizing a stanza and a poem as the site of ever multiplying souls and lyric voices. The room corresponds to the repetitions in the poem, which add words with each repetition. As words and phrases repeat in this poem, with new words at each repetition, potential subjects, objects, and meanings accumulate. Souls proliferate in this poem as they do behind the door of the "stanza" of Paradise. When Vendler asks in *Invisible Listeners* who is in the room, whether the listener is present or absent, she refers to the fiction of the poem, inherited from John Stuart Mill's image of a speaker in a cell, as already voiced in space and time.[38] By casting the poem itself as the "room," Rossetti's poem casts quite a different light on the question of who is in the room, because her "stanza" does not limit itself to a single speaker or listener.

The last stanza of "Echo" suggests that Paradise repeats, and improves upon, earthly life. It articulates a place for bodies and speaking, akin to earthly versions, in Paradise.

> Yet come to me in dreams, that I may live
>> My very life again tho' cold in death:
> Come back to me in dreams, that I may give
>> Pulse for pulse, breath for breath:
>>> Speak low, lean low,
> As long ago, my love, how long ago.[39]

To dream of Heaven would be to repeat, to live "My very life *again* tho' cold in death." The final stanza of the poem imagines an exchange of bodily rhythms intimately in tune with each other. While imagining this exchange, the poem also stylistically enacts it in the intense repetition of these final lines, the commas acting as caesuras that balance repeating words on either side in the last three lines. The pulse becomes a figure for writing, a rhythm that corresponds to the rhythm on the page. Since the poem never cries out for the actual beloved to return, only for an appearance in a dream, the poem in its repetition of the sounds is an echo of the desired dream. Both Hassett and Susan Conley have noted the especially mellifluous quality of this poem, but whereas Conley reads it as a depiction of "a desire that persists into the grave and keeps its speaker bound there," Hassett avers that it "affirms the pleasure of its anguish."[40] That pleasure is possible because the abundant sound effects compensate for the absence of the missing beloved, giving us responsive sounds, rather than absent and present figures that correspond to an "I" and a "thou." In my reading, "Echo" performs the reciprocal feeling it desires, and in doing so it asserts its own repetitions as an echo of the pleasures of earthly life and of Paradise. The repetition of the poem creates a sonorous responsiveness within the poem that its scenario, however ambiguous, can never achieve. The poem itself does not replace what it echoes, but reconstructs it. This poem argues for poetry as a form of repetition rather than of resurrection.

As many have noted, repetition is perhaps the most frequent poetic device that Rossetti uses, and although poems are made of repetitions (after all, what are rhyme and meter if not forms of repetition), Rossetti uses it to an unusual degree. As they do in "Echo," often words, phrases, and sounds re-sound within the same line, within the same stanza multiple times. Eric Griffiths notes that this repetition might first lead to a reader's disappointment, but then defends it on the grounds that its surplus "both enriches its formality, stresses how rule-governed it is, and at the same time releases through the rules the inflection of a quirky, self-determining voice, a voice dutiful to excess and so not only dutiful." Griffiths goes on to suggest that not only is repetition part of Rossetti's distinctive style, which he calls her "voice," but that it is part of the "desire to 'go on saying' of a 'lyric I'" which is "to be understood rather as a part of the grammar of lyric poetry itself, a form of utterance which inherently strives for self-perpetuation and which gives us not snapshots of a particular person's emotional state at any one time but a permanent algebra of human moods."[41] Here, Griffiths acknowledges that there is a difference between the lyric "I" and what he calls the "empirical self." By suggesting that the lyric "I" encodes "human moods," he implies that it participates in universality rather than particularity. Yet his insistence that repetition is essential to the lyric "I" fails to acknowledge an echo that signals lyric intimacies. Another account of Rossetti's use of repetition does more to address repetition's destabilizing effects. Angela Leighton argues that Rossetti's use of frequent repetition creates a sonorousness that empties words of meaning, creating a sound of thinking rather than semantic significance. In discussing the repetition in "Monna Innominata," Leighton writes, "The verbal twitch is so pervasive that it seems like the basis of Christina's work. It is as if she has to press the button of each word twice or three times to make it ring more strangely, more inscapingly—to bring it into question. The biblical echo is there, but the effect is often the opposite of biblical choiceness. Repetition, here, empties rather than fills, baffles rather than informs."[42] It is precisely this strange ringing that reminds us that these poems are not the voice of a singular subjective "I" and that opens up the multivocality of the poem, creating a call-and-response within it. In the case of "Echo," the repetition is a product of the reverberating space between earth and heaven, suggesting that poetry, too, a phenomenon of repetition, exists in a similarly liminal space.

By conjuring a dream vision that is a "speaking silence" in "Echo," Rossetti creates an oxymoron that serves as a useful definition for the contradictions inherent in a nineteenth-century idea of poetic voice. This oxymoron also usefully describes the purgatorial position of the death lyrics. In order to imagine how Rossetti conceives of the afterlife voices of the death lyrics such as "Echo," and indeed poetic voice more broadly, it helps to turn to her devotional prose, where she muses on the voice on earth and the voice in heaven. While this work never explicitly mentions poetry, it nonetheless reflects on the voice and music, concepts essential to poetry. Her approach to voice and music allows us to conclude that for Rossetti poetry was no mere substitute for or imitation of earthly or heavenly voices. Critics often think of poetry as having a voice, as Griffiths does in *The Printed Voice of Victorian Poetry,* where even in the "mute polyphony" of numerous possible intonations, poems produce an imagined voice even if they do not reproduce a real one.[43] For Rossetti, however, voice must be embodied, and therefore poetry could not possibly have a voice. In a remarkable entry in her 1884 devotional diary *Time Flies,* Rossetti meditates on the meaning of recorded voices, wondering how reproduction of the human voice affects its individuality and originality. Rossetti insists on the voice's dependence on the body and therefore on its impermanence, but stops to consider whether a machine can do what words and musical notes cannot:

> For the voice is inseparable from the person to whom it belongs. The voice which charms one generation is inaccessible to the next. Words cannot describe it, notes cannot register it; it remains as a tradition, it lingers only as a regret: or, if by marvellous modern appliances stored up and re-uttered, we listen not to any imitative sound, but to a reproduction of the original voice.
>
> In St. John's vision we read of the "harps of God" but the human voices worthy of such accompanying instruments are the actual voices of the redeemed who sing the new song.
>
> The song indeed is new: but those singing voices are the selfsame which spake and sang on earth, the same which age enfeebled and death silenced.
>
> "And I look for the Resurrection of the Dead."[44]

Following the doctrine of Soul Sleep, this passage assumes that the body and the soul rise to Heaven together on Judgment Day, and that in Heaven the vocal chords produce the same sound that the body on earth produced, but with a new song. Yet in its brief consideration of recording, the passage opens up a paradox. Even as Rossetti asserts that the voice is inseparable from the person, she raises the question of recorded voices, which *are* separated from the people to whom they belong, and yet produce the same sound. The almost miraculously reproduced voice that comes from a phonograph emerges as a way for those on earth to access the heavenly voices of the departed. Rossetti's quotation of the penultimate line of the Nicene Creed, "And I look for the Resurrection of the Dead," points to the potentially quasi-divine function of the technology she marvels over. Her omission of the last line, "And the life of the world to come," suggests, however, that the reproduction of the voice, whether on a phonograph or in the words of a poem, must always fall short of an authentic living voice as Rossetti imagines it in Heaven. In this view, voice, once lost, is irrecoverable. As Chapman suggests, Rossetti would certainly not view voice as an apt trope for the rediscovery of women poets, for as she points out, this trope encourages a misguided fantasy that we can find an "authorial authenticity" and use that as the basis for our reading.[45]

Rossetti insists that even recordings cannot provide that authenticity. In the following entry, Rossetti retracts the heavenly qualities with which she endowed "marvellous modern appliances," and instead dismisses them as "mere clockwork":

> Perhaps one reason why music is made so prominent among the revelations vouchsafed us of heaven, is because it imperatively requires living agency for its production.
>
> For I think that from this connection music produced by mere clockwork is fairly excluded: ingenious it may be, but inferior it cannot but be.
>
> Music, then, demands the living voice for its utterance, or, at the least, the living breath or the living finger to awaken a lifeless instrument.
>
> Written notes are not music until they find a voice.
>
> Written words are words even while unuttered, for they convey through the eye an intellectual meaning. But musical notes express sound, and nought beside sound.
>
> A silent note, then, is a silent sound: and what can a silent sound be?
>
> The music of heaven, to become music, must have trumpeters and harpers as well as harps and trumpets, must have singers as well as songs.[46]

Rossetti entertains and then rejects a fantasy of recording technology as modeling Heaven in its reproduction of the voices of the dead. She remains attached to the idea of the body as the origin of the voice and the locus of the soul, so essential that she suggests that it must accompany the soul to Heaven, its breath and fingers necessary for the creation of heavenly music. Here, Rossetti reads the voice as quite literally the product of a specific person's vocal chords.

Rossetti was hardly alone in conceptualizing the power of sound recording as reproducing the voices of the dead, as Jonathan Sterne's *The Audible Past,* a history of the early development of sound recording, suggests. Yet Sterne shows that the technology at the time did not support these prevalent fantasies of rendering permanent what was transitory. In 1878 the first public demonstration of this technology exhibited a stylus writing on foil sheets that were extremely fragile. Even the wax cylinders used for recordings starting in 1888, four years after Rossetti's meditations on voice reproduction, might easily melt or bend. Early recordings were not as permanent as some imagined them to be. Although she might not have understood the fragility of the foil sheets and later wax cylinders that stored early recordings, Rossetti thought that she had reason to doubt that the phonograph could serve as a model for heavenly voices. Sterne writes that while the fantasy of recording focused on the potential for miraculous permanence, the technical realities accomplished the simpler, but still impressive, feat of repetition.[47] Sterne's argument also sheds light on Rossetti's indissoluble connection between voice and person. He writes: "Because it comes from within the body and extends out into the world, speech is traditionally considered as both interior and exterior, both 'inside' and 'outside' the limits of subjectivity. In contrast, the voices of the dead no longer emanate from bodies that serve as containers for self-awareness. The recording is, therefore, a resonant tomb, offering the exteriority of the voice with none of its interior self-awareness."[48]

Sterne's metaphor for recorded voices, "a resonant tomb," might also characterize the way in which Rossetti conceives of lyric, especially given her propensity to write poems that seem to come from beyond the grave, as "Echo" does. Her consideration of recording in *Time Flies* defines voice and music in a way that excludes poetry from these categories. Poetry might be a kind of music when read aloud, but often poetry is encountered in silent reading. It might in this case fit the definition of "written words," which Rossetti asserts visually impart an "intellectual meaning." Yet as any reader of "Goblin Market" knows, her own poems exceed this idea with their remarkable sound effects. Ultimately, Rossetti's reference to sound in her discussion of the heavenly voice recalls the roots of the word "phonograph": written voice. Although she dismisses recorded sound as a model for the heavenly voice, it presents a compelling metaphor for poetry. Like the recorded voice, poetry can create an illusion of someone speaking, but that illusion does not replace the voice. Rossetti's insistence that words cannot describe the voice nor musical notes register it implies that a poem cannot reproduce the human voice, or indeed give any idea of it. For Rossetti, voice refers to actual sound, not to a person's verbal style. Indeed, for Rossetti, poetry functions, as Yopie Prins puts it in the context of all Victorian poetry, "as a mechanism for the disembodiment of voice, and with similar contradictory effects: sometimes invoking and evoking the spoken word, but also revoking it."[49]

If Rossetti's definition of "person" is so based on the material being, then the "speaking silences" of poetry can be defined as impersonal utterances originating with no person, stretching outside the limits of subjectivity. In *Time Flies,* two different theories of voice emerge that implicitly distinguish the human and the heavenly from the poetic. She defines the human voice as the product of the vocal chords of a living, or resurrected and therefore also living, being, a voice identified with a particular person. From this definition of voice and from her poetic practice, we might infer that Rossetti differentiates the poetic voice from the human voice, defining it as the "speaking silences" of words on the page, a voice without a specific identity, one that can correspond in the abstract to the state of anticipation of the afterlife that Rossetti so often describes in poetry and in prose. In Rossetti's theory, the heavenly voice requires a body for its production but the poetic voice is disembodied, and therefore does not rely on assumptions of a static poetic speaker. The poetic voice remains open to encompass multiple possibilities for its lyric "I"—or, the lyric "me," for the object form of this pronoun is at least as significant as the subject for Rossetti.

For Rossetti, then, the metaphor of recorded sound offers more poetic possibilities than heavenly ones. Repetition and clockwork, features of sound recording, distinguish poetry from prose; they function in rhyme, meter, alliteration, and assonance. As I have discussed, repetition in all of its varieties was one of Rossetti's primary poetic techniques. Rossetti's own repetitions are too sonorous to be considered to have only "intellectual meaning" to the eye, but for her, poetry on the page does not qualify as music. In her meditation on sound recording, Rossetti implicitly addresses two aspects of poetry, the written words and their audible rhythms and tonalities when spoken aloud. In order to understand what poetry is for Rossetti, and her own particular brand of lyric intimacy, we have to see how poetry falls between the categories of "written words" and "music." Although what we might call voice in a poem is disembodied from the human, poems do have their own materiality. In addition to the materiality of the paper on which they are printed or even written, the body of the poem also lies in its meter, which is a visual as well as an aural phenomenon. Meter as a visible phenomenon is not an effect of voice, but a pattern of stress, or multiple possible variations on that pattern, intervals of syllable and accent measured in silent reading. Her question "what can a silent sound be?" is not merely rhetorical, but captures the status of poetry, which can be voiced or not, but whose sounds remain audible in the imagination of the silent reader. Poems, then, can be silent sounds, like the songs Rossetti mentions in *Time Flies* that have yet to find singers.

Despite its potential for being voiced, a poem is not always, or even usually, a voicing. Tricia Lootens argues that in "Monna Innominata," Rossetti "never asserts that her poem fills the silences its preface evokes." Rather, the speaker of "Monna Innominata" "speaks as an heir to their silences."[50] Even though she implies that a silent sound can be nothing, a silent poem, as Lootens suggests, is another story. A poem does not necessarily "speak" for anyone, real or imagined. Unlike the voice, a poem is not tied to a particular person's physical presence. A silence is not an absence of sound, but a potential presence of thought, emotion, tension, movement. The answer to Rossetti's question "What can a silent sound be?" is not necessarily, then, nothing, but something that can still be measured and received.

For Rossetti, poetry has a liminal status, not the product of a human or a divine voice, not only visual or aural, not entirely silent, but unless read aloud not exactly heard either. In "An Old-World Thicket" (1881, *A Pageant and Other Poems*), a poem about purgatory that was written around the same time as *Time Flies,* poetic "music" is a combination of sound and silence and presages the advent of Paradise. Opening with an epigraph from the beginning of Dante's Inferno, "Una selva oscura," the poem depicts a dreamer in a dense forest that at first seems like a land of natural plenitude, with singing birds drinking dew and honey. But the soul in the poem despairs, feeling isolated from the joy she observes and hopeless to regain what joy she had in the past, tormented by what seems like an existential crisis. The birds' songs and the sounds of the landscape in the wind and water then change to correspond to her mood: "The wood, and every creature of the wood, / Seemed mourning with me in an undertone." As the landscape rustles in compassion, she hears a transforming music, whose origin is unclear:

> Without, within me, music seemed to be;
>   Something not music, yet most musical,
> Silence and sound in heavenly harmony;
>   At length a pattering fall
> Of feet, a bell, and bleatings, broke through all.[51]

The sound that is "not music, yet most musical" in this stanza is not heavenly singing, but it heralds Heaven nonetheless, and as such it is a fitting metaphor for the way Rossetti conceptualizes poetry. Although the "fall of feet" refers to the flock of sheep, the context invites a pun on the word "feet," so that what is heard here is the meter of the poem, meter itself fitting the oxymoronic definition of this music as both silence and sound. The description of what the soul hears, a definition of poetry both essential and evasive, does not itself scan easily, however. Do we stress the words "not," "yet" or "most"? The most regular possible reading, "SOMEthing not MUSic, YET most MUSicAL" emphasizes the contradictions inherent in the line with the stress of the word "yet." But other metrical readings are equally if not more plausible, but might lead to an irregular excess of stresses, if, for instance, we stress "not" and "most," suggesting that this line itself is indeed not musical. The suspension of these possibilities holds in harmony the silence and the sound of the line, and of the poem. This stanza reinforces the harmony of silence and sound by emphasizing its own silences in its use of punctuation, with frequent commas, and one semicolon at the end of the stanza's first line that seems unnecessarily to interrupt the syntax of the poem and what would otherwise be an enjambment.

This plurality of metrical possibilities points to the status of the "something not music" as both "within" and "without" the soul. Not only do these silent sounds herald Heaven, but they also blur the boundary of the lyric "me," since they are both internal and external to her, harmonizing her with her environment. This passage comes at a pivotal point in the poem, when the landscape's compassion for the soul's emotional turmoil evokes this not-music that is both "within" and "without." Although before this passage the soul struggled with rage, despair, and loneliness, after it sees a vision of natural harmony in which entities that are not "subjects" engage in a process of mutual exchange. This "something not music" enables an intimacy within the landscape, its elements responsive to the sunlight: "Each water drop made answer to the light." The flock of sheep implied by the "feet," "bell," and "bleatings" is heading homeward, presumably a metaphor for souls proceeding to Heaven.

Another entry in *Time Flies* illustrates the importance of what is "without" the self both for intimacy and for poetry. The pivotal stanza from "An Old-World Thicket" contains an oddly placed semicolon at the end of the first line: "Without, within me music seemed to be; . . ." Yet this strange punctuation enforces a pause that emphasizes that the soul does not will the "music" that leads to her redemption, but that she must be open and responsive to it. As Rossetti meditates on the concept of interruption, she also articulates a poetics of pause:

> An interruption is something, is anything, which breaks in upon our occupation of the moment.
> Now our occupations spring? . . . from within: for they are the outcome of our own will.
> And interruptions arrive? . . . from without. Obviously from without, or otherwise we could and would ward them off.
> Our occupation, then, is that which we select. Our interruption is that which is sent us.
> But hence it would appear that the occupation may be willful, while the interruption must be Providential.[52]

This reflection on interruption is both an idea about how the individual relates to the external world and a poetic principle. This definition of interruption as providential also sheds light on the way in which poems them-selves have a "within and without" like the music of "An Old-World Thicket." Indeed, the pauses and stresses of poetry are an exchange of the "within" and "without." In her essay "Women's Space: Echo, Caesura, Echo," Isobel Armstrong notes that echoes follow a necessary disjunction from the origi-nal sound, so that "the break, the disjunction, is what makes the echo, what makes the sound. The caesura."[53] Armstrong suggests that the logic of the caesura is spatial rather than temporal, allowing sound to reverberate. For Rossetti, the caesura, the interruption, breaks in from without and allows not only space for knowledge, as Armstrong's essay suggests, but separation from the self and space for knowledge of what is other. Rossetti takes these poetic essentials, repetition and interruption, and conceptualizes them in such a way that opens out the poetic voice and creates possibilities for relation and ex-change within it.

While Rossetti defines "voice" as a quality inseparable from particular people, and from their bodies, a *poetic* voice emerges as the opposite of the earthly and heavenly voice. It is impersonal, it exists primarily as words on the page, as potential sound, but also as a visual rhythm of pauses and continu-ities, occupations and interruptions. Although the permanence of the voice that the phonograph offers is a tempting idea for her, Rossetti must reject its "clockwork" as a model for the divine. Instead, the possibility for repeating voices that the phonograph offers is more like her vision of poetry. Poetry, like sound reproduction, facilitates, but does not ultimately fulfill, the fantasy of hearing the voices of the dead. Instead, it establishes a purgatorial space between earth and heaven where the indeterminacy of the voice allows for intimate possibilities that are also particularly poetic, modulating between the real and the ideal. Poetry's status as a kind of contradiction, a silent sound, calls attention to the way in which it blurs the boundaries of subjectivity and voice, so that the difference between "within" and "without" is not so easy to identify. Attention to both what is within and without and to what lies be-tween allows for the kind of exchange that forms Rossetti's ideal of intimacy. By listening for silence, interruptions, "something not music," in her poems and prose, Rossetti encourages the same in her readers, positing an idea of intimacy based not on expressiveness, but on receptiveness.

Intimacy "After Death": Listening, Silence, Knowledge

In looking at one more of the "death lyrics," we can see that by removing these "speakers" from dramatic situations, Rossetti critiques the insufficiency of relationships in the real world, in interpersonal dramatic action, while at the same time gesturing toward an ideal of intimacy that Rossetti presumes is available beyond that world. The critique is already well documented: the women in these poems have been described as "cold," using death to assert autonomy and identity, and therefore feminine power.[54] Yet this very detachment, which I have shown to be one of the cornerstones of Rossetti's poetics, is a precondition for lyric intimacy. These dead or soon-to-be-dead women emblematize Rossetti's approach to poetic voice precisely because, like the poems themselves, they are disembodied. Just as a poem lies dormant waiting to be read, these figures exist in a liminal space between life and death. These poetic explorations of Soul Sleep allowed her to theorize not only about what might constitute an identity or subjectivity after ties to the body are severed, but also what it might mean for a disembodied or attenuated self to exist in relation to another, and how that attenuation can enhance intimacy. In various ways, these poems all refuse any attempt to read a voice within them; they begin with a presumption of disembodiment.

By presenting the lyric "I" as dead, Rossetti refuses to present that "I" as embodied in a dramatic situation. Indeed, the opposite often happens here, where the dead "I" overhears the living, observing them unnoticed.[55] Instead of or in addition to presenting voices, these poems present listeners, whose receptivity to the expressions of others is as important as the words on the page. To present the "voice" of the poem as a disembodied overhearer also calls into question whether there is even an "I" there, or at least how it is different from a person. With the "I" destabilized, Rossetti can present a desire for another, as well as a knowledge of another, as emotion detached from circumstance and situation. While none of these poems represent the kind of idealized intimacy with God that the devotional poems offer, they demonstrate that the distanced, disembodied state creates the conditions for listening, observing, and remaining receptive to another.

Two death lyrics present voices that are listeners as much as they are "speakers," and their capacity to observe signals their intense desire for love. In "At Home," the spirit of a dead person approaches a party at a "much frequented house" and hears the ones she loved talking exclusively about the future and the present, ignoring the past. The exclusion she feels from the revelers who have forgotten her and think only of the present and future indicts the fickleness of earthly relationships. As in "At Home," in "After Death," a recently dead woman's keen observations about the room around her allows the reader initially to imagine the scene, which gives the poem a patina of narrative embodiment instead of lyric detachment. The poem almost immediately undoes this narrative patina however, by raising questions about how the woman describing the scene knows what she knows. Although many of her observations are visual, they do not come from embodied eyes, for her face is covered with a shroud. She notes especially the behavior and even the thoughts of the man whom she declares did not love her but now weeps over her. She demonstrates an extraordinarily insightful knowledge of the man in the room, seeming almost to read his mind:

> He leaned above me thinking that I slept
>   And could not hear him; but I heard him say:
>   "Poor child, poor child:" and as he turned away
> Came a deep silence, and I knew he wept.
> He did not touch the shroud, or raise the fold
>   That hid my face, or take my hand in his,
>   Or ruffle the smooth pillows for my head:
>   He did not love me living; but once dead
>   He pitied me; and very sweet it is
> To know he still is warm tho' I am cold.[56]

It is remarkable that she knows what he is thinking and worth asking how she knows it. We can read her awareness as deduced from the fact that he leans over her and speaks, but if he turns away and is entirely silent, how does she know that he weeps? Even the description of the absence of his touch bespeaks an awareness of the man's state of mind. While a period appears after "head" in the manuscript, in the published version a colon appears in the same position, implying a link between his refusal to touch her hand or shroud or pillow and the assertion that "He did not love me." The colon allows readers to see the dead woman's reasoning process, an intensely thoughtful presence in a room where the other person present thinks of her as absent. Especially in contrast to the forlorn forgottenness of the dead soul in "At Home," the "warmth" of this man signifies not only that he is alive but that he feels for and remembers the dead spirit, even if it is only in the attenuation of pity rather than in the full passion of love. His tears and exclamation of "poor child," an expression that suggests he infantilizes her, signify his pity, while the absence of touch reinforces his failure to love. Yet despite his condescension, her knowledge, a product of reasoning based on the evidence provides a small form of intimate gratification for her. Although it is impossible to know how a colon came to be after "head" instead of a period, it endows the poem with a logic of comfort. The period in the manuscript, however, disrupts this logic. The presence of the period in the manuscript version renders tenuous the link between the man's failure to lift the shroud or ruffle the pillow and the absence of his love. Rather than suggesting a deductive thought process on the part of the spirit, it is an invitation to the reader to draw a causal relation between these nonexistent acts and the lack of love, or not. By disrupting the knowledge that leads even to slight intimacy, the period also casts doubt on the "sweetness" the spirit feels. That the comfort of knowing another's feeling hinges on a punctuation mark suggests how fragile the intimacy is. Even though his pity brings her slight satisfaction, this intimacy is without mutuality. The barrier that allows her to listen but not to respond (except to a third party who reads the poem) implies the difficulty if not impossibility of mutual understanding in human relationships.

There are a number of ways to read "sweet" in this poem, either as genuine pleasure at a crumb of affection, or ironically, as bitterness at this man's emotional shortcomings. The thought process that the poem evokes suggests an attempt to understand the man in a way that is detached enough to imply some sympathy for his tears, even if it is only one-sided. Readings that refuse the possibility of real "sweetness" here also insist on a speaker who breaks free from this insufficient and limiting relationship in order to assert her own identity. Margaret Reynolds's Kristevan/Lacanian reading asserts that this poem declares feminine power and the authority of the female "I," finally in position to deny the man, the "Father," who had once "used me, controlled me, perhaps even hated me" and now "invades" the privacy of her death-room.[57] For Susan Conley, "In these poems, death becomes both an indictment of life and the moment of revenge on oppression, an opportunity, for the dead women to exercise power and control. . . . Death emerges as an act of autonomous self-fashioning."[58] In these approaches, "self" is necessarily linked to autonomy; by recognizing the insufficiency, if not the outright abuse, from this man, the speaker can break free from his hold and assert her own power. But this approach fails to recognize the sincere desire for love that these poems express and ignore the way in which love is necessary to sustain a self, even as a self must relinquish some individuality to gain that love. While it seems maddening or even impossible to a modern reader that anyone could be gratified by the man's insufficient simpering in "After Death," I argue that for Rossetti's poem, it is the understanding of him, rather than his expressions, that is pleasing, and a model for the way that she wants intimacy to happen. Although this ideal does not happen in the "death lyrics," a detached spirit's ability to listen, observe, sympathize, and even feel some small warmth in return gestures toward the ideal that is most evident in Rossetti's devotional work.

The disembodied perception in "After Death," and its spirit's capacity to know what is happening not only in the room but in another's mind without physical sight, emerges as a model for faith in Rossetti's later poetry. In a sonnet that appears in *The Face of the Deep* (1893) and also in *Verses* (1893), Rossetti outlines the conditions for intimacy with God:

> Alone Lord God, we see not yet we know;
>   By love we dwell with patience and desire,
>   And loving so and so desiring pray;
>   Thy will be done in earth as heaven today;
>   As yesterday it was, tomorrow so;
>   Love offering love on love's self-feeding fire.[59]

The "Alone" that begins the sonnet, as well as the sestet quoted above, suggests not the isolation of the speaker but the uniqueness of God. That relationship with God depends on knowing him, even though it is impossible to see him, and knowing, quoting the Lord's Prayer, that His will will be carried out. (There is no knowledge here of what God's will is, just that it will be fulfilled.) In *The Face of the Deep,* this poem appears at the end of Rossetti's exegesis of the first verse of chapter 11 of Revelation, in which John is asked to measure the temple with a reed. Rossetti makes much of the reed, asserting that what is weak is "a measure of what is holy."[60] Rossetti implies in this passage, then, that we can know a strong God by our weak selves, asserting that to be abased is also to be glorified. As is clear in "Monna Innominata," the act of measuring can paradoxically perform this equalizing power that transforms weakness into strength. In "Alone Lord God," the action of knowing is connected to waiting with "patience and desire," and to loving. The repetition of the word "love" in the last line, without possessive pronouns or definite articles, deliberately fails to distinguish between God's love and the worshipper's love, thus equalizing God and the worshipper, in the way that Rossetti's reflection on the reed does. Indeed, Love itself is an active agent as well as an action, a disembodied, abstract entity similar to the speakers of Rossetti's poems. Love means not only waiting, desiring, and knowing, but offering and feeding, giving and consuming. This list of verbs suggests a power dynamic that allows both parties to occupy positions of submission and dominance. The fluidity of subject positions also underscores Rossetti's suggestion that love is about actions rather than objects. The image of the "self-feeding fire" further implies a destruction and rebirth of the self. This love is the product of knowledge without perception, akin to the production of poetic voice without a body. This familiar Rossettian technique in the final line suggests that this state of not seeing, but knowing, waiting, and loving is analogous to the poem that we see on the page, which is an artifact of silence, thought, and desire.

As Lootens and Armstrong attest, by the 1890s, writers of the later generation, such as Amy Levy and Katherine Tynan, felt that Rossetti was out of step with contemporary culture, focused as she was on death and salvation. Lootens argues that critics such as Edmund Gosse associated Rossetti's poetic perfection with the virtues of modesty and purity, holding her up as a counterweight to the commercialism, sexual awakening, and ambitions of fin de siècle women.[61] Surveying responses to Rossetti, Armstrong avers that women writers of the fin de siècle considered her to be "an anomaly, despite what all these poets had learned from her compressed, compact lyric and formal adventurousness."[62] Michael Field's "To Christina Rossetti" epitomizes the kind of aestheticist response that Armstrong and Lootens describe. In this ambivalent tribute poem following shortly after Rossetti's death, Michael Field claims their position as poets of intimacy over what they depict to be the cold, self-imposed isolation of Rossetti:

> Lady, we would behold thee moving bright
> As Beatrice or Matilda 'mid the trees,
> Alas! Thy moan was as a moan for ease
> And passage through cool shadows to the night:
> Fleeing from love, hadst thou not poet's right
> To slip into the universe? The seas
> Are fathomless to rivers drowned in these,
> And sorrow is secure in leafy light.
> Ah, had this secret touched thee, in a tomb
> Thou hadst not buried thy enchanting self,
> As happy Syrinx murmuring with the wind,
> Or Daphne thrilled through all her mystic bloom
> From safe recess as genius or as elf,
> Thou hadst breathed joy in earth and in thy kind.[63]

Just as Rossetti herself proposed an alternate unhappy version of Elizabeth Barrett Browning in her preface to "Monna Innominata," Michael Field imagines a happy Christina Rossetti, erotically fulfilled in an interpersonal relationship. Michael Field criticizes the poet here for idealizing a universalizing union; she does not realize, they claim, that this kind of union allows for no depth, that once the river becomes part of the ocean, there is no possibility to "fathom" it. The poem argues that for a woman's poetry to "breathe joy," the woman poet must not withdraw from others. According to Michael Field, Rossetti sought to escape the poet-muse conundrum by "fleeing from love." They claim that Rossetti fails to comprehend the "secret" that the muse position offers "safe recess." Susan Conley is right to point out that the poem sidelines the idea that Daphne and Syrinx escape ultimately only to transform into tools for the glorification of the men whose violent attacks they would repel: Daphne becomes Apollo's laurel branch, and Syrinx turns into the reeds with which Pan makes his pipes.[64] The poem certainly does present Rossetti as, in Conley's term, an "anti-muse," though I argue that Michael Field objects most strongly to Rossetti's perceived position on intimacy. Their notion of an alternate Rossetti "breathing" joy unites an ideal of intimacy with lyric poetry in the concept of an "air," both a song and the substance of breath; this poem presents the model they wish they had, a model, I argue, that was far more real than they claim. Michael Field's criticism of what they perceived to be Rossetti's attempt to escape from intimacy in both life and in verse misreads Rossetti, who, as I hope I have shown, fully explores how differentiation and distance enable poetic, idealized relations.

Yet the influence of Rossetti's restrained style shows itself in the sympathy Michael Field exhibits in their critique of her. Rossetti critiques Barrett Browning and Michael Field critiques Rossetti by offering alternate visions of the poets that allow for all that they admire in their style, while offering an ideal of an even better poetics. This very style of critique contrasts sharply with their male predecessors, for example, in the "Fleshly School of Poetry" controversy between D. G. Rossetti and Robert Buchanan. In a pseudonymously written review, Buchanan savages what he saw as the "nastiness" of the "trash" Rossetti would put forth as poetry.[65] Rossetti responds not only by defending his work but also by lambasting Buchanan for the cowardice of charging him with "insincerity" from behind a mask.[66] Although Michael Field often considered male poets and critics to be their most important interlocutors, they nonetheless took inspiration from Christina Rossetti's mode of poetic competition and critique.

Although Armstrong recognizes the vogue for "compressed" lyric that Rossetti helped to establish, especially for women poets, no one has yet acknowledged the link between her compact lyrical forms and alternate ideas about intimacy. The chapters that follow will show how silence, thought, and waiting become important thematic and formal ideas, essential for alternate relational dynamics, in the poets that come after Rossetti. The lack of ego that Armstrong finds to be anomalous at the fin de siècle is inseparable from Rossetti's formal innovations, which made it possible for poets after her to think in terms of an "I-thou" dynamic. She led the way for a younger generation, modeling a poetry that made an "other" central to a lyric relation. Her use of repetition, her metrical playfulness established responsiveness within poems that Webster, Robinson, Meynell, and Radford all adapted to their own uses. Rossetti's work created new possibilities for the poets who follow her to consider what lyrical forms can do and how they can create structures of responsiveness, mutuality, and intimacy.

"Appraise Love and Divide"

MEASURING LOVE IN AUGUSTA WEBSTER'S
MOTHER AND DAUGHTER

The measurement of love in sonnets, particularly Victorian sonnets, is a familiar, if underexamined, trope. In chapter 1, I argued that anxiety about "counting up the cost" of erotic love animates Christina Rossetti's poetics of intimacy in her sonnet sequence "Monna Innominata." For her, the solution is to perform a divine calculus whereby lyric selves retain limited individuality in order to reflect and enact God's all-encompassing love. In contrast, Dante Gabriel Rossetti raises only to dismiss the impulse to measure love: "I love you, sweet: how can you ever learn / How much I love you?" a lover asks his beloved in "Youth's Antiphony," one of the sonnets in *The House of Life*. He depicts these words as the idle chatter of romance, filling the space, concealing "Through two blent souls one rapturous undersong."[1] Later in the sequence, he further depicts this question as baseless, for "Not by one measure mayst thou mete our love"; the beloved corrects the lover for ever doubting "love's equality."[2] Most famously, Elizabeth Barrett Browning attempts to answer the question for her beloved, offering to "count the ways" she loves.[3] Numerous sonneteers, including both Rossettis, measure the intervals between the times when lovers meet. These poets are not only lauding the value of their beloveds, but considering how much love it is possible to feel and to express. Even while declaring that their love is infinite and therefore impossible to quantify, they display its magnitude in quantifying metaphors that count love's ways or gauge its duration. Victorian sonnets often consider love to be eternal, but they nonetheless mark its temporal stages, fantasizing about the continuation of love in the afterlife. This impulse to return to—even if only to reject—metaphors of measurement implicates the compulsion to count in poetic conventions that constantly measure sound in meter and rhyme.

Underlying Augusta Webster's sonnet sequence *Mother and Daughter* is the startling proposition that love is a limited resource that can be divided, meted out. Her sequence transposes the concern for how much love is possible, how long love lasts, and how deep it is from the erotic context of the sonnet sequence onto a parent-child relationship. Webster emphasizes that a mother's love cannot escape measurement, for she must track the growth of her daughter, their increasing distance, and the gap between the experiences of mother and daughter that is both pedagogical and nostalgic. Unlike an erotic love, often imagined to continue in an afterlife that is either religious, literary, or both, Webster's concept of a mother-daughter relationship has a painful natural end. Webster sharply contrasts the idealized permanence of erotic love with the constantly changing quality of maternal love. Haunted by fears about the duration of love, the sonnet sequence expresses a compulsion to prove love's depth, comparing it to a still, silent lake and a void "filled to the utterest." Written retrospectively, after her daughter was an adult, and when Webster herself was close to death, *Mother and Daughter* is concerned with the mother's passing, and even in one instance, with the child's. Webster confronts the painful fact of transience in the parent-child relationship, lamenting the passage of time and the distance from her daughter that increases as she ages.

To illuminate the bittersweet relationship between mother and child, Webster must turn to the inherent conditions and contradictions of the sonnet form, which is at once expansive in thought and economical in expression, thought by poets from Shakespeare to Dante Gabriel Rossetti to render permanent a moment even as the meter tallies the time to the poem's end. *Mother and Daughter* declares that while mothers of multiple children must "appraise love and divide" it among the children, loving each with "various stress," the mother of a single child gives all of her love to her child, who "has the whole." Although the sonnets insist that mothers of only children need not measure out their love the way mothers of siblings must, they simultaneously express an anxiety about needing to quantify the strength and duration of this mother's love. Despite this resistance, the use of the sonnet form reflects the compulsion to count the stresses, sounds, and rhythms of maternal feeling. Webster's use of terms like "stress" and "footsteps" refers to the genre, reminding the reader that the poems inevitably measure maternal love as the poet measures accent, syllable, and line. As the sonnets both wish for love's infinitude and doubt it, the meter reinforces this tension, rushing during tropes of stillness, halting with extra stress to slow the passage of time, and interrupting with caesuras; poetic forms themselves "appraise and divide" a mother's love as they express her anxiety. While meter counts the poetic voice of the poems, the poems also address the fleeting quality of the mother's own voice, noting how the human voice measures the passage of time as it ages. Webster asserts that the quest to understand maternal love in sonnets necessarily means she must give its aspects various stress, appraising and dividing the words and sounds that embody the feelings.

Mother and Daughter contains twenty-seven sonnets, and although Webster began work on it in 1881, it remained unpublished at her death in 1894. In 1895 it was published with the subtitle *An Uncompleted Sonnet Sequence,* with an introduction by William Michael Rossetti. The poems were presumably ordered by Webster's husband, Thomas. In his introduction, W. M. Rossetti avails himself of the prevailing commonplaces about women's poetry by praising the poems as "genuine" and the feeling therein as "beautiful and natural."[4] Rossetti goes on to acknowledge Webster's reputation in the pantheon of poetesses, alongside Barrett Browning and Christina Rossetti, yet, strangely, he spends the rest of his short introduction suggesting that Webster's verse drama about Emperor Caligula, *The Sentence,* is her best work and marks her greatness as a poet. This curious introduction, in which Rossetti could only praise a work with explicitly "masculine" themes, suggests that while Rossetti admired Webster a great deal, he could not find suitable comment for *Mother and Daughter,* besides platitudes, and was blind to its complex treatment of maternal feeling. In her book that looks at Webster's works in the context of what relatively little is known about her life, Patricia Rigg connects the emotional complexity of the sequence to Webster's personal experience to explain why she worked on *Mother and Daughter* for thirteen years but never finished it.[5] I would argue in light of Rossetti's introduction, however, that Webster may have been fully aware that the public would not know quite what to do with it.

In recent returning critical attention to Webster, particular notice has gone to her dramatic monologues, especially poems like "A Castaway" that argue for women's rights. However, after the publication of her last collection of dramatic monologues, *Portraits,* she turned entirely to writing in shorter lyric forms. Webster began writing the sonnets around the time she published her first short lyrics, the "English Rispetti," in *A Book of Rhyme* in 1881. Although it appears that she worked on the sonnets from this time on, Webster had not completed *Mother and Daughter* when she died in 1894. A number of recent critics have offered astute readings of *Mother and Daughter.* They have usefully drawn thematic connections to the sequence's precursors, and have sparked debates about how Webster responds to thematic sonnet conventions, but none have marked the significance of Webster's emphasis on measuring love. For Webster, the inevitable measurement of maternal love is inextricable from the counting inherent in writing and reading sonnets. Webster refers to sonnet conventions—a mediation between presence and absence, the attempt to preserve a fleeting moment, and the measurement of sound in meter—in order to illuminate the need to quantify love.

Webster's concern with measuring maternal love was both a formal issue and a cultural one. After investigating the sonnets about love for an only child, I turn to the advice literature of the period, which reveals anxieties that a mother could love her child too much by exhausting her own emotional resources too soon, but also that a mother could provide too little love, especially if she is preoccupied with other pursuits. One competitor for a mother's love, of course, is her husband, and I turn to other poems in Webster's oeuvre to examine her critique of marriage and ideas of it in light of the way that love must be rationed within a family. I go on to show how other Victorian female sonneteers raise the complicated calculus of love's proportions when a new person enters a life. The question of how much love a mother can give is inextricable from the question of how much time a mother has with her child, a quantity that changes as the child grows up. Finally, I consider how *Mother and Daughter* distinguishes the permanence of the poetic voice from the singularity and mortality of any human voice. I give special attention to metrical readings of *Mother and Daughter* because the conflicts between what the mother wants and what she can both give and get manifest in a conflict between what the words of certain poems say and what their meter suggests.

"Scarcely a Mother": Counting Children

Mother and Daughter considers "how much" a woman can be a mother by taking on the detractors of a mother of an only child. Those detractors tell her, "You are scarcely a mother, at that rate. / Only one child!"[6] The poems defend having only one child in several ways. At first, in the same poem in which the rebuke appears, Webster suggests that a mother of many children cannot love any individual child as much as that child loves her, for the children love her singly. For their mother, Webster asserts that one child can somewhat compensate for the loss of another. A mother with a "household crowd," the poem suggests, would not grieve as much "were her first-born folded in his shroud," for she would have "more sons to make her heart elate."[7] Many mothers would certainly take issue with this assertion, particularly Alice Meynell, who felt, despite her own "household crowd," that when she lost a child God now had something for which to ask forgiveness.[8] Nonetheless, siblings, Webster implies, do not have the unique, irreplaceable love of their mothers.

You think that you love each as much as one,
    Mothers with many nestlings 'neath your wings.
    Nay, but you know not. Love's most priceless things
Have unity that cannot be undone.
You give the rays, I the englobed full sun;
    I give the river, you the separate springs:
    My motherhood's all my child's with all it brings—
None takes the strong entireness from her: none.

You know not. You love yours with various stress;
    This with a graver trust, this with more pride;
This maybe with more needed tenderness:
I by each uttermost passion of my soul
Am turned to mine; she is one, she has the whole:
    How should you know who appraise love and divide?[9]

This sonnet defends having an only child on the principle that love is, like a river's water or the sun's light, vast but nonetheless divisible and therefore quantifiable and limited. While mothers of more than one child must "appraise love and divide," perhaps giving more of one sort of love to one child or another, depending on her needs, the mother of an only child must perform no such calculation. Presumably, these mothers of "many nestlings" were at some point mothers of only children after the birth of their first, but that uniqueness, the poet suggests, was undone with the birth of the second. The defensiveness of the diction here, along with the insistence on the wholeness and oneness of the mother's love for her daughter, point to an anxiety about the very calculation she describes. As we will see in chapter 4, writing about the second person singular, Alice Meynell asserts that she prefers the intimate address of "thou" to "pointing the rude forefinger of 'you.'"[10] Indeed, in its repetition of the word "you," this poem deliberately points a rude forefinger, which stands in stark contrast to the "thou" with which the poems address the daughter.[11]

Echoing this defensive tone in the meter, the poem addresses other mothers with various metrical stress. Several lines use trochaic and spondaic substitution, and so the stress not only varies from line to line but is sometimes in excess. Reciting the words "you know not," repeated twice and echoed throughout, a reader may stress any or all three words, as in YOU know NOT, or you KNOW not, or YOU KNOW NOT. The most stressed version of these words in fact puts four stresses next to each other, or two spondees, to read "Nay, but YOU KNOW NOT. LOVE'S most PRICEless THING" and "YOU KNOW NOT. YOU love YOURS with VARious STRESS." The spondees and sharp caesuras in this poem act almost as a blunt rhythmical weapon. The excess appears not only at the level of accent but in the number of syllables as well; four of the fourteen lines, including the final two, carry eleven instead of the customary ten syllables. It is as though the poem emphasizes that in receiving the whole, the daughter receives more than enough love—there is extra. At the same time, the extra syllables invite attempts at elision to help the line fit the meter, so that "uttermost" can be pronounced "ut-most" and "the whole" as "th'whole." It is no accident that words signifying fullness are the words that are cut short. While the sonnet insists that an only child is better off with the mother's "strong entireness," the meter suggests that there *is* such a thing as too much. In his reading of Webster's sonnet sequence, John Holmes inquires whether the daughter of such a mother might not "experience her mother's love not as an ideal but as an oppressive imbalance."[12] In the daughter's near-silence in the sequence, Holmes identifies a potential daughterly rejection of her mother's encompassing love and an invitation to critique the mother instead of sympathizing with her. Certainly, his reading points to the sequence's implication that it is possible to love too much.[13]

Although Webster herself cautioned against biographical readings in her essay "Poets and Personal Pronouns," many readers of this sonnet sequence surely would have known that Webster had only one child, and may have been tempted to read these poems as a defense of this fact. Indeed, Patricia Rigg reads the sequence biographically on the grounds that Webster focuses on mothering an only child and that Webster never published the sequence in her lifetime.[14] If a reader extends a biographical reading, Webster's status as a professional poet, a critic, and an adamant defender of women's education and women's professionalism suggests that she surely must have divided up her time and her thoughts between her child and her own interests.[15] Webster's questions about how we measure and compare a mother's love implicitly challenges the conventional wisdom about motherhood in the period. Readers responding that a mother *can* love many children with equal intensity might be forced to consider who and what else a mother might love besides her children. If a mother can share her love among her children and husband, can she not give her emotional energy to other pursuits as well?

Even if we take Webster at her word that "as a rule, I does not mean I," then it becomes clear that however much the poems might have been informed by personal experience, the focus on an only daughter usefully reflects on both the singularity of love in sonnet conventions and the unsettling prospect that love is quantifiable.[16] On the one hand, the sequence revels in the idea that a mother's love is infinite. On the other hand, the very idea that it is infinite for one but not for more suggests that however many children a mother has, she must divide her emotional resources between her child and other people or pursuits. How a mother measures her love has important implications for the women's rights that Webster passionately championed.

Webster's ambivalence about measurement—the rejection of counting that coincides with the compulsion to do it—complicates the received wisdom of Romanticism. Percy Bysshe Shelley famously disparaged the "unmitigated exercise of the calculating faculty" in his "Defence of Poetry."[17] Shelley suggests that too much measurement and attention to utility denies "eternal truths" and in doing so generates social and political inequality. Shelley opposes rationality, utility, and calculation against poetry and the imagination: "A poet participates in the eternal, the infinite, and the one; as far as relates to his conceptions, time and place and number are not."[18] Shelley downplays the mathematical elements of meter, for he insists that "poetry" may also be written in prose and that meter, while it is "to be preferred," is not essential as long as "harmony" is preserved.[19] On the surface, Webster's phrase "appraise love and divide" seems to agree with Shelley's account. The word "appraise," with its connotation of worth as well as number, sits especially uneasily next to "love," the idea of assigning worth to a child an especially ugly accusation. The association of "appraise" with "divide" also implies that to measure is to sunder one thing or person from another.[20] Yet a metrical reading of Webster's poem reminds readers that meter *does* measure, and that the "calculating faculty" *is* necessary for poetry. As we shall see, in Webster's sequence, the "calculating faculty" extends to the balancing act that a mother, even of only one child, must do within her family and over time. For Webster, time and number inevitably insert themselves into the world of the poet.

"Ungoverned Springs of Tenderness": Calculating Mothers in Victorian Culture

Questions specifically about a mother's emotional obligations were circulating in other literary as well as nonliterary texts from mid- to late century. Two critical works identify starkly different views on Victorian attitudes about motherhood. Angela Leighton characterizes verses about motherhood from the period as almost entirely treacly, including works by poets known for emotional complexity or subversive politics such as Christina Rossetti or Dollie Radford. Leighton suggests that the scant poetry directly addressing motherhood in the nineteenth century tended to represent its subject with "picturesque religiosity" or by "infantilizing" it.[21] She focuses on Alice Meynell's poems about motherhood as defying this tendency and also cites

Mother and Daughter in passing: "It is as if the subject is the last to get free of that sentimentalism of the heart which weigh heavily on women's poetry as a whole. The child in these verses is rarely older than a baby (Augusta Webster's *Mother and Daughter* sonnets make an interesting exception) and the mother rarely expresses any feelings beyond those of absolute love or grief."[22] While for Leighton motherhood is the last bastion of unabashed sentimentality in women's poetry, the view of motherhood in the advice manuals, medical texts, and sensation fiction that Sally Shuttleworth examines is quite different. She focuses on the ways in which these texts enforce patriarchal bourgeois power by stressing the need to control the potential excess of feeling, even of insanity, in mothers. For Shuttleworth, the language of biological imperatives in these texts—a woman can only be fulfilled by giving birth to and raising a child—dominates. The texts she examines nonetheless fear that these imperatives might be corrupted. Concerns about a range of feelings in mothers, from the infanticidal to the eroticism of breastfeeding, threatened the sentimental ideal.[23] The difference between these two approaches is in their focus on separate genres. Leighton draws attention to the function of poetry as a celebratory and consolatory genre, while advice manuals and sensation fiction tend to bring to light that which should be feared and avoided. Webster complicates this function of poetry, particularly the poetry of maternity, by allowing her sequence to express fears in an emotionally realistic way, one that diverges from sentimentality as well as from the alarmist "demonic" images of mothers that Shuttleworth considers.

Although some of the anxieties that Shuttleworth mentions have no place in Webster's sonnet sequence—breastfeeding as erotic self-pleasuring, for instance—she does address the fear that mothers can love to excess, citing the necessity to measure maternal love articulated in Sarah Stickney Ellis's *The Mothers of England* (1843). Ellis critiques the "uncalculating" mother who cannot dole out her love in the right proportion: "Strange anomalies in the characters of what are called *amiable women,* have done much to convince me, that sound principle and common sense, with unquestionably a due proportion of warmheartedness are in the long-run more conducive to individual, as well as social happiness, than those ungoverned springs of tenderness and love, which burst forth and exhaust themselves, without calculation or restraint."[24] Ellis's vocabulary pertaining to love centers on a lexicon of measurement: "proportion," "governed," "calculation." For Ellis, "ungoverned springs" of love damage a child's moral character. Turning a positive trait into a negative one, Ellis criticizes the "amiable" mother. According to Ellis, a child with too much love does not learn to be grateful or generous and takes for granted the good feelings and good things granted to him. Indeed, feelings and things are of the same type for Ellis; both maternal approbation and sweetmeats can be given with harmful abandon. Ellis illustrates this idea with a quite literal example of measurement. When teaching a child to share, "the parents should actually take what is offered—not merely that tiny crumb which the tender mother breaks off, and with disproportioned thanks pretends to eat."[25] The "amiable," "uncalculating" mother is a bad one because she does not constantly make her own expressions of affection into teachable moments.

By 1881, the first known date of composition of any of the *Mother and Daughter* sonnets, some advice manuals had shifted their tone. W. H. Wigley, in *Thoughts for Mothers* (1881), declares that a mother's love is measureless and her influence unlimited. Likewise, Frances Power Cobbe asserts, "Fear, my friends, to make your children unhappy, and to love them too little. But never fear to make them too happy or to love them too much!"[26] Cobbe and Wigley both insist, as Ellis does, that the mother is responsible for the child's moral education. Wigley suggests that mothers focus their attention on their children and refuse the distraction of other pursuits. She critiques women's efforts at social and political engagement, disparaging the prominence of these pursuits: "We might fairly describe the age in which we live as 'the age of Ladies' Committees.'"[27] The author disapproves of such committees for taking mothers away from their children. Nor should mothers become overly concerned with servants, finances, or "our love of reading or music or painting."[28] Dara Rossman Regaignon and Barbara Thaden's approaches to advice manuals note a trend that implores mothers to leave less child care to nurses and servants and to give more attention to their children. Both Regaignon and Thaden read this trend as a turn away from a tendency in the middle and upper classes to leave much child care to hired help. This trend, they assert, helped to create an ideal of motherhood in which a self-sacrificing woman, queen of the domestic realm, takes charge of her children's physical, emotional, and spiritual well-being.[29] Of course, just because the advice was circulating does not mean that it was followed; nonetheless, I turn to these sources to indicate that Webster's sonnet sequence drew on prevalent anxieties about maternal feeling.

Webster agrees that what often seems imperative for women in polite society is in fact an extraneous distraction. However, in *A Housewife's Opinions,* Webster argues that making and receiving social calls interferes not only with parenting but also with the vocation of a literary artist. In this respect, protecting both literary and parental work, Webster departs from these advice manuals.[30] These books shift from mid- to late century as the fear of overbearing love gives way to an exhortation that a mother cannot love her children too much. The desire of the mother in Webster's sequence for immeasurable maternal love is largely in line with this shift, but the anxieties in *Mother and Daughter* also reflect some concerns of Sarah Stickney Ellis. As my reading of sonnet 25 above shows, the undercurrent of the meter allows for the possibility of too much love. Other sonnets, in contrast, bemoan the feeling of love being fully spent. As I go on to show, two of Webster's dramatic monologues and two of the sonnets from *Mother and Daughter* critique the idea that love can and should be infinite.

Measuring Love in Marriage

Other works in Webster's oeuvre address the relationship between marital and parental love more directly than do the sonnets. Several of her dramatic monologues also consider the question of whether there is enough love to go around. The ways in which other poems address this topic can usefully account for its near-absence in *Mother and Daughter*. Although *Mother and Daughter* does not express the related fear that maternal excess will alienate a husband, Webster took on the subject in her dramatic monologue "The Happiest Girl in the World."[31] In this monologue, a young woman contemplates her impending marriage and wonders whether she loves her fiancé well enough. She worries that her love is not feverish or "real," and wishes that she could "love him to his worth." The speaker of this monologue, in a phrase reminiscent of Swinburnian poetics and aestheticism, ardently desires to feel "that subtle pain of exquisite excess."[32] At one point in the monologue, she says she is afraid to have children, for it would reduce the love she does have for her future husband:

> And is it selfish that I cannot wish,
> That I who yet so love the clasping hand
> And innocent fond eyes of little ones,
> I cannot wish that which I sometimes read
> Is women's dearest wish hid in their love,
> To press a baby creature to my breast?
> Oh is it wrong? I would be all for him,
> Not even children coming 'twixt us two
> To call me from his service, to serve them;
> And maybe they would steal too much of love,
> For, since I cannot love him now enough,
> What would my heart be halved? Or would it grow?
> But he perhaps would love me something less,
> Finding me not so always at his side.[33]

This monologue attests to the influence of the very sorts of texts that Ellis and Wigley wrote, which the Happiest Girl claims she "sometimes read." She falls victim to the advice manuals' attempt to regulate feminine emotion in their prescriptions about how women should feel. With the weight of the emotional obligation to want a baby, and the sense that this desire should emerge out of her love for her fiancé, the speaker secretly struggles with the simultaneous requirement to give all of her love to her fiancé and, if she had a child, to give all of her love to her child. She perceives love as a quantity; it can be stolen or halved, and it can grow or lessen. Just as the mother of the sonnets does, the speaker assumes that if the objects of her love multiply, she must divide that love among them.

With its ironic title, "The Happiest Girl in the World" illustrates how women suffer in their attempts to conform their feelings to the illusions and ideals of culture at large. Recently, critics have emphasized Webster's rebuke of such expectations in her dramatic monologues. Christine Sutphin argues that Webster represents the title character of "Circe" as vocalizing an erotic desire that can never be fulfilled. At the beginning of the monologue, Circe bemoans the monotonous beauty of her island and wishes for some change, which she perceives is on the way, for a storm is brewing and she sees the speck of Odysseus's ship on the horizon. Ending before the arrival of the ship, the monologue is full of anticipation. Webster's Circe articulates a desire for a man who will recognize that she will be entirely satisfying, a recognition, the poem implies, that she thinks he will be as satisfying to her:

> Where is my love? Does someone cry for me
> Not knowing whom he calls? Does his soul cry
> For mine to grow beside it, grow in it?
> Does he beseech the gods to give him me,
> The one unknown rare woman by whose side
> No other woman thrice as beautiful
> Could once seem fair to him . . .
>
>   . . . .
> . . . whom once found
> There will be no more seeking anything?[34]

Circe will want Odysseus to be that man, but he cannot because he will inevitably continue his quest. Sutphin asserts that Webster suggests, but does not dramatize, the disappointment that Circe must eventually feel in order to emphasize how unrealistic her expectations are: "I would argue that one effect of Webster's choices is to undermine a powerful myth of heterosexual romance: that lovers are all in all to each other, that once love is found, they need nothing else. Webster's Circe wants something impossible and she does not realize its impossibility—yet."[35] The dynamic that Sutphin notices is even more complicated than this, for the monologue ends with Circe anticipating disappointment with the shipwrecked sailors, expecting her potions to turn *all* the men into pigs and thereby to reveal their true natures. She does not foresee that one man will not turn into a pig but will disappoint her nonetheless, abandoning her because even her love cannot quench his perpetual thirst for adventure.

If Webster critiques the idea that an erotic relationship or a marriage must be fully satisfying to the exclusion of all else, then she often embraces this idea, to the extent of adopting its poetic tropes and conventions, when it comes to a parent-child relationship. The sonnets are more open to an ideal, I suggest, because the mother in them is fully and painfully aware of the ideal's limits. While the desires of the Happiest Girl or of Circe clearly conflict with what they can reasonably expect, the mother in the sonnets is self-aware enough to know that what she wishes for is not always what will be. Many of the mother's desires are ideals to be celebrated but rarely and briefly achieved. The mother's desire, for instance, to relive her youth with her daughter can be satisfied only as a temporary illusion. In dramatic monologues, Webster uses dramatic irony to critique the societal expectations that shape the desires of these women. In contrast, her lyrics use a series of poems to depict change over time. She embraces a Petrarchan version of a mother-child relationship because the very changing nature of that relationship must undermine the ideal of it. While most of the sonnets in *Mother and Daughter* do idealize and yearn for a plenitude of love, one sonnet in particular offers the same type of direct, biting critique found in the dramatic monologues.

Sonnet 11, entitled "Love's Mourner," works against the very kinds of conventions that appear in the advice manuals—and that Webster argues against in her dramatic monologues—but puts these oppressive conventions in the minds of men. This sonnet claims that men fail to understand women's love for children by presuming its constancy. Men err in their idealization of a mother's and a wife's love as perfectly steady and fail to recognize that change over time can diminish a woman's feelings. The mother seems to wish that men's idealizations were right and bemoans the tragedy that they are not. The poem expresses pain at the fervor of love degrading into something less than passionate unconditional attachment:

> 'Tis men who say that through all hurt and pain
> The woman's love, wife's mother's, still will hold,
> And breathes the sweeter and will more unfold

For winds that tear it, and the sorrowful rain.
So in a thousand voices has the strain
      Of this dear patient madness been retold,
      That men call women's love. Ah! they are bold,
Naming for love that grief which *does* remain.

Love faints that looks on baseness face to face:
      Love pardons all; but by the pardonings dies,
      With a fresh wound of each pierced through the breast.
And there stand pityingly in Love's void place
      Kindness of household wont familiar-wise,
      And faith to Love—faith to our dead at rest.[36]

Obligated to confront faults and forgive, love decays into a habit that re-
sembles kindness more than passion. Here, the loyalty shown to the child
and the husband is more a product of the memory of love than of continually
renewing or constant love. In this poem, the abundance that the mother in-
sists on in sonnets 25 and 26 is represented as a man's illusion. That plenitude
is a "dear patient madness," itself the product of a canon of male poetry, the
strain of "a thousand voices." Time itself, and the exposure to faults that it
brings, whether a child's or a husband's, here seems to "appraise love and di-
vide" in spite of the mother's ardent wishes. As love changes over time, as the
ideal is bruised by "winds" and "sorrowful rain," it transforms into something
resembling grief, at its own loss perhaps, for it is only a "remembered ghost."

While "Love's Mourner" is meant to correct a misconception about women
perpetuated by men, it also draws attention to the ways in which other poems
in the sequence participate in the ideals of love perpetuated precisely by Pe-
trarchan love poetry. It undermines the poems at the end of the sequence that
defend the "strong entireness" of the mother's love.[37] Indeed, "Love's Mourner"
explains the defensiveness of sonnet 25, for it is working against not only
other mothers' criticism but also the mother's own knowledge of her struggle
to reconcile the complex nuances of her love. The sonnet sequence depicts a
struggle between the impulse to expose the painful realities of maternal love
and the impulse to elevate them. In praise of maternal love, Webster takes re-
course to the familiar Petrarchan tradition, relying on it even as she modifies
it. In her defense against the criticism of mothers of siblings in sonnet 26, she
cannot help but to cast maternal love in the conventions of male lovers:

      Of my one pearl so much more joy I gain
            As he that to his sole desire is sworn,
      Indifferent what women more were born,

And if she loved him not all love were vain,
Gains more, because of her—yea, through all pain,
All love and sorrows, were they two forlorn—
Than whoso happiest in the lands of morn
Mingles his heart amid a wifely train.[38]

The mother aims to convince others of her constancy by comparing herself to a young man who has eyes only for his beloved. Lee Behlman identifies this sonnet's tropes and dynamics as the most Petrarchan in the sequence, with its allusion to the pearl, and its emphasis on the way this love excludes all others.[39] Webster transforms men's misconceptions passed down by "a thousand voices," suggesting that a woman's love is only constant insofar as it is like a man's. Here, in contrast to "Love's Mourner," the man's love is constant, and she measures her love as a mother against it. Yet the mother-child bond here not only is likened to an erotic bond but replaces it, for the sonnet leaves no room for the child's father: "And who but we? We, darling, paired alone? / Thou has all they mother; thou art all my own." The explicit comparison of maternal to heterosexual love reminds us that the bond between the parents is absent here. In this pointed absence, the fears of the Happiest Girl are realized. As sweetly profound as the attachment to the daughter may seem, the exclusion of the husband from the mother-daughter dyad reveals that the Happiest Girl's projection of her future is not the product of the naive musings of an ingénue who has absorbed too much conventional wisdom. In this implicit replacement of the beloved by the daughter, Webster implies a realistic fear that there will not be enough love for the entire family; too much love for a child means insufficient love for a husband. Moreover, by placing this absence of the beloved of the heterosexual bond—the husband and father—within a particularly Petrarchan sonnet, Webster suggests that love itself is ultimately as limited as the sonnet form; no matter how capacious its themes, it still has only fourteen lines.

Responding to the Sonnet Tradition

In the late nineteenth century, a discourse about measuring love was circulating not only in the culture at large—as conduct manuals attest—but also within a tradition of sonnet writing that flourished in the period. Webster's sequence was published posthumously in 1895, just as the fashion for the sonnet sequence was waning at the dawn of modernism. She began to write it, however, in 1881, an important year for Victorian sonnet sequences that saw the publication of Christina Rossetti's "Monna Innominata" and a new, longer version of D. G. Rossetti's *The House of Life. Mother and Daugh-*

ter is among the last of the great Victorian sonnet sequences. Yet within the nineteenth century, there is no single sonnet tradition. While there remain disputes about whether or not there are separate male and female traditions, other critics group sonnets according to such categories as "amatory," "devotional," "meditative," and "political."[40] Scholars such as Stuart Curran and Amy Billone identify a Romantic and a women's tradition that begins with Charlotte Smith.[41] Those who write about Webster disagree about her place within these various lineages. Several argue that Webster uses her sequence to critique Petrarchan conventions. Both Laura Linker and Marianne Van Remoortel suggest that simply by virtue of transforming the lover-beloved relationship into a mother-daughter relationship, Webster undermines the gendered assumptions of amatory sonnet sequences by male poets.[42] Van Remoortel considers Webster's sonnet sequence as a successor to D. G. Rossetti's *The House of Life,* arguing that Webster critiques his (and other male poets') use of procreativity as a metaphor for artistic creativity. For Van Remoortel, Webster reclaims the literal terms of motherhood and restores the concepts of presence and unity to the sonnet sequence.[43] Melissa Valiska Gregory reads the formal discipline of the sonnet as corresponding to the moments of maternal discipline within the sonnets. Arguing that the requirements of the sonnet form make the daughter's spontaneous song into something artificial, she suggests that formal discipline does damage to their intimacy.[44] Whereas Van Remoortel and Gregory see Webster as critiquing sonnet conventions, Lee Behlman argues that her use of Petrarchism is "opportunistic and adaptive. . . . [It is] an archive of language and a set of characterological and narrative patterns she uses to reframe literary motherhood."[45] This proliferation of criticism demonstrates the number of lenses through which we can understand nineteenth-century sonnets, all of them useful, but each one to some extent excluding the view from the other. Here, I focus on a feature of the sonnet form with which Webster was especially concerned, and which coincided with the questions she uses to ask about the nature of love: its propensity to count and its evident limitation of size.

Webster's quandary with measured love has its roots in two other Victorian sequences that adapt a masculine formal tradition to a woman's voice: Barrett Browning's *Sonnets from the Portuguese* and Rossetti's "Monna Innominata." Looking at these predecessors can help to explain why Webster chose the sonnet form and how she understands the mechanisms of measuring love. The concept of love as all-fulfilling is embedded in a set of powerful conventional associations that Alison Chapman refers to as "sonnet ideology." According to Chapman, nineteenth-century sonnets elevated the amatory Petrarchan sonnet over Shakespearean sonnets and sonnets on other subjects, and prized an ideal of the completeness, unity, and purity of thought that the compact form was thought to embody.[46] Chapman discusses *Mother and Daughter* as the embodiment of the sonnet ideal of plenitude and completeness in its vision of maternal love.[47] However, I argue that Webster challenges this very element of sonnet ideology.[48] Indeed, as I will show below when I discuss Webster's accounting of time, she uses a language of debt and credit that is reminiscent of Shakespeare's sonnets. Even as Webster's sonnets express a wish to make the fullness of maternal love eternal, they are forced to acknowledge the constraints that mortality places on that love and the experience of it. While questioning amatory sonnet ideology, I agree with Behlman that Webster also uses and refigures it; by casting *Mother and Daughter* in a form associated with the erotic, she both celebrates the erotic element of maternal love and reveals its startling intensity.[49] This comparison also questions whether the love object must be singular or plural. She interrogates cultural commonplaces in which an erotic love is assumed to be singular, and in which a mother's love is idealized, paradoxically to be both infinite and repeatable, without limit for each and every sibling. Webster's examination of these commonplaces responds to accounts of counting from Christina Rossetti and Barrett Browning.

Although many critics have emphasized that Webster follows Christina Rossetti and Elizabeth Barrett Browning in adapting the sonnet form to a feminine voice, few have considered how these poets also refigured the sonnet's modes of measuring love. In chapter 1, I have shown how Rossetti's "Monna Innominata" asks how a woman ought to balance her love for a man with her love for God. Margaret Reynolds has shown how Barrett Browning's sequence struggles with the question "How much do you love me?" For Reynolds, it is a disempowering question—for women especially because a male figure often asks it—since the answer can only attribute worth to the asker and not to the respondent. Reynolds asserts that Barrett Browning takes two approaches to the question: "In the early sections of *Sonnets from the Portuguese* she plays out the old version of the measuring fairytale. She treats herself as a commodity and works out her price, her value, how much she is worth, before she allows the question, which makes her worthless, to be asked. But in the latter part of the *Sonnets* she sets up a new relation, a new version of sexual commerce, where she is an equal trader, driving a hard bargain."[50] According to Reynolds, Barrett Browning focuses on the question of measuring love in order to claim a place for a woman's voice and to establish a model of equal and reciprocal exchange in a heterosexual relationship. She reads sonnet 43, "How do I love thee?," not as quantifying love, but as a "measure of the self," focusing on "me" despite the repetition of "thee." As such it values the woman and her agency, escaping the Petrarchan "old regime."[51]

While I agree with Reynolds, I argue that Barrett Browning does more than this; she comments on an economy of feeling within the self and between selves, rather than on individual worth. It is important to note that after questioning the methods of measuring love, and the importance of exchange, Barrett Browning *reaffirms* the need to measure love. Indeed, she must gauge her own love in order to assert the very agency as a lover that Reynolds says the poem expresses. Measurement is essential because feelings, sonnet 43 suggests, are never entirely new. Within the catalog of methods of measurement in this poem—"depth, breadth, and height," "the level of everyday's / most quiet need," terms of moral value such as "freely" and "purely"—comes the benchmark of previous experience. In counting the ways, Barrett Browning enumerates the permutations of her feeling to the extent that her emotions are recycled from the past: "I love thee with the passion put to use / In my old griefs." In calling attention to her "old griefs," Barrett Browning reminds readers of the beginning of the sonnet sequence, in which she discusses those griefs and their place within a new erotic relationship. She does so in order to establish continuity for the sequence and for the life it represents. Following Barrett Browning in measuring present emotions against past ones, Webster declares that her daughter's present corresponds to the mother's past. Webster, however, modifies the idea to suggest that feelings can be shared from one person to another, across generations. Rather than recycling feelings within a single person to accommodate a new situation, when a daughter recapitulates a mother's feelings, as Webster imagines her daughter will, she compares her daughter's future to her own past.

Both Rossetti's and Barrett Browning's modes of evaluating love establish a dynamic where love repeats itself, and by doing so continues. Even for Rossetti's sequence, in which the love is unrequited, and in which the final sonnet depicts empty-handed despair, something remains to replace what is lost, even if it is only silence. (As I show in chapters 1 and 4, for Rossetti and for Alice Meynell, silence is much more than nothing.) For Barrett Browning and for Rossetti, poetic repetition renders love, whether requited or not, permanent. Mapping the idealized focus of an erotic relationship onto a parent-child relationship, Webster's *Mother and Daughter* contrasts pointedly with her female predecessors' sequences by anxiously insisting on the certainty of time passing, asserting not only that death will finally separate her from her child, but that each passing year alters their love, coloring it with the pain of loss. That the daughter's present is the mother's past is the source of melancholy anxiety. All of these sonneteers emphasize their chosen form when they focus on the repetitiveness of love, for they write in what Erik Gray calls "the most codified and imitative of all lyric traditions."[52] But whereas Barrett Browning and Rossetti are often reassured by their poetic measurements of love, despite their initial trepidation, the very prospect of measuring love unsettles Webster for it reinforces the fact that maternal love goes through stages and inevitably confronts loss. Indeed, Webster reverses the progress of Barrett Browning's sequence. In the first poem of *Sonnets from the Portuguese*, the speaker mistakes the arrival of Love for Death: "'Guess who now holds thee?' Death I said. But there / The silver answer rang . . . 'Not Death, but Love.'"[53] Thus the sequence begins and ends by replacing death with love. *Mother and Daughter*, on the other hand, confronts death's eventual replacement of living maternal love. Webster contradicts the assumptions that erotic love is the most likely context for a unique love of only one other and that maternal love should naturally accommodate plural objects. By making the husband and father an innocuous and negligible presence in the sequence, and by rebuking the mother of many siblings, Webster strenuously decries competition for love. Yet whereas Rossetti and Barrett Browning ultimately resolve the problem of competition, Webster never does.

By writing a sonnet sequence about maternal love, Webster questions an amatory sonnet ideology that claims that sonnets present an ideal of plenitude and completeness of feeling. Even as Webster's sonnets wish to make the fullness of maternal love eternal, they are forced to acknowledge their formal limits and the constraints that mortality places on that love and the experience of it. Webster challenges the transcendence that previous sonneteers idealize. She writes about motherhood in a sonnet sequence in order to represent a generically familiar longing for permanence while at the same time troubling the convention that a sonnet renders eternal a single moment. By casting *Mother and Daughter* in a form associated with the erotic, Webster reveals the startling intensity of maternal love, and questions expectations of lovers and parents.

Sonnets about maternal love are not without precedent. Chapman argues that Christina Rossetti's sonnet to her mother displays the reciprocity, longevity, and fullness of maternal love as superior to the unrequited model of Petrarchan erotic love.

> Sonnets are full of love, and this my tome
>   Has many sonnets: so here now shall be
>   One sonnet more, a love sonnet, from me
> To her whose heart is my heart's quiet home,
>   To my first Love, my Mother, on whose knee
> I learnt love-lore that is not troublesome;
>   Whose service is my special dignity,

And she my lodestar while I go and come.
And so because you love me, and because
   I love you, Mother, I have woven a wreath
Of rhymes wherewith to crown your honoured name:
   In you not fourscore years can dim the flame
Of love, whose blessed glow transcends the laws
   Of time and change and mortal life and death.[54]

In honoring her mother, Rossetti stresses not only that this love is more dignified and less troublesome than erotic love, but that it is uniquely and reliably unchanging. I argue that whereas in her sonnet to her mother, Rossetti casts their love for each other as limitless, Webster investigates the dissonance between that ideal and inevitable restrictions. What seems here to be Rossetti's confidence in the permanence and transcendence of the mother-child bond might also be read as the ardent wish of a daughter, like the daughter's idealization of her mother's voice in *Mother and Daughter.* Chapman also notes that Dante Gabriel Rossetti dedicated to his mother the opening sonnet of *The House of Life,* where he declares that a sonnet is a "moment's monument." He enclosed an illustrated manuscript of this sonnet in a copy of David Main's *Treasury of English Sonnets* given to his mother for her eightieth birthday. The Rossettis' sonnets dedicated to their mothers contrast pointedly; whereas Christina's emphasizes transcendence, Dante Gabriel's stresses the melancholy of loss. Webster incorporates influences from both into her sequence, expanding on the ideals of a loving daughter and the melancholy fears those ideals are meant to deny.

As I will discuss in the following section, Webster elaborates on the comparison between maternal and erotic love that Christina Rossetti's sonnet to her mother invites, considering maternal love *as* a form of erotic love. I want to dwell first, however, on the importance of measurement to the sonnet form's depiction of eros. Even in the sonnet to her mother, where Rossetti declares love to be beyond the materiality of time, she cannot escape the impulse toward measurement. She emphasizes her mother as her first love and calls attention to the natural human lifespan of fourscore years. The former is a signifier of the love's importance and the latter a barrier that the love must transcend. "Time and change and mortal life and death" cannot dim love's glow, but the poem still relies on the yardstick of time to express the quality of love. Even if love transcends time, it must be measured against it. Even here, the urge to quantify is inseparable from the desire to convey the importance of a love. Rossetti tries to sidestep this logic by using the depersonalized word "glow," which might belong to her, her mother, or to no one, an unembodied light disconnected from the lifespan of Rossetti's mother. Rossetti's attempts to defy the measurement of love have the opposite effect, only retrenching the inevitability of it. Indeed, the dynamic of presence and absence endemic to sonnets can often imply the measurement of time, as in the first sonnet of Rossetti's "Monna Innominata": "for it is over then. / And long it is before you come again."[55] Lovers and beloveds are only too keenly aware of inevitable moments of departure; the insistence on permanence of erotic love in so many sonnets is really just the corollary to current or future absences. Because a mother cannot participate in these fantasies of an infinitely static relationship with her daughter, Webster must find her own strategies for anticipating absence.

Maternal Voice

Similarly with Rossetti's reflection on the recorded voice in *Time Flies*, *Mother and Daughter* asserts that the very attempt to capture the human voice—in this instance, in a sonnet—must always fail, rendering the poetic distinct in its repeatability and permanence (a poem, in contrast with a human voice, lasts as long as the paper on which it is printed, and lends itself to endless repetition, silently and out loud, by various readers). Webster uses this paradox to underscore the mother's fears that her own voice's deterioration with age will ultimately reduce its emotional power with her daughter. In contrast, the daughter idealizes her mother's voice as an instrument of intimacy between them:

> My darling scarce thinks music sweet save mine:
>   'Tis that she does but love me more than hear.
>   She'll not believe my voice to stranger ear
> Is merely measure to the note and line;
> "Not so," she says; "Thou hast a secret thine:
>   The others' singing's only rich, or clear,
>   But something in thy tones brings music near;
> As though thy song could search me and divine."[56]

For the daughter, the nearness she hears in the music of the mother's voice is her own feeling of closeness to her mother. The closeness and the difference are enacted in the poetic structure, which position the two quatrains as two parts of a dialogue between mother and daughter. According to the mother, the daughter's love clouds her ability to hear, and she cannot judge her mother's voice with the objectivity of the "stranger ear." Hearing love, rather than the voice itself, the daughter confounds the mother with her song in her claim that it could "search me and divine." Only the mother herself can seek and accurately guess what is in the daughter's heart, but the daughter's use of these verbs suggests that for her, her mother's voice and her person are inseparable. While the daughter notes the qualities of her mother's singing, the mother herself notes the quantities; for her it is "merely measure to the note and line." Webster's use of the word "measure" here reminds reader that its musical definition coincides with is mathematical one; a measure of music exists as a standard unit and is defined by its length. The voice's very measurability points to its ordinariness and detracts from its supposed divinity. The mother also measures the ultimate duration of her voice when she anticipates the deterioration the coming years will bring to it.

In the sestet, the mother responds to her daughter's idealization of her voice with her own knowledge of its mortality. She breaks from the dialogue of the octave to apostrophize her own voice:

> Oh voice of mine that in some day not far
>   Time, the strong creditor, will call his debt,
> Will dull—and even to her—will rasp and mar,
>   Sing Time asleep because of her regret,
> Be twice thy life the thing her fancies are,
>   Thou echo to the self she knows not yet.[57]

Although Webster writes in the Petrarchan form, her themes here are very Shakespearean. The fear of time's effects on an older lover and young beloved recall the "young man" sonnets. In sonnet 2, particularly, the speaker implores the young man to procreate so that he may be able to say "'This fair child of mine / Shall sum my count.'"[58] Yet while for Shakespeare the existence of a child or a poem is an effective replacement—it "sums" the "count"—for Webster, that substitution entails loss. The child's experience will "echo" the mother's, and she will lose the confidence she has in her mother's perfection. By using the voice to figure poetry, rather than the page, Webster insists that it can represent but not compensate for the inevitable losses that come with time.

In Webster's sonnet, time, figured as a creditor, makes the human voice subject to an accounting. The logic of the poem works like an equation: for the daughter, the mother's voice equals the mother's love; for the mother, her voice equals death. In this calculation, then, love, like the voice, is represented as a limited resource that, measured or not, will eventually run out. The daughter's illusion about her mother's voice cannot last, and she must notice it "rasp and mar." The mother begs her voice in vain to reverse Time's effects, but in its performance of a poetic and metrical voice, it is itself an instrument of Time. The meter in this sonnet obeys the iambic pentameter almost to the syllable. Only when she addresses her complaint to her own voice does the meter's regularity waver. Line 10 follows a trochaic substitution with a spondee and a pyrrhic: "TIME, the STRONG CREDitor, will CALL his DEBT." In the final line, the mother confirms the daughter's sense that her voice can "divine," for she casts it as an "echo to the self she knows not yet," the sound that the daughter's mature voice will resemble. The voice does know the daughter both intimately and objectively, in a way the daughter cannot yet understand. Here, Webster's distinction between human voice and poetic voice aligns with Rossetti's in chapter 1. The human voice is the sound made by an individual body, and is subject to that body's wear and tear. The poetic voice exists in the multiple possibilities within the forms of the poem that might suggest, but do not produce, sound. In this way the mother can use a poetic voice to address her human one.[59]

Although Webster distinguishes the poetic voice from the human voice, she suggests that both types of voice indicate emotional attachment and can be measured. In her view the poetic voice engenders the feelings of an imagined other within the reader, establishing a reader's sense of identification. The poetic voice can be repeated in multiple readings, and thus its emotional potential lies in this possibility for identification for multiple readers; the poetic voice's repeatability is what makes it permanent. In contrast, the human voice, as the daughter's love for her mother's voice attests in the sonnets, brings out love for the specific person whose voice, and voice in that moment, to the hearer, is inimitable. Because inimitable, it is also limited and must eventually end.[60] Webster insists on the distinction in her essay "Poets and Personal Pronouns," which instructs readers not to read the poetic "I" as the voice of the poet herself: "As a rule 'I' does not mean I."[61] Careful to point out that characters in poetry are not like those in novels because they are not as "sharply definite," Webster asserts that even when situated in a particular epoch, readers require that poetic personas be suitable to "always and everywhere, no matter under what disguise of date and story."[62] Webster presents poetry as the genre of empathy, for its readers should be made to feel that the feelings expressed could be their own:

> We look to the poet for feelings, thoughts, actions if need be, represented in a way which shall affect us as the manifest expression of what our very selves must have felt and thought and done if we had been those he puts before us and in their cases. He must make us feel this not only of what we ourselves, being ourselves, could come to think and do in like circumstances, but of what no circumstances could possibly call out in us. . . . Not many have it in us to be Iagos, but we feel sure that, if we were to be an Iago, we should be *that* Iago.[63]

Whereas fiction allows for and might even encourage objectivity, poetry invites identification. Webster implies that the identification that comes from reading can move beyond individual boundaries, so that even if someone were never a mother or a woman, he might feel that he would be *that* mother represented in the sonnets. This is not to suggest that all mothers must feel alike, but that the poetry must be so persuasive as to engender its feelings in the reader. This approach to poetic voice is an inherently instructive one, meant to enlarge a reader's range of emotional possibilities, especially for women, for it suggests that although this voice does not necessarily represent *me,* it might represent *you.* This rationale may explain why the sonnets may be *for* the daughter but are not often addressed *to* the daughter. Even when the mother identifies with the daughter, she does not address her.

An address to the daughter would have had two poetic effects that Webster wanted to avoid. One reading of such an address would situate the daughter as a silent listener in the manner of dramatic monologues. The evocation of the dramatic monologue, for which Webster was well known, would have undercut the meditation on presence and absence that the lyric voice affords. An apostrophe to the daughter would have put special emphasis on her absence and on the need to make her present in poetry. At the same time, by apostrophizing entities of herself, in an address to "the voice" or to "my music," Webster can draw attention to the mother's ever-impending absence and to the melancholy of this knowledge even when she depicts moments full of presence and youth.

Indeed, the sequence opens with a shifting address to "the voice" that emphasizes the sadness of time's passage. While Webster distinguishes the mother's voice in poem 13 as the product of human vocal cords, she represents the poetic voice as a spring bird in the poem that opens the sequence:

> Young laughters, and my music! Aye till now
>   The voice can reach no blending minors near;
>   'Tis the bird's trill because the spring is here
> And spring means trilling on a blossomy bough;
> 'Tis the spring joy that has no why or how,
>   But sees the sun and hopes not nor can fear—
>   Spring is so sweet and spring seems all the year.
> Dear voice, the first-come birds but trill as thou.
>
> Oh music of my heart, be thus for long:
> Too soon the spring bird learns the later song;
>   Too soon a sadder sweetness slays content;
> Too soon! There comes new light on onward day,

> There comes new perfume o'er a rosier way:
>   Comes not again the young spring joy that went.[64]

Although the poem begins with an exclamation drawing attention to the sounds that the mother and daughter make, the voice is quickly depersonalized and referred to as "the voice" rather than "my voice." As "the bird's trill," the voice is a poetic convention, but it is also the voice of an illusion of the eternal present, of a joy that "hopes not nor can fear."[65] Identified with the "dear voice" of the daughter, the bird's trill represents the daughter's unawareness of what the future holds. The daughter's frame of mind is the mother's impossible ideal, for she wishes in vain that the "music of my heart" may remain longer than the song of the "spring bird," which changes too soon with the season.

This poem establishes a structure that many poems in the sequence adhere to: the octave presents an ideal of the present moment followed by a sestet that reminds both mother and reader of the disappointment of the future, confirming that the present passes. More than the death or transformation of feeling, elsewhere the mother fears death itself. The most stark of these—one that Theodore Watts particularly appreciated—contemplates the inevitable death of the mother and in doing so anticipates the death of the daughter.[66] While the mother's demise seems "Death's natural hest," "To know she too is Death's seems misbelief / . . . / . . . Life is Death begun: / But Death and her! That's strangeness passing grief."[67]

Because the mother experiences the passage of time in a way that the daughter cannot yet, the daughter's impulse to measure the quality of the voice conflicts with the mother's impulse to account for the quantity. By extension, they use different standards to understand their lives and their love for each other. This conflict is not just between the two but within the mother's discourse throughout the sequence, for while the mother wants to preserve the present and focus on the quality of the voice, she cannot help but think in terms of quantity, measuring the years. The nature of the genre of the sonnet sequence reflects this divergence; it records the quality of a moment and attempts to preserve it, suggesting narrative in its sequentiality.

Measuring Time

In *Mother and Daughter,* Webster struggles to reckon with time as an agent of perpetual change at the same time as it functions as a repetitive force, and whether the way love happens in time is sequential or cyclical. I turn now to Webster's "English Rispetti" in order to consider how Webster used poetry to measure time, but also as a point of contrast. Whereas the sonnets suggest that the primary effects of time are aging, separation, and loss, the rispetti are much more optimistic about the effects of time. They group poems into seasons to suggest a cyclical passage of time, but at the same time, they conclude with a lonely "Winter" rather than with the renewal of spring. Webster subtitles the "English Rispetti" as "Marjory," perhaps to alert readers that the poetic voice cannot be identified with the author, but also perhaps to unify the lyrics within a persona, even one only defined by a name. Marjory expresses the same wish as the mother in the sonnets does, for she wants time to stop and to preserve the moment: "And I would keep the blossoms and the song, / And I would have it spring the whole year long."[68] The sequence of rispetti presents a narrative of affective attachment and loss: Marjory falls in love and marries, has a child, and then loses her daughter to marriage and her husband to death. Rigg argues that these poems compare natural time to human time in order to use the renewal of natural cycles as a way to express the infinitude of human love. Even as they convey this, however, these poems represent the way love changes over time, and particularly the way in which the love of a child affects the love of a married couple.[69]

The rispetto that depicts early love, "The Heart That Lacks Room," recalls both "The Happiest Girl" and *Mother and Daughter* in its concern for measuring love. Here, Marjory is the opposite of the Happiest Girl, for she fears that she loves too much, and that her heart will break because it cannot accommodate the intensity of feeling.[70] At the same time, this fear relates an awareness that her love will change:

> I love him, and I love him, and I love:
> Oh heart, my love goes welling o'er the brim.
> He makes my light more than the sun above,
> And what am I save what I am to him?
> All will, all hope, I have, to him belong;
> Oh heart, thou art too small for love so strong:
> Oh heart, grow large, grow deeper for his sake
> Oh, love him better, heart, or thou wilt break![71]

The first line displays the excess of feeling in its repetition. This excess is disordering as well, for it keeps the meter of the first line from being regular. It could be scanned in a number of ways, emphasizing only the word "love" (and thus with a dearth of stresses), or alternating the stress in different patterns between "I" and "love" and "him." The meter becomes more regular after this line, as if to say that if the verse can accommodate this repetition, even if it misses a few beats, surely her figurative heart will have the capacity for her expanding love. Indeed, this love becomes essential to her sense of self, not only here—"And what am I save what I am to him?"—but later in the series where she declares their identities to be mutually dependent: "To think if we had passed each other by; / And he not he apart, and I not I!"[72]

In "Baby Eyes," the infant is an extension of Marjory's love for her husband, since she will recapitulate his looks and his facial features. Indeed, this is the index whereby she measures the baby's love:

> Blue baby eyes, they are so sweetest sweet,
>   And yet they have not learned love's dear replies;
> They beg not smiles, nor call for me, nor greet,
>   But clear, unshrinking, note me with surprise.
> But, eyes that have your father's curve of lid,
> You'll learn the look that he keeps somewhere hid:
>   You'll smile, grave baby eyes, and I shall see
>   The look your father keeps only for me.[73]

In the tone of its opening line, this poem replicates the "treacle" that Leighton finds in many nineteenth-century women's poems on motherhood—it is difficult to say "sweetest sweet" without adopting a babyish tone.[74] But the poem immediately departs from "treacle" by emphasizing what the baby cannot do, and that the relationship cannot yet be reciprocal. The baby will embody the father both because she resembles him and because she will imitate him. The baby will learn "love's dear replies" from her father, since she will use his facial expressions for intimacy.

In the later stages of the narrative, the child continues to correspond to a phase within the relationship of the married couple. The "Autumn" and "Winter" sections of "English Rispetti" each contain a pair of poems entitled "We Two." In "Autumn," these poems are about growing older together. One emphasizes the union of the parents, which remains even after the children develop their own independent lives:

> We two, we two! the children's smiles are dear—
>   Thank God how dear the bonny children's smiles!—
> But 'tis we two among our own ones here,
>   We two along life's way through all the whiles.[75]

By contrast, in "Winter," the "We Two" poems are about widowhood and the continuation of love after the death of the beloved. Here, they are directly preceded by "The Daughter," in which Marjory presents her daughter with her wedding veil and marriage advice: "Thou hast Love's rose, and tend it without fail."[76] The loneliness that the poems express originates in the absence of both the daughter and the husband, and her address to her daughter is tinged with bitterness: "Fly forth and mate: and 'tis long life alone." The "We Two" poems form a pair, one feeling bereft, missing the "blossom-time and song" of the earlier part of the sequence, and reflecting on the strangeness "To think we two have nothing now to share." The second one responds with hope: "Surely he feels my being yet; and I, / I have no thought but seems some part of his."[77] This hope for some mutual feeling of understanding beyond death marks Webster's love poems about marriage apart from the sonnets about maternal love. To wish to see the daughter in the afterlife would be to wish, even at some distant point in time, for the daughter's death, which is unimaginable. Webster's own love poems on marriage, following Barrett Browning's, wish for unification in the afterlife and in doing so cast the love as permanent.

Any sense of permanence in *Mother and Daughter* lies in the repetition between the older and the younger generation's experiences. While time creates distance between the mother and daughter, it can also establish intimacy in the way they repeat each other across generations, so that the present mother echoes the future daughter's "self she knows not yet." The kind of time that allows this nostalgia is rhythmic and repetitive rather than sequential. In sonnet 17, the mother displays the intimate knowledge that her daughter senses in the previous poem:

> And how could I grow old while she's so young?
>> Methinks her heart sets time for mine to beat,
>> We are so near; her new thoughts, incomplete,
> Find their shaped wording happen on my tongue;
> Like bloom on last year's winterings newly spring
>> My youth upflowers with hers, and must repeat
>> Old joyaunces in me nigh obsolete.
> Could I grow older while my child's so young?[78]

Just as the mother's present echoes the daughter's future, the present daughter's youth recalls the mother's past. This poem uses its own "mere measure" of the mother's song to represent rhythmic responsiveness between mother and daughter. While some poems fear the measurement of time, this one embraces it, aiming to cast it in a positive light by saying that the daughter brings back the mother's youth. This gauge of time is not of its passing but of its rhythms. When "her heart sets time for mine to beat," counting rhythms is hardly a process of fear, or a division of love, but rather the very means of bringing mother and daughter closer together. The figurative rhythm of the heartbeats is as essential to their mutual understanding as are words.[79] Moreover, when the daughter's "heart sets time for mine to beat," this counting of rhythms counteracts the process of aging that the mother gauges throughout the sequence.

Van Remoortel contends that in the latter part of the sequence the mother rejects the "convoluted and hackneyed" language of Petrarchism, in favor of wordless communication. Citing the line about heartbeats, she avers that the mother "generat[es] a mother-tongue that is more about closeness and rhythm, about wordless understanding and unisonous heart-beats, than about signification and difference. . . . Only the pulsation of the iambic pentameters remains, like the beating of the heart mentioned in the text."[80] However, in sonnet 17, as in sonnet 25 discussed above, the meter does not communicate the same message that the words do. Webster reminds us that just as the human voice and the poetic voice are not the same thing, poetic meter and the rhythms of the heart are not the same either. The iambic pentameters of this poem *do not* consistently pulse like a heart; rather, right after the mention of the heart, they are weighed down with extra stress: "We ARE so NEAR; her NEW THOUGHTS, INcomPLETE, / FIND their SHAPED WORDing ON my TONGUE." The spondaic and trochaic substitutions in these two lines do not allow the reader to experience the lines themselves as regular as a heartbeat. While the mother and daughter's "wordless communication" may be in their heartbeats, the wordless communication of the poet's meter suggests weight, gravity, slowing down. Moreover, the idealization of maintaining youthful vigor with the merger of heartbeats only lasts a short while, for the following sonnet describes how "in the heyday of our prime," "suddenly we note a touch of time, / A little fleck that scarcely seems to mar; / And we know then that some time since youth went." Deliberately measuring the poem's meter can both briefly halt and dramatize what Webster describes as "the slow advance of time."

The daughter's development brings about the mother's fears about how her own feelings change over time. Webster also figures these fears rhythmically. While the poems at the end of the sequence vehemently resist measuring maternal love, earlier poems express fear of the changes in the love between mother and daughter, marking them in meter and song. In sonnet 8, the mother notes how the passage of time changes feelings about developmental stages:

> And yet, methinks, sad mothers who for years,
>   Watching the child pass forth that was their boast,
> Have counted all the footsteps by new fears
> Till even lost fears seem hopes whereof they're reft
> And of all mother's good love sole is left—
>   Is their Love, Love, or some remembered ghost?[81]

The poem laments the danger that accompanies new progress; fear limits the hope and pride that constitute the joy of maternal love. By the time that fear can resolve into hope, the moment for hope is past, and the mother is bereft of it. This poem speaks to the dangers of measuring love, not for the child, but for the mother. A pun on "footsteps" reveals that she counts her emotions in poetry as well as in the delicate balance of learning to walk. The meter in this poem is much surer than in "You think you love each as much as one." The iambic rhythm dominates; occasional substitutions are used for emphasis or to stir meaningful ambiguity, as in the last line where a reader might stress "their LOVE" or "THEIR Love," the latter suggesting that while the mother's love remains, the child's does not. The mother's love, praised with such certainty at the end of the sequence, here is reduced to "some remembered ghost," a vestige of the past like the fears that become hopes, both of which are feelings to be mourned as they outlast their relevance. Because a mother's love is constantly changing, from pride to protectiveness and worry, to hope, she must count each developmental change, but as she does so the quality of her love is perpetually transformed.

The "English Rispetti" do little to cloud the expectation of sentimentality in the sonnet sequence's reception. Indeed, as W. M. Rossetti's introduction suggests, the contemporary reception of this sequence does not indicate an awareness of its nuance or of its dark foreboding. In his review of *Mother and Daughter* in the *Athenaeum,* Watts focuses on the sonnets that are most idealistic, paying no attention to sonnets that challenge and undermine these ideals. The softer side of the sequence appeals to Watts, who uses his review as an occasion to praise maternal love as a subject for poetry, as much as to praise Webster's sonnets:

> For here, when once the sweet womanly vanities of the mother
> have become merged in maternal joy and pride, the charm of entire
> companionship—which no father can fully feel—seems to shed
> a marvelous kind of glow over all the pageantry of life. There is no
> phase of sexual love, nor even, perhaps of paternal love, that is so
> satisfying in its beauty as this . . . the spectacle of a loving mother
> surrounded by the daughters whose adoration of her grows with
> every advancing year. Never has the sacred bond between mother
> and daughter been more beautifully depicted than in the sonnet
> sequence before us.[82]

Watts misses the point in numerous ways, not only in conjuring an image of plural daughters when the sequence goes on at length about the daughter as an only child, but in what he neglects to notice about the sequence's focus on development *as* separation. This review says as much if not more about the state of ideas about motherhood in 1895—it remained the fulfillment of womanhood, generally thought to be aesthetically and emotionally satisfying rather than complex and trying—than it does about Webster's lyrics.

Webster's sequence brings together cultural anxieties about measuring maternal love with short lyric forms' paradoxical resistance to measuring time, even as they count their beats in meter. In doing so, she represents a more nuanced and complete view of maternal love than had previously been seen in women's poetry. In these sonnets, maternal love resembles erotic love in its intensity. At the same time, the sonnets cannot idealize a perpetual union, because to do so would both stunt the daughter's growth and imagine her death. The sonnets waver on the question of the constancy of maternal love, for while they assert that maternal love is both intensely consuming and limited, some sonnets acknowledge that family life can devolve from passion to habitual kindness. Webster casts this particular mother's love as different from that of many other mothers because she is not obligated to "appraise love and divide" and thereby budget her love among siblings. Yet Webster does exactly that in the meter of her poems, recognizing that love cannot escape measurement. The metrical feet of the poem as well as the "approaching sound of pit-pat feet" must mark the passage of time and its effects on a mother and daughter's love.

3

The Strain of Sympathy

A. MARY F. ROBINSON, *THE NEW ARCADIA,* AND VERNON LEE

In her third volume of poetry, *The New Arcadia and Other Poems* (1884), A. Mary F. Robinson aimed to test how poetry might ethically bind its readers. Writing about rural poverty, she strove to compel readers to feel the same outrage she felt at the conditions she witnessed. To do so meant stretching the formal bonds of verse, writing in meters meant to strain the ears of her readers. The poetic strains in which she wrote embodied the conflict she felt between the aesthetically appealing qualities of lyric poetry and the dire needs she observed in the poor. Robinson wrote the following lines in *The New Arcadia* in an effort to reconcile a conflict she perceived between her poetic vocation and her compulsion to help people in poverty:

> Others shall learn and shudder, and sorrow, and know.
> What shame is in the world they will not see.
> They cover it up with leaves, they make a show
> Of Maypole garlands over, but there shall be
> A wind to scatter their gauds, and a wind to blow
> And purify the hidden dreaded thing
> Festering underneath; and so I sing.[1]

In this collection of poems on a series of characters living in rural England (many of them abandoned by the exodus to the cities), Robinson sought not only to raise awareness about rural poverty caused by the grave agricultural depression that took root in the 1870s, but also to create sympathy both for its subjects and between poet and reader. The pleas in *The New Arcadia* for a sympathetic response to suffering questioned the ethics of aesthetic experience, intentionally straining readers' ears and minds beyond well-known sentimental—and indeed profoundly moving—poetic pleas for help, such as Elizabeth Barrett Browning's "The Cry of the Children" (1844), which protested child labor in the factories and mines, or Thomas Hood's "The

Song of the Shirt" (1843), which sought to heighten awareness of the plight of seamstresses.

The lines cited above from *The New Arcadia* rang sour to the ears of critics who had praised lines like these from her first volume of poetry, *A Handful of Honeysuckle:*

> A man passed playing a quaint sweet lyre,
> His strange face young though his hair was grey,
>   And his blue eyes gleamed with a wasting fire
> As he sang the songs of an ancient land,
> Sad singing no hearer could half understand.
>   Can this have been Thou, O Apollo?[2]

In its fascination with the seductive power of music, synesthesia, classical tropes, and mythic figures, Robinson's first volume of poetry seemed to conform to an ideal of aesthetic poetry pleasing to critics. Early reviews of Robinson's work helped to establish her reputation as an aesthetic poet, praising her mastery of form: "Miss Robinson has a considerable mastery of verse, she has style. . . . Her collection is infinitely superior to most handfuls of lyrical honeysuckles."[3] E. C. Stedman, the American arbiter of poetic trends, refers to her as "the young songstress who of all seemed to be most hopefully and gallantly regarded by her fellow poets and the surest among new aspirants to fulfill the predictions made for her."[4] The very journals, then, such as the *Athenaeum,* the *Saturday Review,* and the *Spectator,* which had praised the form and style of *A Handful of Honeysuckle,* dismissed *The New Arcadia* as unmusical, with strained rhythms and repellent subject matter. They failed to see, however, that having become famous for mellifluous lyricism, Robinson cultivated jarring, discordant prosodic and lyric techniques in her third volume in order to jolt her readers out of their complacency and to stimulate sympathy for the sufferings of rural poverty.

I turn to the term "sympathy" in this chapter in order to distinguish the poetic possibilities that Robinson sought from the relational dynamics created by Rossetti, Webster, and Meynell. In my use of the term, "sympathy" can be defined as "pity or compassion," which Rachel Ablow has aligned with a standard concept of the term in studies of the Victorian period.[5] This definition highlights sympathy as a one-sided relationship. As Robinson was acutely aware, the middle-class sympathizer can try to understand what a poor person feels, but the attempt to feel it herself will always fail, and the object of sympathy will not respond with mutual concern. Readers might feel a sense of intimacy with the position of the poet, however, in observing poverty with horror. Robinson hoped that this kind of relation between poet and reader would create an ethical bond in the reader akin to the ethical impulse that Robinson herself felt.

However one-sided the sympathetic dynamic might be in addressing poverty, Robinson dedicated *The New Arcadia* to her intimate friend Vernon Lee (Violet Paget), the art critic, essayist, and fiction writer, in order to demonstrate that these ideas about sympathy emerged from a genuinely intimate dynamic. Writing in response to their personal conversations, Robinson dedicated her collection of poems on poverty to Lee after Lee had dedicated "A Dialogue on Poetic Morality"—a work equally concerned with the ethical responsibilities of aesthetics—to her several years before. In this remarkable essay, collected in *Belcaro* (1881), Lee theorized how the acts of producing and consuming art could themselves be moral by creating pleasures that approached the feeling of sympathy. In their intellectual and affectionate exchange, Robinson and Lee considered how art could generate sympathetic compassion and understanding in the reader. Robinson strove to put her own version of these theories into practice in *The New Arcadia*. By dedicating their works to one another, Robinson and Lee made their private intimate relationship part of the public lives of their works. Their relationship fits within the idea of intimacy that I have described so far in this book; they engaged in a mutual exchange of ideas but never identified with one another. Indeed, their vigorous debate about how the aesthetic could be ethical both recognized differences and, as I will argue, admitted of influence and change but never a wholesale transformation of ideas.

Not only did Robinson and Lee forge their intimacy around questions of ethical aesthetics, but their social world was engaged in these issues as well. Although Robinson and Lee were not deeply involved in philanthropy in the early 1880s, nor were they allied with radical causes, they were seriously engaged with the artistic ambitions of aestheticism, whose leading lights formed part of their social circle, and whose indulgences—which were routinely satirized in journals such as *Punch*—they questioned in *Belcaro* and *The New Arcadia*. Robinson had come of age in her family's London salon, which had been graced by such well-known aesthetes as Walter Pater, Oscar Wilde, and John Addington Symonds, as well as women poets recognized and admired in their day, such as Amy Levy, Mathilde Blind, and Augusta Webster.[6] In 1881, when Robinson commanded considerable respect as a rising star among younger poets, she introduced Lee to these distinguished friends and acquaintances.

At the time, the figures associated with aestheticism diverged in their attitudes to social and ethical questions. Recent criticism has identified multiple strands of aestheticism, characterizing it as an influential cultural trend that insisted on the central value of art and beauty, both to the exclusion of all else, as in the phrase "art for art's sake," and as a means of democratization through popular culture.[7] Similarly, aestheticism has also emerged as a development that expressed—sometimes in politically contentious ways—dissident sexualities.[8] A further political position within aestheticism, one identified largely with the teachings of John Ruskin and William Morris, held that those living in slums could benefit from exposure to art and beauty, which would not only rescue them from the ugliness of their own lives but enliven their moral sensibilities. Ian Fletcher, though he hardly took this side of the movement seriously, styled it "missionary aestheticism"; more recently, Diana Maltz has examined the breadth of aesthetes' uneven—and at times condescending—campaigns to "bring beauty to the people."[9]

These politicized accounts of aestheticism certainly contrast with the most familiar theoretical aspect of the movement associated with Walter Pater, who insisted in both the preface and conclusion to *Studies in the History of the Renaissance* (1873) that beauty is and should remain morally neutral, and that aesthetic pleasure neither emerges from nor inspires moral concerns. He writes, "The theory or idea or system which requires of us the sacrifice of any part of this [aesthetic] experience, in consideration of some interest into which we cannot enter, or some abstract theory we have not identified with ourselves, or of what is only conventional, has no real claim upon us."[10] Not surprisingly, Pater's concern for characterizing aesthetic experience and his insistence that impressions remain isolated in the mind that has them earned his school of thought a reputation for solipsism. Although critics such as Jonathan Freedman and Linda Dowling have argued for the political liberalism and inherent democratization implicit in a Paterian position more broadly, Pater had deliberately little to say about how art might address poverty.[11]

Maltz has disclosed how the tensions between Ruskin's politically committed and Pater's morally neutral positions affected Oscar Wilde, who encountered both men at Oxford in the mid-1870s. The antagonism between the two becomes evident in *The Woman's World,* the progressive journal that Wilde edited from 1887 to 1889, which published the work of many up-and-coming female aesthetes. On one hand, the journal expressed skepticism about aesthetic philanthropy, fearing that it might naively attempt, as Maltz quotes Wilde, "to solve the problem of poverty . . . by amusing the poor."[12] On the other hand, Maltz shows that articles endorsing aesthetic philanthropy risked paternalistically trying to manage the inner experience of the urban poor, or adopting an attitude of voyeurism toward those one would purport to help.[13]

None of these alternatives satisfied Robinson, who was powerfully conscious of the suffering of those less fortunate than she, felt compelled to help, and worried that her aesthetic ambition was irrelevant to this compulsion. As she wrote to her mentor John Addington Symonds, this desire to help the needy conflicted with the complacency that both religion and art presented:

> The religion in which I have been brought up no longer helps me
> and I must renounce what I have no more faith in; but I feel hurt
> unhappy even wicked at renouncing. . . . My soul often feels very
> lonely especially since I have lost the personal god on whom I utterly
> relied. . . . I only want to be good and some use in the world. . . . I
> think I am growing more thoughtful for others. At least I know I of-
> ten feel the love of the whole unhappy world and a passionate long-
> ing to help it that burns like a fire in me like a real physical fever. But
> it is so easy to feel unselfish. I often feel passionately unselfish but I
> live a life that is narrow, selfish, self-centered so that I hate myself.[14]

This passage shows that her religious crisis (she was raised Anglican) was also an aesthetic one, for she felt writing poetry to be an element of that selfish life that obstructed her altruistic impulse.

A year after she sent this letter to Symonds, Robinson turned to Vernon Lee as her lonely soul's companion. As they wrote together and responded to each other's work, the passionate relationship between Robinson and Lee became a crucible for their bold attempt to establish an ethical aesthetics. In a letter, Lee tried to convince her intimate friend that by writing her poetry she was "of some use in the world," and challenged her to continue to write beautiful poetry despite their skepticism about both Paterian and Ruskinian perspectives on art's relation to social inequality: "You have woken up from false aestheticism, you have recognized the opposite danger of wasting your artistic gifts from ardour to be practically useful; then why do you not calmly take up your position and make up your mind to do your utmost in the line for which you are appointed."[15]

Jointly, Lee and Robinson aimed to establish an alternative to the sort of aestheticism that was often accused of solipsism. Here, I argue that Robinson's *The New Arcadia* offers another way for art to confront poverty, one in which those who want to help must try to understand the perspective of the other, and to acknowledge the importance of the attempt despite the impossibility of fully doing so. Robinson wrote *The New Arcadia* not only to expose the difficulty of rural poverty but also to question how poetry might engender that sympathy in a way that avoids the paternalistic, controlling attitudes that, as Maltz observes, underwrote much aesthetic philanthropy.

Moral Cravings: *Belcaro*'s Ethical Aesthetic

Robinson met Lee in 1880 and spent the fall of that year in Florence at "Casa Paget," and for the next eight years both of them were close intellectual and emotional companions. Thereafter, Lee spent summers with Robinson in London, and Robinson spent part of the year in Florence. They developed ideas together, reading and critiquing each other's work, sharing not only artistic pleasures but also, as Lee wrote in a letter, the greater "pleasures of affection." Lee even suggested in a letter in 1881 that had she been a man she would have asked Robinson to marry her.[16] When, in 1888, Robinson decided to wed the Frenchman James Darmesteter, and effectively broke off their companionship, Lee was heartbroken and suffered a breakdown. At this point, Robinson moved to Paris and concentrated on writing prose rather than poetry. Both writers seemed to have lost, for a time, a muse of intellectual and artistic inspiration.[17]

Before I analyze a number of poems from *The New Arcadia*, I wish to investigate the ways in which Robinson's exploration of poetic sympathy emerged out of her own sympathetic process with Vernon Lee. Lee, as I have mentioned, wrote Robinson's fantasies and anxieties about poetic sympathy into the final essay of *Belcaro*, "A Dialogue on Poetic Morality." But Lee also argued *against* what she saw as Robinson's overconcern for practical moral good, in the process critiquing aestheticism's overly materialistic approach as well. Although a number of recent studies have addressed Lee's writings on aesthetic experience and sympathy, or empathy—the term she developed in the 1910s from the German psychological research of Theodor Lipps and Karl Groos—no one has yet considered the degree to which A. Mary F. Robinson left a lasting influence on Lee's investment in both relational theories and practice of aesthetic philanthropy.

In writing about their relationship, both Robinson and Lee create a public idea of their intimacy in order to shape the way that readers respond to their works. By describing their own responsiveness, including ways in which they disagree and come to agree, and by suggesting that one writer's words might end up in another writer's work, they invite readers to respond to them similarly, to absorb their ideas and perhaps make them their own. In her brief memoir of her writing process with Lee, "In Casa Paget," Robinson presents herself as subject to Lee's influence. She idealizes the atmosphere of intensity but also of cozy warmth in which they shared ideas:

> From early dawn to dewy eve, we appeared to exist merely in order
> to communicate to each other our ideas about things in general. . . .

We were always writing in corners, Violet and I. She at a carved table on large vellum-like sheets; I huddled in a shawl on the chimney step, my inkpot neighboring the firedogs, a blotting-pad upon my knee. I cannot say we wrote in solemn silence. Impressions, forecasts, reminiscences, quotations from Michelet or Matarazzo, subjects for ballads, problems for essays, aesthetical debates and moral discussions would burst forth, in the midst of our occupations, from the couch in the corner, from the writing table, or (much more rarely) from the warm seclusion of the chimney step.[18]

Lee's presence here is expansive, her writing spread out on the table, and she proclaims aloud her most startling insights. Robinson, on the other hand, withdraws into her chimney stoop, absorbing Lee's proclamations, only rarely speaking from her place of "warm seclusion." Although Robinson characterizes herself as absorbing Lee's wisdom, Robinson's letters to Symonds demonstrate that their conversations originated as much with Robinson's concerns as with Lee's, if not more so. Within the roles that Robinson defines, their words mingle. Robinson implies that their spoken words find their way to the page just as often as what they write might be read aloud. In this atmosphere, they write as individuals, but always in response to one another. The intimacy of this exchange of ideas requires receptiveness to others. As I will show in my reading of *The New Arcadia,* Robinson sought to cultivate this kind of intimacy with her readers, even if she knew that only a one-directional sympathy was possible with the impoverished subjects she wrote about.

Just as Robinson's brief memoir invites readers into her intimacy with Lee, the introduction to Vernon Lee's *Belcaro* invites the reader to put herself in the position of Mary Robinson. Its opening paragraph is written as though it is a manuscript sent to her, creating an impression of the published version that what the readers encounter is not really for their eyes:

A little while ago I told you that I wished this collection of studies to be more especially yours: so now I send it you, a bundle of proofs and of MS., to know whether you will have it. I wish I could give you what I have written in the same complete way that a painter would give you one of his sketches; that a singer, singing for you alone, might give you his voice and his art; for a dedication is but a drop of ink on a large white sheet, and conveys but a sorry notion of property. Now, this book is intended to be really yours; yours in the sense that, were it impossible for more than one copy of it to exist, that one copy I should certainly give to you. Because these studies represent the ideas I have so far been able to work out for

myself about art, considered not historically, but in its double rela-
tion to the artist and the world for whom he works; ideas which it
is my highest ambition should influence those young enough and
powerful enough to act upon them; and this being the case, my
first thought is to place them before you: it is, you see, a matter of
conversion, and the nearest, most difficult, most desired convert,
is yourself.[19]

By proclaiming her wish for the work to exist as a unique unit, Lee calls at-
tention to the fact that it is not. Lee seems to acknowledge grudgingly that
the book must be printed in multiple copies in order to emphasize that what-
ever its cultural forces, art acts on individuals. In acknowledging Robinson as
her "most desired" convert, she reveals that she desires many more converts
as well. The dedication allows her to make her own work evidence of her
relational theory of art, to make public the private relations that helped to
form the ideas that appear here. As she proclaims her topic to be the "double
relation" of art, she declares that this very book and its author have double
relations, to one particular person and to the public. This introduction posi-
tions the reader as an outside observer of the relationship, via the book, of
Lee and Robinson, but it also offers readers the opportunity to participate in
a network of relations around art. A "converted" reader, and especially one
who might develop her ideas and go on to influence others, can put herself
in Robinson's position and can congratulate herself on being "young enough
and powerful enough" to do so. Readers of this book are in the dual position
of being influenced and observing the influence between Robinson and Lee.
In a letter to Robinson, Lee explains, "I like to think of you when I write;
sometimes in a way to write at you, things which perhaps I shall never ask you
to read. It is merely the pleasure of the imaginary company."[20] Pulled into the
dialogue by the address of the dedicatory introduction, the readers too can
enjoy the "pleasure of the imaginary company" as they read.

Lee writes the introduction as though it were a note appended to a manu-
script so that the book might still feel "alive." Once ideas are written and
printed, they are "removed out of all this living frame-work . . . [and] made
quite lifeless and inorganic."[21] These ideas emerged in conversation, while
composing, and Lee writes that she attempted to maintain this atmosphere:
"I have always felt that some one else was by my side to whom I was show-
ing, explaining, answering. . . . It is the constantly felt dualism of myself and
my companion."[22] Even as it specifies a particular companion, this sentence
invites readers to participate as "companions" of the book, bringing it to life
in their own responses. Lee explains that the title of *Belcaro* comes from the

name of a castle near Siena that Lee and Robinson visited together. Lee writes that during the composition of this book she was haunted, in the way one might be by a melody, by the memory of the day they spent together there. Not only does the dedication explain the title of the book, but it also argues that one person's ideas cannot always be so easily dissociated from another's. She writes that the "fragments" she presents in these essays always came from being in relation to something or someone else, with works of art or in conversations with friends. Although Lee says that the title does not describe the contents of the book, Belcaro becomes a figure for the place of intellectual conversation and the exchange of ideas, as well as a place whose beauty enriches the pleasure of those conversations. For Lee, beauty facilitates dialogue, and the sense of togetherness in conversation enriches their aesthetic appreciation of the landscape.

The role of the aesthetic, however, is precisely the point of contention in "A Dialogue on Poetic Morality." In it, Cyril (who roughly corresponds with Robinson) declares that he has burned his poems and intends to write no more because poetry cannot accomplish any moral good. As he sees it, poetry no longer has a political impact, no longer reaches "poor overworked souls" who could find relief in it, but merely contributes to the surfeit of aestheticist sensuality. Baldwin (who is in many respects Lee's persona) replies to Cyril's dilemma by asserting that right living demands the elimination of evil and the creation of good. In his view, while activists, doctors, and philanthropists remove pain, only the artist can create the good on a large scale, because the artist produces pleasure for more people than are in her immediate surroundings. Cyril responds by saying that it is not worthwhile to bring pleasure to an aesthetic audience he fears will be hopelessly effete. As I will show, in her poetic solution to this problem, Robinson entreats her audience not to take poetic pleasure for granted; indeed she withholds it from them in order to make her point. Whereas Lee's essay seeks to define morality in relation to art, Robinson is less concerned with such a definition and more concerned with ethical practice: how, in both creating and consuming art, one's thoughts and actions are moral.

Given that Belcaro emerged out of Lee's private conversations with Robinson, it is fitting that the last essay in the book should be in the form of a Platonic dialogue. Lee's use of the dialogue form allows readers to see the process of intellectual intimacy in action, as the speakers modify their ideas in response to each other. Dialogue also enables Lee to air more extreme views than would be acceptable in the standard essay form, and permits those extremes to play out to their logical conclusions. The exchange of ideas between two voices opens space for skeptical ironic reading, so that the reader can occupy a third position that synthesizes the competing ideas in various ways. Dialogue therefore foregrounds the processes through which intimacy arises, by making differences and similarities apparent, and by exploring where divergence of opinion can be overcome and where it remains. Lee can at once be extremely critical of aestheticism, criticize Robinson's critique of it, and laud the principle of art for art's sake that stands at the center of it. Cyril complains,

> "The artist may be nobly and generously employed, and yet, by some fatal contradiction, the men and women who receive his gifts are merely selfishly gratified. He might not, perhaps, be better employed than in giving pleasure, but they might surely be better employed than in merely receiving it; and thus the selfishness of the enjoyment of the gift seems to diminish the moral value of giving it." . . .
>
> [Baldwin responds,] "So, your sense of the necessity of doing good is so keen that you actually feel wretched at the notion of your neighbours being simply happy, and no more, for an hour. Why, my dear Cyril, if you condemn humanity to uninterrupted struggle with evil, you create evil instead of destroying it." . . .
>
> "I can't make it out. You seem to be in the right, Baldwin, and yet I still seem to be justified in sticking to my ideas," said Cyril. . . . "You have always preached to me that the highest aim of the artist is the perfection of his own work. . . . But then an hour later, I have met the same idea—the eternal phrase of art for art's own sake—in the mouths and the books of men I completely despised."[23]

This passage clearly signals Lee and Robinson's shared fashioning of an aestheticism based not on individual experience but on response and exchange.

For Cyril, the worst aspect of aestheticism is that it has transformed, in a negative, socially irresponsible way, the audience for poetry. He claims that poets used to write for those readers who had "struggle and misery" and genuinely needed the repose of poetry. Now his audience is made up of "a lot of intellectual Sybarites, shutting themselves out, with their abominable artistic religion, from all crude real life; they [the poems] would be merely so much more hothouse scents or exotic music (*con sordino*) to make them snooze their lives away."[24] From his perspective, the problem with the aestheticist audience is that in their obsession for material things and the sensuous gratifications they bring, they become closed off to the world. In order to fulfill their vocation more responsibly, he contends, poets must create a new kind of audience for poetry, one that renounces soporific perfumed prettiness.

In response to Cyril's concern about his audience's reception of his poetry,

Baldwin raises the equally important question of how poets influence their audiences, by telling him that the poet can awaken current readers from their slumber and enliven them to moral questions. Readers benefit, he argues, from the poet's greater sensitivity, from which readers learn to weigh ethical questions. Baldwin argues that poets are particularly significant in the present age, when numerous influences vie for readers' attention. Whereas Cyril borders on characterizing the age as degenerate, claiming it lacks politically compelling causes, Baldwin sees the pluralism of the age as positioning its people on a precipice between degeneration and aesthetic salvation.

> "It was not the development of the natural sciences, but rather of the historic and ethnographic which upset people's ideas; it was the discovery of how our institutions, moral and social (hitherto regarded as come straight from heaven), had formed themselves, and how they were subject to variation. . . . The utterly confusing effect of our modern literary eclecticism, our comprehension and sympathy with so many and hostile states of civilization, our jumbling together of antique and mediaeval, of barbarous and over-ripe and effete civilizations, our intellectual and moral absorption of incompatible past stages of thought and feeling, with the follies and vices inherent in each;—sum up all this and you will see that, with our science and our culture, our self-swamping with other folk's ideas, we are infinitely less morally steady than the good sceptics of the days of Voltaire."[25]

At first, Baldwin understands the overwhelming eclecticism of the age—with its seemingly incoherent diversity of specialized forms of knowledge—as presenting a unique opportunity to the poet. While Baldwin appreciates the way in which the proliferation of ideas has inspired doubts about the rightness of established ideas, he also sees this proliferation as leading to dangerous uncertainty, and it is against such uncertainty that poetry can serve as an antidote. Baldwin explains why it might seem to Cyril that there are no noble causes left to write about: the age is simply too confused to identify them. Baldwin points out the dangers of modern "literary eclecticism" but at the same time seems to celebrate it. In the idealized version of this characterization, no longer do thinkers and writers struggle in the stranglehold of convention. An understanding of other peoples and periods has shed new light on Western traditions and allowed modern Western people to see the folly of some of their institutions.

Yet the more Baldwin talks in this vein, the less tolerant he appears. Sharing ideas gives way to a destabilizing "self-swamping with other folks' ideas."

His account of "modern" times degenerates as it develops. At first the new approaches of history and ethnography lead to a greater, and more illuminating, understanding of the variation between cultures. As the account continues, doubt becomes "utterly confusing," sympathy is misplaced with "hostile," "barbarous," and "over-ripe" civilizations, and study leads to the "absorption" of the vices of the other. In the effort to convince Cyril that theirs is an appropriate climate for the work of the morally concerned poet, he seems more and more attached to convention. In trying to show how the poet can rescue readers from moral confusion, if not degradation, Baldwin seems to slip off his own precipice back in to the presumably more morally stable mid-century that he—and implicitly Vernon Lee—criticize.[26] Such nostalgia testifies to the difficulty of finding a middle ground where debates around aesthetics were so highly polarized.

Lee attempts to work her way out of these contradictions by theorizing a kind of pleasure that removes itself from a sexual taint. Lee's complex position relating morality to art, which emerged during her involvement with Robinson, is linked to an idealized contradictory sexlessness that Kathy Psomiades sees in Lee's novel *Miss Brown,* which came out in 1884, the same year as *The New Arcadia.* In the novel's explanation of its protagonist Anne Brown's status as one of a group of women born "not to have been women . . . women without women's instincts, sexless," Lee insists also on her altruism, one "whose field is the whole of the world in which there is injustice, callousness, and evil . . . made not for man but for humankind."[27] For Lee, sexlessness created space for selflessness. Moreover, sexlessness puts authors in the position to think and do primarily for others. This standpoint is important in an era when, as Seth Koven notes, the form of philanthropy in which the well-to-do occupied slums for a time also allowed them to explore alternative sexualities.[28] In a way, Lee's thinking is the reverse of the models Koven discusses—an alternative sexuality, or more specifically a sexual "style" as Psomiades calls it, which strives to create room for a fresh mode of philanthropic thought and action. Purified of the encumbrance of traditional heterosexual relationships, the sexless artist might direct her energies to other people. Lee's critical perspective on pleasure, and her concomitant insistence on "purity," forms part of what Kathy Psomiades refers to as Lee's lesbian aesthetics.[29] Although Anne Brown was by no means modeled on Mary Robinson, the selflessness of a "woman without woman's instincts" was a trait that Robinson clearly sought out, as is evident in her letter to Symonds and in *The New Arcadia.* Though it is impossible to say which woman's ideas influenced the other, it is clear that ideals of selflessness and sympathy, and the aesthetic embodiment of these ideals, emerged in the crucible of their relationship.[30]

By casting herself and Robinson as aestheticist male characters in the "Dialogue on Poetic Morality," Lee reappropriated a version of masculinity, one that prized productivity and virility, for female aestheticism. In a milieu where men at times wove fantasies around forms of exotic, perverse, or vengeful femininity in order to unsettle cultural norms, Lee reclaimed the "energy and strength" that the male aesthetes had supposedly forfeited for her own masculine versions of women. That "masculine" strength included challenges to one another's ideas and attempts to influence one another that were a part of their intellectual sympathetic process. This couching of the feminine in masculine terms further complicates Psomiades's argument that Lee connected aesthetic experience to desire between women, both being part of her "purity polemic."[31] The ideal of productivity that Lee claims for women helps to define the purity that she simultaneously claims for aesthetic experience and for relations between women. The very process of conversion links "masculine" productivity, desire between women, and aesthetic experience into a complicated, even contradictory, ideal. By transposing her female companionship with Robinson into a dialogue between men, Lee was able to denounce in her characters' voices what she saw as the "effeminate, selfish, sensual mysticism"[32] of the male aesthetes, but also to mock men who dismissed women's poetry. Baldwin is forced to acknowledge that "there are such multitudes of poetesses that Nature may sometimes blunder in their production, and make one of them of the stuff intended for a poet."[33]

Baldwin's, and Lee's, contradictions are useful in establishing a renegade gender politics, one that legitimizes both Lee and Robinson as writers, circumventing the ideological traps of the woman poet. Yet Baldwin's tendency to take his arguments to their logical conclusion risks reiterating the problems with ethical aesthetics. On the one hand, Lee values the formal qualities of artworks for the simple pleasures they bring and condemns morally focused readings of artworks for getting in the way of this pleasure; yet on the other hand, in the figure of Baldwin, she moralizes against "sensuous stimulation." She wants to liberate art and the relations around it and at the same time seeks to impose ethical conventions on those relations that are just as strict as the ones she inveighs. The contradictions in Baldwin's discourse therefore speak to the problems in Lee's claim that art can indeed have moral value without moral meaning. Although Lee insists in earlier essays in *Belcaro* that consumers of art should appreciate works for their pure beauty, Baldwin exists in the dialogue as one logical extreme of that view, one that necessarily falls back into Victorian conventions of morality. Christa Zorn notes that in "A Dialogue on Poetic Morality," Lee seems to hold literature to a higher moral standard than visual art when she claims that because poetry is a "lifelong struggle for purity," the poet must have a sense of right and wrong.[34] This moral sensibility is to the poet what colors and sound are to the artist and the composer. Baldwin concludes the essay by saying, "I do not think that the poet's object is to moralize mankind; but ... the poet is the artist, remember, who deliberately chooses as material for his art the feelings and actions of man; he is the artist who plays his melodies, not on catgut strings or metal stops, but upon human passions; and whose playing touches not a mere mechanism of fibres and membranes like the ear but the human soul, which in its turn feels and acts."[35] It is these feelings and actions that Robinson attempts to influence with *The New Arcadia*.

"Others Shall Sorrow": *The New Arcadia*

Whereas Lee wanted to establish a "pure" aestheticism, Robinson circumvented Lee's contradiction by creating an aesthetic experience that questioned pleasure, suggesting that social conscience is more necessary to ethical aesthetics than Lee allows. Robinson did not share all of Cyril's prejudices nor did she accept all of Baldwin's (or Lee's) somewhat contradictory advice in her response. She was not entirely converted by *Belcaro,* but like *Belcaro, The New Arcadia* was an effort at conversion. By questioning whether poverty eclipses even the possibility of aesthetic pleasure, these poems respond to Lee's claim that the poet must create good. They respond, as Cyril does in the "Dialogue," to Lee's assertion that aesthetic pleasure is democratic, available to all, by suggesting—contra Lee—that it is in fact the case that the poor do not have the time and energy for the aesthetic. Resisting Lee's ideal of conversion, Robinson acknowledged a difference between the sort of intimacy she had with Lee as a fellow writer and companion and the sympathy she felt for the impoverished subjects she writes about. Whereas her feelings for Lee were reciprocal, her sympathy for her subjects was not, and they feel nothing for her; she can acknowledge the pain of their poverty, but she cannot feel it herself. Her sympathy for them offers no mutuality; for the poet, it marks a clear—and indeed painful—division between subject and object.

Such anxieties about the nature of sympathy have a literary history that goes at least as far back as the eighteenth century, when, in what is sometimes called the "Age of Sensibility," both poets and novelists, such as Thomas Gray, Charlotte Smith, Frances Burney, and Laurence Sterne, came to view fellow feeling as a requisite virtue. At the same time, these authors, among others, questioned whether sympathy for those less fortunate was more for the benefit of the sympathizer or her object. Patricia Meyer Spacks has written that for the poets of this age, "the notion of sympathy registered the unease of a culture wishing and not wishing to confront its own inequities, but also the discomfort of individuals both preoccupied with their own feelings and possessed of a sense of obligation to look outside themselves."[36] By the end of the Age of Sensibility, certain writers, namely Frances Burney and Laurence Sterne, approached the topic satirically, mocking characters who pride themselves on their own perceived compassion, however ineffectual it might be. In contrast, some nineteenth-century works emphasized sympathy's tangible material benefits, even while acknowledging its dangers. For instance, in George Eliot's *Daniel Deronda,* Daniel's sympathy morally benefits Gwendolen, but, as Leona Toker has shown, her very hunger for his sympathy threatens to drown out Daniel's own beliefs and interests in their exchanges: "When the listener takes over some of the speaker's burden of pain, part of the listener's own personality shrinks."[37] Hoping that readers would take on a "burden of pain" that might lead to political action, some women poets of the period, such as Amy Levy and Augusta Webster, believed that they might further their early feminist agenda by generating sympathy for female characters in dramatic monologues.[38]

While Robinson inherited many of these hopes and anxieties, her work differs from her predecessors' by casting the problem of sympathy as an aesthetic one. She tries to reconcile her contradictory impulses at once to question the possibility of poetic sympathy for poverty, to validate its political significance, and to do so in her use of the genre. While disconnected from those she writes about by class, she is connected to them by shared feelings of helplessness, which she is able to dramatize in her use of lyric form. *The New Arcadia* includes a set of ten poems, many of which are narratives about characters who would be good candidates for dramatic monologues: street performers, vagrants, a poor spinster thought to be a "witch," a fallen woman, a "village idiot," the desperately murderous. Instead, all but one are in the voices of observers who try to imagine the experiences of those whose stories they tell, but at the same time recount the experience of witnessing horror. The sympathy these poems attempt to elicit is for the observers' guilt, frustration, helplessness, and sadness as witnesses as much as it is for the poor themselves.

Much recent critical theory has taught us that the gaze ensures that the observer comes to possess the observed and to control the object in the act of observation. The gaze on the poor in *The New Arcadia* models a complex and different structure of power that incorporates the fantasy of mutual understanding and aid with an anxiety about that fantasy's impossibility. Robinson makes it clear that she is powerless to do anything to alleviate the suffering of her subjects and powerless to understand their pain fully. In her lyrics, the gaze is defined by her lack of control, her helplessness. Her poems juxtapose the pleasure and plenitude of art with the pain of deprivation. While wholly acknowledging the privileged class position of her poetry, Robinson disavows the power of the figure of the poet, claiming that words are "weak as water," in order to bring the polarities of poetry and poverty closer together.

The opening stanza of the "Prologue" to *The New Arcadia* emphasizes the invisibility and helplessness of the poor. Robinson calls attention to the Victorians' awareness that it is the migration from rural areas to the cities that has led to poverty, overcrowding, and squalid conditions, leaving rural life intact. While these poems are meant to correct that misconception, they address willful ignorance more broadly. The repeated negations create a sense of the void that characterizes the experience of poverty but also the world's experience of social deprivation. This stanza links the lack of agency that its passive voice suggests to a lack of knowledge, not only on the part of the well-off, but of the poor themselves as well:

> Not only in great cities dwells great crime;
> Not where they clash ashore, and break and moan,
> Are waters deadliest; and not in rhyme,
> Nor ever in words, the deepest heart is shown.
> But, lost in silence, fearful things are known
> To lonely souls, dumb passions, shoreless seas,
> And he who fights with Death may shrink from these.[39]

The verb "known" here has no subject; it is unclear who knows. The use of the preposition "to" that follows "known," instead of "by," creates the impression that the lonely souls' knowledge of their own "fearful things" is indirect and unconscious. Their "dumb passions" are inarticulable; the emotions cannot even speak to the consciousness within the soul. Lost in "shoreless seas," these lonely souls are unable to reach out for help, they have nothing to grab hold of, and their sorrows engulf them. The suffering of those in rural poverty may be, as Lee's Cyril says, "unsingable"—not because it does not merit song but because it is impossible to comprehend fully and is therefore lost in silence. By saying that it is impossible for words or rhyme to show "the deepest heart," the poet challenges herself to do just that while proclaiming the failure of her chosen genre.

The "Prologue" thus attempts to legitimize writing poetry as a response to poverty but not without expressing doubts about the endeavor. The formal twinning of "rhyme" and "crime" indicts poetry, accusing it of neglecting or even obscuring those in need. Moreover, the allusiveness of the "Prologue" declares a need for a new type of poetry to address what has been silent and ignored. The second line calls to mind two canonical Victorian seaside poems from the previous generation: Tennyson's "Break, break, break" and Arnold's

"Dover Beach," in which "ignorant armies clash by night." Both of these poems, to some extent, address the inability to put thoughts into words—insofar as the only means of expression lies in echoing the melancholic sound of the sea. These lines are the first and only reference to sound in the "Pro-logue." By referring to these poems' absorption in elegiac rhythms of the tide, Robinson declares that their well-known metaphor is inadequate to her task of representing misery and loneliness. Moreover, in refusing to provide any reassuring echo to evoke the plight of the landlocked rural poor, her prosody conspicuously thwarts lyricism. Indeed, the use of pentameter and enjamb-ment makes the "Prologue" feel like blank verse, or even like prose, though it is in stanzaic form with a constant rhyme scheme.

While the poem's formal structures push against their own status as po-etry, these striking lines—even if suspicious of poetic rhetoric—continue to signify poetically. The poem calls upon other senses to represent emotion and, by extension, the form of sympathy that preoccupied Robinson's imagi-nation. In the place of sound, it offers the sensation of weight, another way of conceiving of the stresses of poetry, a felt sense that is an alternative to sound. The poet's sorrow becomes tactile in her effort to communicate the pain of her observations:

> And I have heard long since, and I have seen,
> Wrong that has sunk like iron into my soul,
> That has eaten into my heart, has burned me and been
> A pang and pity past my own control,
> And I have wept to think what such things mean
> And I have said I will not weep alone,
> Others shall sorrow and know as I have known.[40]

As Robinson acknowledges the pain of those in poverty, she experiences a frustrating helplessness, and yet she remains determined that others should feel what she feels. Noticeably, the poet transforms what she witnesses into her own sensory perception. What is heard becomes a visceral effect in her own figurative body, and therefore in the body of the poem. With its irregular anapests and dactyls and its shifts between falling and rising meter, especially in the second, third, and last lines, the iron weight of the wrong is dramatized in the stresses of the poem, and extra syllables that burden the line. These ef-forts to make the verse carry such heavy weight respond to the enduring fear that the poem expresses: that poems are only "The froth of the world a song, as water weak."

Symonds was unconvinced by these efforts, writing that although he con-sidered *The New Arcadia* a stunning work, he doubted whether her "anapestic lines in the iambic stanzas" were "always successful." "They seem to me," he added, "sometimes to have driven the iambic rhythm so far away, that *it* becomes intrusive on our ear."[41] That Symonds would make this criticism demonstrates that the poem's strenuous prosodic attempts to announce itself as poetry also constitute the poem's resistance to its own form—in other words, its refusal to be a metrically conventional work.[42]

But the "Prologue" does something more than to suggest that the genre of poetry remains inadequate to its representation of human suffering. It also stands as a dialogue with itself, declaring at one moment that words are weak, incapable of showing the "deepest heart," but at another holding English pastoral accountable for its deceit, for willfully eschewing responsibility to represent rural life honestly.[43] Nature appears as the perennial topic of poetry, but one that offers no consolation: "Alas! Not all the greenness of the leaves, / Not all their delicate tremble in the air, / Can pluck one stab from a fierce heart that grieves." In this view, an appreciation of beauty, aesthetic or natural, is ineffectual in the face of material deprivation. Robinson indicts the pastoral in particular when she writes: "You see the shepherd and his flocks a-field, / Hunger and passion are present there, no less." Thus Robinson sets out to reconceive what she sees as the genre that misleadingly idealizes Arcady. In the passage I cite at the opening of this chapter, the wind is a material force meant to sweep away the pastoral show of Maypole garlands. The force of the wind signifies poetic force: by writing a candid account of the rural poor, the poet asserts that she can at least attempt to wipe away the shame of their condition. If people are poor, the "Prologue" asserts, at least they should have the right to their dignity: "I know that you will help, you will let them be / Foreseeing, noble, wise, and even as ye." By restoring dignity to her subjects, the poet also erases her own shame at her inability to help them in what she regards as more substantial ways.

The poet instructs her readers not to enjoy the poem, lest we miss the point. Robinson seems afraid that her own reputation as an author of sweet, delicate, refined verses might get in the way of her message:

> For I do not sing to enchant you or beguile;
> I sing to make you think enchantment vile,
> I sing to wring your hearts and make you know
> What shame there is in the world, what wrongs what woe.[44]

Here she disavows a particular kind of aesthetic pleasure that comes from obscuring realities in order to indulge in fantasies. Poetry that enchants and beguiles weaves an illusion, a fantasy within which the reader can escape; it provides the pleasure of being deceived. Whereas enchantment is a sort of enjoyment that leaves a reader isolated in his own fantasies, the "Prologue" implies that the readers of *The New Arcadia* will receive the benefit of sympathy and its melancholy pleasures. This disavowal of enchantment also implicitly rejects erotic pleasure, and thereby embraces the "sexless" aesthetic that Lee promotes in *Miss Brown*. The poet's rejection of aesthetic seduction clears the way for ethical outrage; she is explicit in her hope to "purify" rather than eroticize both her subjects and her readers' minds.

Robinson's use of form illustrates her uncertainty about what the effects of poetry in the world really are. Just as Lee's manipulation of the dialogue form makes a single work into a conversation, Robinson aims to establish not only a conversation with her readers but also a conversation within her poems. *The New Arcadia* explores the uncomfortable juxtaposition of primarily middle- and upper-class pleasures in the arts, especially poetry, with their knowledge of those who are afforded no such pleasures. Its message must be in verse in order to elicit the jarring reality that art and abject poverty exist in the same world. As it declares to "sing," the "Prologue" announces a new sort of discordant lyricism, one that deploys modern, jarring rhythms to correspond to the modern realities—class consciousness, moral uncertainty— that Vernon Lee refers to in her "Dialogue on Poetic Morality."

As we have seen, *The New Arcadia*'s meters are often deliberately strained so that its rhythmic effects embody both the difficulty of witnessing another's pain, and the anxiety that poetry cannot console. Familiar with the audience for her previous volumes of poetry, Robinson confronts an audience whose expectations of poetry "A Dialogue on Poetic Morality" parodies. *The New Arcadia* attempts to create out of these readers the audience that Cyril complains does not exist. Robinson chastises her audience for their blindness to the poor, but at the same time focuses on herself and on her speakers as a model audience. They exhibit a range of responses from horror to self-blame. In the process of modeling responses, Robinson hopes to generate a socially conscious sympathy, both for the poor and for the witnesses of the poor. Lee's "Dialogue" therefore emerges in these poems in the questions about the ethics of reading and writing poetry. Robinson responds to Baldwin's plea to Cyril that he is made for writing poetry by writing poetry about the very ambivalence that Cyril expresses. *The New Arcadia* renders the conflict between the practical and the poetic impulses in its discordant lyricism, inviting readers to feel the strain of sympathy.

While both Lee and Robinson sought a middle ground between an overly moralistic approach to art and effete aestheticism, they engaged the task differently. Whereas Lee essentially put a moral spin on the same old aestheticist premise about the supreme value of beauty, Robinson addressed the potential conflict between aesthetics and ethics. But it would be a mistake to see this volume as a work of social criticism.[45] Despite its clear project of making readers aware of poverty, the collection does not seek an understanding of the problem's origins and potential solutions, nor does it call readers to action. Rather, the poet certainly asks for sympathy for her subjects, but even more fervently she asks for empathy for herself as their witness.

A sampling of the characters in the collection demonstrates the significance for Robinson of isolation as one of the primary hardships of poverty. As we will see, the girl in "The Scapegoat" is orphaned by the death of her father and abandoned in a hovel by her brothers. As a result she has no recourse but to become a "fallen woman." The couple in "Man and Wife" become so destitute that they have no choice but to go to the workhouse—that place of Dickensian urban misery—where they cannot even take comfort in each other's presence, since they must be confined to separate dormitories. That loneliness echoes what the poet herself claims to feel upon witnessing these injustices. Especially in poems like "The Hand Bell Ringers," discussed below, Robinson demonstrates her awareness that she sees her subjects through the filter of poetic convention. In this way, these characters mirror the poet's feelings much more so than she mirrors theirs.

First-person voices, some of them dramatic, appear periodically throughout *The New Arcadia*. Earlier, I referred to the "I" of the "Prologue" as "the poet" because while it is in the voice of a writer explaining the work we are about to read, it is not simply Robinson herself either. By comparison, "The Hand Bell Ringers" facilitates the transition between the poet-as-observer and the neighbor-as-observer in the poems that follow. The speaker of that poem, like the one of the "Prologue," studies her less fortunate subjects; but at the same time, she lives in proximity to them and studies her own feelings about them. With the exception of "Man and Wife," a dramatic monologue in the voice of a wife who must go to the workhouse with her husband, all of the following poems have an observing "I."

Commenting on these poems in later years, Robinson declared that she observed her subjects not only as a poet but also as a community member. Robinson proclaimed that "Tim Black, the Scapegoat, and most of the personages of the New Arcadia, lived on a common in Surrey near my garden gates: all of them are drawn from human models."[46] Even as she describes the nearness of these people to herself, there is a material dividing line between them that distinguishes their space and their class: While they all lived on a common, she remained behind her own garden gates. While they inhabited public space, she observed at a distance (the possessive of "my garden gates" indicates the privacy of personal property and its seclusion). This alternation between separateness and nearness is clear in *The New Arcadia*. The community observers in the poems are clearly not Robinson herself. The speaker of "Cottar's Girl" is a doctor who discovers that parents have murdered their own daughter in order to hide the shame of her illegitimate pregnancy. Robinson uses the "I" to such an extent that some poems are as much dramatic monologues about the poetic experience of observing crime as they are narratives of the tragedy of poverty. By writing an observer's dramatic monologue, she brings the ambiguities and complexities of sympathy for the abject other into the spotlight.

The poem that follows the "Prologue," "The Hand-Bell Ringers," offers a more subtle instruction on how to read the poems in this collection. It uses the figure of a window at night to superimpose images of a warm, comfortable drawing room onto Christmas carolers singing in a cold, barren landscape. The poem develops a scene of domestic light, from the fire and the lamps reflected onto and through indoor plants, especially a red geranium and cactus-crimson, with the "waste of endless black" outside. The ringers' faces are "dim and brown," becoming visible only as the room's light reflects from their bells and illuminates them. As with the specific characters of the poems to follow, they require the poet's light in order to become distinct, even human: "Till slowly the figure, barely guessed, / Grows human; the face grows clear."[47] Looking out the window, the speaker sees her own image reflected onto what she sees outside:

> My ribbon breast-knot dances across
>   The leader's solemn brow,
> The moon-globed lamps burn low in the moss,
> And my own pale face, as it seems, they toss,
>   With the ringing hand-bells now.[48]

While the speaker has her window in which to see her reflection, the ringers control another reflective surface with their bells. The "leader's brow" also becomes a screen onto which the speaker's chest is superimposed. They are reflected onto each other, but mismatched in height, their faces unable to come together. The speaker's face is broken into fragments and tossed about in the dark unfamiliar landscape outside. This figure recalls the "pang and pity past my own control" from the "Prologue." By giving her feelings over to another, by feeling for another, she loses control of herself. In the process of looking at the other, the self fragments into many moving, altering versions.

If the "Prologue" was not clear enough on this point, then the final lines of "The Hand-Bell Ringers" inform readers that the poet is well aware that these poems are as much about her distance and isolation from those with whom she would sympathize as they are about the poor themselves. Although she knows she looks on the outside world, she says, "Yet I see no less in the window-glass, / The room within, than the trees and grass, / And men I would study without."[49] She cannot look at them without seeing her own world. And it is this self-reflexivity, and the poet's fear of her own potential narcissism, that makes this volume so original as a body of poems that, if not overtly political, remains highly politicized.[50]

Whereas "The Hand-Bell Ringers" addresses how an observer's own view of herself obstructs her view of others, "The Scapegoat" goes so far as to assign blame to that obstruction. "The Scapegoat" tells the story of a young girl who is orphaned by her father and then abandoned by her brothers to live alone in a hovel. Since the misery of loneliness (a theme in these poems perhaps even more so than poverty) is worse even than the violence of her brothers, she would rather "feel her cold fingers kept warm in a sheltering hand, / Than crouch in the desolate house." As a result, she falls into prostitution. The speaker watches her, wondering who is to blame for the girl's downfall:

> Yet, now, when I watch her pass with a heavy reel,
>   Shouting her villainous song,
> Is it only pity or shame, do you think, that I feel
>   For the infinite sorrow and wrong?
>
> With a sick, strange wonder I ask, Who shall answer the sin,
>   Thou, lover, brothers of thine?
> Or he who left standing thy hovel to perish in?
>   Or I, who gave no sign?[51]

The speaker interrogates her own feelings about the girl. In asking whether she feels only pity or shame, she opens the way for more complex feelings without naming them. Perhaps even in her pity she disdains the girl, or perhaps she has a lurid fascination with her. Her wonder is "sick" and "strange" not only because she wonders about her own guilt in not giving a "sign," but because her thoughts turn away from a pure interest in the girl and towards herself. Whereas the first two thirds of the poem attempt to empathize with the girl, imagining the desperation she must have felt, these last two stanzas turn toward the speaker's feelings about herself.

The address shifts between stanzas, between "you" and "thou." The "you" in the penultimate stanza seems to refer to the reader, especially since the girl is referred to in the third person. Yet the last stanza addresses the girl directly. The second line of the last stanza seems to ask whether the girl herself, her lover, or her brothers are to blame. The "he who left standing thy hovel" is an oblique reference to civic authorities who might have destroyed the shack and "placed" the girl someplace else. The list of people to blame for the girl's downfall suggests that it was a joint effort, that the blindness, cruelty, or desperation of a number of different people contributed to her misery. This stanza stresses the interconnectedness by way of guilt of the well-off, the lover, the village council, the speaker / poet, and the fallen woman, her father, and her brothers.

The speaker puts herself up for blame, but is unclear about what for. In listing those potentially responsible for the girl's fall, she puts herself last, saying, "Or I, who gave no sign?" To whom was she to give this sign, and what sort of sign should it have been? The ambiguity of this line signals at once the observer's despair that she cannot do anything to help and her feeling that she must do something. The only sort of sign she can give is to point, to say figuratively, "Look." As the "Prologue" suggests, the poem as "sign" becomes political in its imperative tone. This line changes the poem from a lament into a questioning, "What could I have done?" This poem is the would-be sign, addressed presumably to middle-class readers, consumers of aestheticist poetry. The speaker associates the power of her own observation with some guilt for the girl's situation. There is a certain indulgence in that guilt, for it allows the speaker to feel connected to the girl. That sense of responsibility creates sympathy, and the sympathy and guilt expressed are the "sign" that constitute the fulfillment of the speaker's perceived social duty.

The poem underscores that sympathy by matching its own rhythm with that of the girl's gait on her way through town. Sense is sometimes sacrificed to create this effect; the missing article with "lover" preserves the halting meter of the poem. Though not all of the poems' meters are as strained as they are in the "Prologue"—some are in a more conventionally jaunty tetrameter—the meter of "The Scapegoat" is studiously strained, stretching an ordinary alternation between tetrameter and trimeter into an alternation between pentameter and trimeter that limps along. As in the "Prologue," anapests and dactyls alternate in the lines themselves to contribute to a halting sense of rhythm. At the level of the foot and the line, the meter avoids any felicitous rhythmical thrust. It is as if the lurching of the feet of the verse imitates the "heavy reel" on which "The Scapegoat," both girl and poem, walk. This metrical effect allows the *poem* to feel *with* the girl, to echo her rhythms, even though the observer herself cannot identify with the girl.

In "The Rothers," a mysterious sign forebodes evil rather than prevents it. "The Rothers" tells the story of two daughters of a landed gentry family in decline who are orphaned by their father's equestrian accident. When he dies, their only remaining family member, Miss May, comes from France to take care of them. When they grow up and get married, they have no use for Miss May, but Miss May has no place to go, so she is to spend three months at each woman's home. The women are resentful of their obligation to her and will tolerate her for no longer than the three-month limit. The speaker is on her way to visit her neighbor and friend Miss May, who has fallen ill, but discovers on the way that the time has come for her to go from one woman's home to the other. Maud and her husband, Thorn, had loaded her on to a cart to take her to Florence's home. The speaker sees the Thorns driving a cart with something that looks like an animal under a blanket. When she approaches them, she sees Miss May's gray head rocking back and forth and realizes that she is dead.[52]

The sign in this poem comes not from the poet, but from the ultimate observer, God, to the speaker on earth below: "God sees our sins; for a sign I saw / Set in the western skies one day— / White over Rother, white and pale."[53] Just before she recounts seeing her friend's body in the cart, the speaker gives an elaborate description of an eerie sunset that she interprets as a sign of God's wrath—a wrath that mirrors her own. The "strange white light" changes the colors of everything that it falls upon, bleaching trees and flowers of their brilliance. It reduces the dimensions of everything she sees, making hills, buildings, and landscape into flat shapes. What she sees leads her to question how an artist would render such a strange sight:

> I fell to wonder, by some chance
> Of a sketcher's fancy—how would fare
> The tones of flesh in that strange white glare?
>
> A freak of the painter's cautious eye
>   Which notes all possible effect—
> I scarcely daub, but I love to try—
>   So, full of the whim, I recollect,
> I stretched my own right arm and gazed
> At the hand, quite black where the full light blazed.[54]

The speaker's concern with pure form, the quality of the light and how to render it, suggests that the aesthetic should embody sympathy, rather than engender it. It is as though nature has produced an artificial effect; the flesh tones in the strange light would appear too unreal, "A freak of the painter's cautious eye." The speaker's own hand, turned black portends her own possible shame, though she does not admit guilt in the way that the speaker of "The Scapegoat" does. Yet while the light distorts the speaker's hand, it shows the true character of Maud and Thomas Thorn, "livid, and clear, and plain." In particular, the light throws into relief Maud's "bitter-sour" mouth.

The death of Miss May also signifies the death of kindness and sympathy. Her charges having rejected her intimate care, there can be no beauty; the world becomes drab and two-dimensional, human flesh turns gray. The primary argument of this poem, then, is not just that one should be kind to family members or that one should repay generosity. Rather, the poem argues that without mutually caring relationships or even one-sided sympathy, there can be no art, no beauty, no pleasure. At the end of the poem, she says that the moral "'Do good, and it is done to you'" is all fine and good, but that her experience leaves her enraged and bitterly unforgiving. She cannot "forgive and forget" but leaves instead this moral: "Touch pitch and be defiled, I say." The sunset that she thought might be interesting to be painted leaves her feeling defiled, her hand black after touching the figurative "pitch" of Miss May's murder.

The "signs" in these poems—ambiguous, as in "The Scapegoat," natural and from God in "The Rothers," and an effect of reflection as in "The Hand-Bell Ringers"—suggest that while these crimes or wrongs are a result of the cruelty of individuals to each other, they also have a more metaphysical significance. By choosing this mode over more explicit social criticism, Robinson declares, in spite of all the questioning of the value of poetry within these poems, that the poetic is essential. Throughout the collection, the abject subjects whose stories it tells grasp toward intimacy and beauty. Even though the poems acknowledge that those in poverty hardly have the resources to appreciate beauty, Robinson suggests that they nonetheless desire it. In "Man and Wife," there is a wistful beauty to the wife's opening description of the landscape that she will leave behind. It has the stark barrenness of approaching winter:

> The bracken withers day by day,
> The furze is out of bloom.
> Over the common the heather is gray,
> And there's no gold left on the broom.

Yet the wife declares that she will miss the "wild rough sea of furze" when she leaves it for the workhouse.[55]

"Men and Monkeys" goes so far as to imply that there is an animal instinct toward the aesthetic. In contrast to some of the other wintry, barren landscapes, this poem portrays the countryside in bloom, with "every gust of breeze, / A light loose-petalled blossom shower."[56] The speaker, who lies dreaming in the grass, watches Italian vagrants go by, the "monkey, man, and peasant lass," looking at nothing but the dust their feet kick up in the road. They are clearly too exhausted to take notice of the landscape. Yet the speaker notices that the monkey pays attention to it: "suddenly I heard / The monkey mimic the singing bird, / And snatch a trail of flowering may."[57] This animal's "delight" in the surroundings suggests that there is some hope for his masters. Beautiful surroundings, such as the "wild rough furze" in "Man and Wife," the apple blossoms in "Men and Monkeys," and the lilac boughs in "Cottar's Girl," throw the sufferings into relief. Without their abject desolation, these simple pleasures would be available to the characters of these poems. This point both refutes and supports Lee's argument that the democratic nature of art stems from a universal human ability to appreciate beauty. Robinson acknowledges more than Lee does that material need gets in the way of aesthetic pleasure, but she agrees with Lee that such pleasure does not require education and cultivated taste.

This distant, even lost, appreciation of beauty competes with these poems' ambivalence about beauty, their resistance to being beautiful, their refusal to satisfy readers' expectations. Robinson refuses to make these poems enchanting in order to make their subjects more immediate; she does not want beauty to hinder understanding. She makes it unavailable to her audience, as distant from them as it is to her subjects. This collection embodies two conflicting approaches to the aesthetic. The first, more closely resembling Lee's approach, appears in the characters' grasping at pleasure, their dim awareness of beauty in the landscapes that surround them. Poems such as "Men and Monkeys" and "Man and Wife" express a wish that the pleasure of beauty be available to everyone. The second approach disavows the pleasure of pure beauty, arguing that this pleasure blinds people to the plight of the rural poor. In place of charming, beautiful poetry, Robinson presents a discordant song, one that attempts to awaken readers by denying them the poetic pleasure they expect. In her verse, Robinson creates a poetics that corresponds to the helplessness, guilt, and frustration in witnessing, but not being able to help, those in dire need.

Critical Reactions to *The New Arcadia*

Lee responded to *The New Arcadia* in her letters by casting Robinson's aesthetic conflict as a stage in the development of a new style. She referred to *The New Arcadia* as "your most important work in my eyes; and even supposing it to the mere transition, development work, it must have developed in you a power of [undecipherable] and movement which you did not dream of in your pre-Raphaelite days."[58] In her biography of Lee, Vineta Colby writes that on her first visit to London, Lee especially enjoyed satires of the "humourless aesthetes of Pre-Raphaelitism" and found the Pre-Raphaelites she met (William Rossetti, for instance), as well as other aesthetes, to be excessively caught up in their overwrought décor and dress. Lee implied that Robinson's "pre-Raphaelite days" lacked substance and subtlety, and in other letters referred to her early poetry as "high art," their code words for "the excesses that turn serious culture into vulgarity and banality."[59] While Lee viewed Robinson's third volume as a necessary correction to her "false aestheticism," and an important outgrowth of Lee's own "purity polemic," she also considered the realism of *The New Arcadia* an overreaction both to Robinson's older work and to the influences evident in that work.

Although Lee wished the style of the poems to be more like Robinson's older ones, she congratulated Robinson on the way in which her versification echoed the thoughts expressed in the poems. Lee described the poems' merits in the manner in which she described her own essays in *Belcaro:* "[The poems] have a quality of construction which seems no construction, of being seemingly loosely strung together, almost conversational, which has always struck me, in the few precious cases in which I can remember it, as one of the rarest and most piquant artistic merits. I speak for . . . the memorable way in which the verse seconds the intellectual construction. So also the Bell Ringers."[60] This characterization of her own book of essays as "loosely strung together" and implicit praise of Robinson's work for resembling her own was a product of the dynamic that Lee established between the two of them. She admired the "construction that seems no construction" because she disdained the overwrought, highly stylized quality of aestheticist art. Lee understood the poems' dialogue between meaning and meter, just as she understood that her own and Robinson's writing were in dialogue.

Lee measured her praise of *The New Arcadia* against what Robinson had produced in the past and what she expected of her in the future. Using more tact with her close friend than she did with many others, Lee encouraged Robinson to keep writing, while still commenting on what she saw as the book's failures. Upon receipt of the volume, she wrote in her 1 April 1884 letter to Robinson, "I think this book is an immense stride in advance a much finer, nobler, worthier, more even book than either of the two others. . . . I nevertheless feel persuaded that you are destined to do much more. . . . And I believe you will one day reacquire certain qualities of your first book which you have lost in this." Whereas Robinson altered her verse, creating a discordant lyricism in order to investigate the moral possibilities of poetry, Lee still seemed to want her morality and her beauty too. In her letter responding about *The New Arcadia,* Vernon Lee warned of an unfavorable response from the critics: "That the critics, up to their chins in Swinburnism or Gos-sism[,] should receive this coldly . . . would not surprise me in the least, and I think, my love, you must be prepared to be told you are a failure."[61] Lee un-derstood the book to be a criticism of aestheticism and believed that as such it could not be well received. Yet its critique was so new that it found allies neither among conservative critics nor with ardent devotees of the aesthetic movement.

The New Arcadia was indeed generally panned in the press by reviewers who not only found its subject distasteful but who had also become quickly accustomed to the metrical mastery of the delicately drawn landscapes and wistful love poems of Robinson's earlier volumes. The sense of repulsion at the possibilities of its own medium, the need to protect the poems from po-etry's more dangerous pleasures, may well have been, in part, what elicited the negative notices. These reviewers chafed against the "rough wild sobs" for which she prepared them in the "Prologue." The Saturday Review wrote, "It is perhaps idle to object to the poet's determined perversion of the chief function of a singer as expressed in the prologue, seeing that her aims are very successfully realized."[62] This review, as well as others, found that the poems' didacticism obstructed the potential felicity of its form. Similarly, the Specta-tor singled out the "Prologue" for particular criticism: "We do not think that any unsophisticated reader can fail to feel the strain in these verses,—a strain which manifests itself in a refusal to say simple things in a simple way, and in a deliberate choice of metaphor and language whose very far-fetchedness and exaggeration seem meant to conceal the want of body in the thought and emotion beneath."[63] The strain is undoubtedly there, especially in the "Prologue," but, as I hope to have shown, it represents the tension between the expectations of beauty in poetry and the effort to represent what is ugly with power and weight. Behind the notices that criticized the "strained" or "forced" quality of The New Arcadia lay the assumption that poetry, especially by women, should appear effortless. Although Symonds dismissed the crit-ics of the volume, saying that "their abuse is a compliment to your versatil-ity," his encouragement did not change the fact that the book fell largely on deaf ears.[64]

New Arcadian Legacies

The disparaging reviews of The New Arcadia and the lukewarm praise she received from her mentors Vernon Lee and John Addington Symonds convinced Robinson to return in several subsequent volumes of poetry to the more purely aestheticist style of her earlier work. At least one poem in Robinson's next volume of verse, *An Italian Garden,* reveals bitter disappointment at *The New Arcadia*'s poor reception. In "A Ballad of Forgotten Songs," dedicated to "V.L.," Robinson views the version of herself that wrote *The New Arcadia* as dead. In the Envoy to this poem, Robinson addresses Vernon Lee directly, rejecting her encouragement:

> Vernon, in vain you stoop to con
> The slender, faded notes to-day—
> The Soul that dwelt in them is gone:
> Dead are the tunes of yesterday![65]

Despite this bitterness, the "soul" of her "faded notes" lives on in later works. Ultimately, the ideas behind *The New Arcadia* split into two directions. Her exploration of metaphysical, epistemological questions about the knowledge of others' sorrow and the fear of isolation became ultra-lyrical, while her prose allowed her to write about the practical difficulties of the lower classes. In "The Workman's Diet of Paris," she compares the budgets of working men across the centuries, comparing the price of meat and other goods, trying to understand the economics of need. M. Lynda Ely notes that Robinson's 1903 collection of essays, *The Fields of France,* also offers social critique. Her commentary on the poor must remain within the confines of prose, while sympathy becomes a more abstract concept for her.

An Italian Garden returned to the dreamy poetics of Robinson's earlier volumes. Ely characterizes this volume as "a return . . . to the pastoral ideal that she had so repudiated in *The New Arcadia.*"[66] While *An Italian Garden* is more similar to Robinson's earlier volumes, it is hardly a disavowal of the principles of *The New Arcadia.* Rather, in *An Italian Garden,* Robinson abstracts the themes of *The New Arcadia,* rendering metaphysical the question of how one can know another's pain. The sorrow in *An Italian Garden* is so abstract, so disembodied, that the sorrows at the loss of love, at feeling isolated, at the sufferings of another, or at the forced silence of a poetic message, are difficult to distinguish. While certain "flower" poems in this volume may seem like an iteration of a "pastoral ideal," more often these poems portray a withering landscape characteristic of *The New Arcadia.* Nature is not idealized so much as it is bereft of color and energy. The word "pallid" appears often, as in these lines from "Aubade Triste": "For, pale, beyond the pallid trees, / The dawn begins to break"; or from "Death in the World": "The great white lilies in the grass / Are pallid as the smile of death."[67] A study in grays, in shades of pale, these lines are reminiscent of a Whistler painting, marking not only the dominant melancholy of the volume but also its return to aestheticist modes of representation, which rely on symbols and impressions. The melancholy becomes spiritual rather than material, and Robinson deals in nuance rather than in color.[68]

At the end of *The New Arcadia,* the poet retreats into silence, in a poem entitled "Song" that refuses to sing: "I have lost my singing-voice; / My heyday's over." This poem lacks the imperative that energizes the "Prologue," expressing a fear that singing is futile: "Wherefore should I stop to tell / The pang that rends me?" That silence becomes a frightening world in itself in "Invocations" from *An Italian Garden.* Here, music and silence mingle:

> O song in the nightingale's throat, O music,
> Dropt as it fell by a falling star,—
> All of the silence is filled with thy pain
> Listening till it shall echo again.
> O song in the nightingale's throat, O music,
> Thou art the soul of the silence afar![69]

Although music is absent, beckoned by apostrophe, its pain lingers in the silence. No longer attached to particular people or to narratives, as in *The New Arcadia,* pain exists here only as a lyric figure, coming from the nightingale. Yet the pain of the music now silent might also be that of the preceding volume. The third and last stanza asks a question that underlies all of *The New Arcadia.* Here, the silence of the music becomes the silence of Death. Death in this poem, as in others in this volume, is not any particular death, but an abstraction of death, inscrutable and mysterious: "O silence of Death, O world of darkness, / Shall we perceive thee or know thee at all?" In *The New Arcadia,* variations on the word "know" appear throughout the "Prologue"; but in the "Epilogue," Robinson concedes that her subjects seem locked away from the understanding of others. The last line reads: "Nor, should one cry, would any understand." The poems of *An Italian Garden* echo the sympathetic concerns of *The New Arcadia* in epistemological terms.

The conflicting rationales for reading Robinson's work in recent scholarship reflect her ambivalence about what sort of poetry would fulfill at once her desire to be thoughtful of others, her acute sense of internal states, and her attraction to impressionistic beauty. Ana Vadillo, for example, reads Robinson's poetry of the 1880s and early '90s as formative of British symbolism and influential for Arthur Symons's important essay "The Decadent Movement in Literature" (1893), rewritten six years later as "The Symbolist Movement in Literature."[70] For Vadillo, Robinson's symbolism involves a preference for visionary reality, spiritual truth, and inward contemplation. Vadillo characterizes Robinson's core philosophy as "the negation of physical experience in favor of the disembodied soul," and she notes its relation to Pater's emphasis on individuals' impressions in isolation. While Vadillo only mentions *The New Arcadia* in passing, Ely chooses to focus on it as Robinson's effort to prove herself as more than a dreamy aesthete. In order to "re-present" Robinson to current audiences, Ely traces the course of Robinson's career, aiming to rescue her from her contemporaries who focused on the charm of her physical presence (she was widely regarded as an immensely attractive personality) at the expense of her poetry, and who would see her literary success as only an extension of that charm.[71] The special attention that Ely gives to *The New Arcadia* in order to provide evidence of Robinson's seriousness as a poet implies a dismissal of the aestheticism that Vadillo elevates as a form of proto-modernism.

Indeed, the emphasis on inward experience in what Vadillo calls Robinson's "immaterial poetics" accompanies her diminished confidence in intimacy and sympathy. She retreats into an isolationist view of the self, but rather than reveling in the pleasures of the lonely senses, she bemoans this condition. The sestina "Personality" conceives of the self as walled in, the words of the poem closing in on themselves, encircling the poem like walls:

> As one who goes between high garden walls,
> Along a road that never has an end,
> With still the empty way behind, in front,
> Which he must pace for evermore alone—
> So, even so is Life to every soul,
> Walled in with barriers that no Love can break.
>
> And yet! Ah me! How often would we break
> Through every fence, and overleap the walls,
> And link ourselves to some beloved soul,
> Hearing her answering voice until the end,
> Going her chosen way, no more alone,
> But happy comrades, seeing Heaven in front.[72]

The poem vacillates, hoping for intimate redemption, as in the second stanza, but ultimately siding with the first, the speaker lamenting that she must "sing within my walls." The poem closes with the speaker singing in spite of the prison of self, hoping for some unknown listener: "I trust the end and sing within my walls, / Sing all alone, to bid some listening soul / Wait till the day break, watch for me in front!" The only hope in this poem for sympathy is at limit points, in the action of breaking, at the end, in the front. Here, as in Christina Rossetti's poetry, it isn't so much beauty that hinders sympathy, but the self. This understanding of the self as limiting and imprisoning explains what Vadillo calls the immateriality of much of Robinson's poetry, especially in *An Italian Garden*. Sympathy, for Robinson, becomes an ideal, a poetic dream, rather than a social reality.

Between the initial raves of her first volume in 1878 and Hannah Lynch's lament in the *Fortnightly Review* in 1902, "deploring the poet's long silence," Robinson's star as a poet rose and quietly fell.[73] The inward turn in "Personality" may be a response to the overwhelming lack of support for *The New Arcadia*. The disparaging critiques in the press may have been easier to bear had it not been for the mixed reviews from Robinson's mentors, Lee and Symonds. In retrospect, however, it is clear how forward-looking the volume is. Because it expressed anxiety about the possibilities of poetry while experimenting with form, because it offered an ethical challenge *as* aesthetic experience, *The New Arcadia* began to break through existing binaries between a pious, moralistic, conservative tone in literature on the one hand, and the aesthetic celebration of sensual experience on the other hand. Had Robinson developed what she began in *The New Arcadia,* she would surely have enriched a debate that seemed largely divided into these two camps. Ironically, her conversations with Lee, who was so sharply critical of aestheticism but at the same time steered Robinson toward writing "beautiful" verse, may have ultimately arrested Robinson's poetic development. Later, Robinson must have known that this style would soon be outmoded, for at the dawn of the twentieth century, turning her attention to essays and historical studies, Robinson adopted Lee's primary form, still, in some ways, responding to Lee's influence even after their intimacy had come to an end.

For her part, Lee advanced her own thought to some degree under Robinson's lingering influence. Lee continued to consider comradeship and social interaction essential to creative production, as Dellamora stresses.[74] After her relationship with Robinson dissolved, Lee took up with Kit Anstruther-Thompson, whose physiological responses to artwork became the basis of Lee's psychological aesthetics in the 1890s. In her examination of Lee's intense collaboration with this intimate companion, Maltz suggests that Anstruther-Thompson distracted Lee's focus from the social and ethical concerns that had previously occupied her. Their joint project, which began as art-appreciation gallery tours for underprivileged audiences, devolved, Maltz writes, into "decadent amusement."[75] Later still, Lee developed a passionate interest in suffragism and, in the midst of World War I, she became an outspoken (and unpopular) advocate of pacifism. Throughout the rest of Lee's long career, sympathy (and then, more specifically, empathy) remained a central component of her aesthetics, while the dialogue proved a mainstay in her

writing, with Baldwin serving as the title character in her next book of dia-
logues, and the guiding presence in the third, *Althea* (1894). Then again, the
characters in her dialogues understandably would change. When she pub-
lished *Althea,* Cyril was no longer present, Althea, who resembles Anstruther-
Thomson, having taken his place. Even if Robinson's later pursuits do not,
Lee's long career following their relationship attests to the importance of inti-
macy in the aesthetics of the fin de siècle and into the early twentieth century.

"Be Loved through Thoughts of Mine"

ALICE MEYNELL'S INTIMATE DISTANCE

To many, Alice Meynell's writing seems impersonal, detached, and restrained. The formally careful, abstract, sometimes precious qualities of her writing both in poetry and in prose seem for critics to constitute a world apart. Her praise of silence in her poetry and of "so many significant negatives" in "A Remembrance," a tribute to her father, seems to refuse the need for emotional and linguistic expression. Her most famous poem, "Renouncement," about restraining thoughts of the beloved, seems to denounce passion. Her devotion to the Catholic Church and her fascination with the laws of verse are seen as part of her penchant for discipline. This view of her work as detached often maintains an opposition between the emotional and the intellectual, as does Vanessa Furse Jackson, who writes that Meynell's writing has a "high spiritual but low emotional temperature." Similarly, Angela Leighton maintains that Meynell's rigor refuses intense emotion: "Renunciation remains, in much of Meynell's poetry, like an unbreakable bar to passion." These views are consistent with those of many of her contemporaries. For instance, Osburt Burdet called her work "intense but detached." G. K. Chesterton wrote that in her meditations "things did always detach themselves from vague environment," and that "She never wrote a line, or even a word, that does not stand like the rib of a strong intellectual structure." While these interpretations point to an undeniable quality of Meynell's work, they have established a view of Meynell that fails to take into account her deep concern with personal, literary, and imaginative relations.[1]

In this chapter, I argue that in every genre, Meynell was deeply engaged in questions of how people and poems relate. Meynell prizes distance and silence precisely because they create possibilities for intimacy. Meynell's writing importantly distinguishes between detachment and distance. Whereas detachment severs bonds, distance makes room for them. Distance allows one subject to see another's difference clearly. It keeps one subject's fantasies of the other from overshadowing the reality of the other, even if that reality is never fully scrutable. Distance maintains boundaries between selves so that those boundaries may be intersubjectively crossed. Meynell's prosody even maintains boundaries in its insistence on the metrical foot to measure verse, as opposed to simpler accentual meter. This understanding of distance undoes the opposition between the intellect and the emotions in some Meynell criticism, accounting for the tendency in Meynell to be "impassioned *about* the bars."[2] Because separation and order are a precondition for bonds, they ignite passion. The threat of emotions running wild is the threat of falling into solipsism.[3]

Alice Meynell takes many of her cues from Christina Rossetti—the prizing of silence, religious devotion, careful mastery of poetic form. Whereas Rossetti insists on willing self-negation and the instability of the lyric "I," Meynell requires distance between subjects. That distance creates space in which subjects—real, imaginative, and poetic—must remain distinct in order to connect with one another. While both were deeply religious, Rossetti's work emphasizes the spiritual life while Meynell's also asserts the significance of social life. While it seems intuitive that speech connects and silence refuses connection, for Meynell, silence creates room in which two subjects establish separate identities. Only with that separation can they form a bond; otherwise their link would be mere unification or absorption. At the same time, her emphasis on distance acknowledges that it is never possible to fully know the other and it thereby cultivates respect for that unknowability. Silence is the embodiment of that unknowability both thematically and in her own poetics.

Others' descriptions of Meynell's silence are distinct from her own. Even those who appreciated her silence in her own day seem at times to have misunderstood it. George Meredith's letters reveal that Meynell could often be silent in social situations as well as in poetic motif: "You write of your not being a talker. I can find the substance I want in your silences and can converse with them."[4] For Meredith, silence did not equal detachment; rather, it was the basis for secret, intimate, but most likely imagined conversation. These phrases from Meredith's letter focus on himself: "I can find . . . I want . . . [I] converse." By seeking and finding what he wants, Meredith does not emphasize unspoken communication but rather interprets the silence of the other in terms of the observer's fantasy. The "substance" is his, not hers, and his conversation is in fact one with himself.

Meynell's poems often treat the inaccessibility and silence of works of the past, as in "To a Lost Melody," or in "To Any Poet," where silence is "the completest of thy poems, last, and sweetest." A poem written at the end of her career, "To Silence," declares that silence shapes melody, sculpts sound, and creates meaningful pauses. As a forming force, it is at once a power of unification and separation. It separates words and makes them mean as a whole. That which separates the words connects them. In "To the Beloved," silence brings lovers together, but words sever the possibilities that silence raises:

> Thou art like silence all unvexed
>> Though wild words part my soul from thee.
> Thou art like silence unperplexed,
>> A secret and a mystery
> Between one footfall and the next.[5]

In this poem, silence embodies all that is unknown, mysterious, and therefore desired. In contrast to the silence that affords space for fantasy in Meredith's letter, the comparison of the beloved to silence in the poem characterizes the relation as open and expansive. The rest of the poem presents silence as poetic and figurative connective tissue, permeating everything, itself "mingling" with speech and song. The simile cited above is a part of an extended metaphor comparing the beloved to silence, establishing the other as ever-present, yet always to be discovered. While the poem is circumscribed by silence and therefore limited, silence itself is infinite, made audible only by the interruptions of words, and ever-present, mysterious, and calm, just as the poem wishes the beloved to be.

Just as silence creates space that establishes boundaries around the subject, solitude is necessary for intimacy. It provides a sense of perspective that constant togetherness would never allow. Meynell's essay "Solitude" considers its topic within the context of social life. Socioeconomic class produces various experiences of solitude. Whereas solitude is readily available at opposite ends of the spectrum of civilization, to the "wild man" and to "the man for whom civilization has been kind," for the many in between those poles, "solitude is a right foregone or a luxury unattained."[6] Meynell insists that solitude must be available to everyone, "to be found in the merest working country," and that "a thicket may be as secret as a forest" and that solitude may be enclosed in the smallest of spaces. For those who have not even these smallest means of escape from others, "the best solitude does not hide at all." Meynell resists the opposition between solitude and society, insisting instead that intimacy and companionship cannot exist without solitude. Those who live in crowded conditions where solitude is scarcely available can hardly have satisfactory relationships: "There are many who never have a whole hour alone. They live in reluctant or indifferent companionship, as people may in a boarding-house, by paradoxical choice, familiar with one another and not intimate."[7] Engaged companionship and meaningful intimacy require the recognition of self and separateness that comes from being alone. Without a measure of self-conscious detachment, intimacy can only approach mere familiarity. Indeed, Meynell understands closeness and distance to be measured quantities in the way she conceptualizes and uses poetic meter. Just as her essay "The Rhythm of Life" understands emotional life to be metrical, emotions subject to the periodicity of tides, Meynell's use of meter draws lines and words together and pulls them apart with pauses.

The idea that solitude, separation, and silence enable social and interpersonal bonds departs from critics' conception of these qualities as an escape for Meynell from a hectic family and professional life. Some current critics have reincorporated the sense of distance in her writing and in her poetic persona into their understanding of Meynell's personal life in order to understand her life and work as a whole.[8] They often see the issue from a feminist perspective, one derived from Virginia Woolf's *A Room of One's Own,* viewing Meynell as a beleaguered woman who had to create space in her writing because she did not have it at home, from her family or from the writers who constantly sought her attention. Meynell has often been characterized as a distant woman, someone whose thoughts and feelings were not fully accessible to those who loved her, and whose attention and time were precious commodities. This impression of her is due, in part, to biographical fact. In addition to editing two weekly journals with her husband, and writing for those journals as well as others, she was mother to seven children. She was the epitome of a working mother a century before it was the norm, and her resources were doubtless taxed. In an often-recounted anecdote, she had to escape into the privacy of a locked bathroom in order to be able to write.[9] Yet both in private and in public, Meynell was incredibly sociable; Ana Parejo Vadillo has documented the significance of Meynell's house in Kensington as a literary salon as well as Meynell's own circulation in that neighborhood's artistic and literary community.[10]

Some of the most significant figures in that community are in part responsible for Meynell's reputation of aloofness. The literary men who keenly admired her, the poets Francis Thompson, Coventry Patmore, and George Meredith, all made demands on Meynell's time and energy, but all praised her silence and distance. Coventry Patmore, who preferred her prose to her verse, wrote a poem to her, "Alicia's Silence," which praised, "all your mild and silent days / Are each a lyric fact."[11] I have already shown one way in which George Meredith idealized her silence. Francis Thompson, the poet whom the Meynells rescued from addiction and destitution, wrote in his review of her 1893 book *Poems,* "The footfalls of her Muse waken not sounds, but silences."[12] Meynell's close friendship with Coventry Patmore ultimately ended because Patmore wanted more from Meynell than their marriages to others would allow. Badeni's biography of Meynell depicts Patmore's desires as insatiable, his expectations wildly unrealistic. It is impossible to know whether Meynell seemed detached because the men she was close to in the literary world wanted so much from her, or whether they were drawn to her unavailability. Whatever the case, her friendships with Patmore, Thompson, and Meredith, and the infatuation that these men professed for her contributed to the myth of Alice Meynell as a woman just out of reach, always at arm's length in personal relationships.

Despite the range of demands others made on her, Meynell maintained a public image of herself as a composed, aloof, domestic angel. Talia Schaffer argues that Meynell's reputation for distance and silence enabled her to construct a literary persona that both satisfied the dominant mores of late Victorian Britain and subtly challenged them: "Meynell's silence and loneliness became her essential claim to power and precision and enviability. By constantly refraining from speech, she intimated the existence of reservoirs of thought too sacred to expose to the multitude."[13] Although Schaffer is astute in recognizing Meynell's construction of her poetic persona, she also contributes to the assumption that silence and distance signify withdrawal. Schaffer argues that Meynell's writing is wholly solitary, pointing out that that there are "virtually no essays where she depicts two or more people in social contact" and that "Meynell's visionary world is solitary and silent."[14] Yet this very detachment, which others have interpreted to be a sign of her antisociability or her desire for solitude, is in fact a sign of sociability. Her work sets forth a theory of social life in which restraint is essential, for it creates space for others. Restraint, for Meynell, is a sign of respect for others and for shared resources, the most important of which is language itself.

In the chapter that follows, I explore the different kinds of relationships, the types of self and other, that Meynell addresses in poetry and in prose. First, I show how Meynell's literary criticism indirectly champions her own tempered style and its connection to a life overflowing with professional and social pursuits, a life full of other people. A style incorporating critical distance, she argues, entails more sensitivity to others, to oneself, and to literary resources than more aggressive styles do.[15] In essays on Jane Austen and Elizabeth Barrett Browning, Meynell addresses the effect of seclusion on women authors. Since the publication of *A Room of One's Own,* it has been taken for granted that seclusion is necessary for literary production. In fact, without naming her, it repudiates Meynell's argument to the contrary that solitude can be counterproductive.[16] Meynell suggests, however, that there can be too much of a good thing, that without regular involvement with others, writers, especially women writers, lose perspective, on themselves as well as on the rest of the world. The chapter begins by addressing Meynell's engagement with her own literary foremothers. Here, I argue that Meynell finds sociability essential to writing and that a measure of distance is crucial for sociability. I go on to define intimate distance as a question of perspective, of understanding how one looks at the other. The following section examines how Meynell's poetry conceives of relations between poets, between poets and readers, between readers and figures or characters, and between readers and poets and poems in the abstract. In these relations, literary artifacts are figured as subjects in their own right, separate from their authors and readers, while at the same time they are poets' products and their inspirations. Finally, I turn to Meynell's poems and essays on children and mothers in order to show how the attitude in them, which has been noted for its modern ambivalence, incorporates, and is perhaps a source for, the dynamic of separation and closeness.

"A Gentle Self-Denying Practice": Sociability in Meynell's Criticism of Women Writers

In an essay that bears the title of the column that she wrote for the *Pall Mall Gazette* between 1893 and 1898, "The Wares of Autolycus," Meynell remarks upon the tensions of country social life revealed in the publication of *Charades Written a Hundred Years Ago by Jane Austen and Her Family*. Meynell finds the charades themselves without wit, their publication a sign of mere author fetishizing. Meynell implies that it is not the charades themselves but the fact of them and their dullness that suggest the complexities of interpersonal dynamics in the Austen home. Meynell writes, "One and all must have been playing a game more difficult than charades — the courteous game of pretending to be amused. Without that gentle and self-denying practice it is hardly possible for people to abide together in any kind of seclusion. In that day all country life was inevitably secluded."[17] According to Meynell, the game of charades, and the polite appearance of amusement it requires, appear on a scale of social development that begins with admitting boredom with one's companions without compunction and ends in the ideal of not being bored with them at all. For Meynell, restraint from voicing judgments in such circumstances is a sort of social lubrication. Silence preserves the dignity of others by not revealing their silliness or stupidity. As she points out in "The Wares of Autolycus," a pun on "handbill" that divides the word into its two parts and acts out their literal meaning might not be very clever, but one must respect it in order to preserve whatever delight the pun-maker might get out of it. Self-denial creates social harmony. Meynell calls attention to the fact that she has no such obligation to keep silent on the subject of the Austen family's charades, and her critique is sharp. However, her comments here leave tantalizingly open the question of what Meynell's own celebrated silences might signify, what sharpness they might hide.

Indeed, Meynell finds that Elizabeth Barrett Browning did not temper her sharpness often enough and attributes her sometimes aggressive style to too much time spent in solitude. A devoted and sympathetic reader of Barrett Browning and a collector of her papers, Meynell nevertheless did not hesitate to measure Barrett Browning's shortfalls against her triumphs. In her introduction to Barrett Browning's *The Art of Scansion,* Meynell writes that Barrett Browning is at her best when she is "pacing softly in the strictest measure of the bonds that all true poets so love — the bonds of numbers, stress, quantity, rhyme and final shape" and is more uneven in her blank verse, which is "nearly swaggering, certainly swashing and martial."[18] In the introduction to *Prometheus Bound and Other Poems,* Meynell tempers her praise of Barrett Browning with a critique of her style. After praising "The Cry of the Children" for the social and political work it does, Meynell criticizes Barrett Browning for a "too emphatic revolt against her time, a too resolute originality."[19] She characterizes her verse, especially in *Aurora Leigh,* as "tense," "defiant," and "violent." Meynell is clear here about her own feeling that this sort of style is not the best for any sort of poetry, even political poetry.[20] She deeply admires Barrett Browning, but when her style is assertive or "menacing," it detracts from the "steadfast eagerness for righteousness" and her "passion for truth," which draw Meynell to her work. Meynell connects Barrett Browning's literary style to her social existence: "It is difficult not to attribute something of this resolute style to the seclusion of the years in the course of which Mrs. Browning's literary habits were formed. Nothing but the secrecy of a dark sick-room and a sofa could give a sensitive woman the strange courage of Elizabeth Barrett's poems. . . . She was bold in her hiding place — very bold, for example as a letter writer."[21] Meynell offers Barrett Browning's letter-writing habits as proof of the connection between social behavior and literary style. By connecting Barrett Browning's style in letters to that in her poetry, Meynell implies that writing poems is akin to addressing an unknown audience; both carry the risk of losing self-awareness. To correspondents she had never met, Barrett Browning did not mince words, writing "emphatically-finished sentences." According to Meynell, this style gave way to a more genteel one when Barrett Browning "rose from her sofa, stood at a husband's side, received friends."[22]

This essay says at least as much about Meynell's own struggle with solitude and sociability as it does about Barrett Browning. Like critics of her own work, Meynell considers biographical fact and literary analysis to be mutually reinforcing. However, the pitfalls of that approach are evident here, for this essay and one on Christina Rossetti that I read below both clearly filter their assessments of their authors through Meynell's own biases. For instance, Barrett Browning's poems are good when they have a "pause of style" and flawed when they have too much "dash." Meynell's own preference for the subtle over the aggressive, for the disciplined over the raw, accounts for her assessment of Barrett Browning's style. It expresses Meynell's belief that feelings, thoughts, and opinions must be tempered for the sake of one's audience. Whereas other critics of Meynell's work have discussed her sense of discipline as something she valued for its own sake, a view consistent with her attraction to the rigors of Catholicism and poetic metrical law, Meynell also valued discipline as necessary for social and literary interaction. To Meynell, abrasive writing denotes a failure to understand one's own character and the expectations of one's audience.

Meynell considers the overly bold, overly Byronic style of Elizabeth Barrett's letters to correspondents she had never met was a result of taking on a persona that she wished them to imagine for her. Meynell argues that secluded women writers in particular, not only Elizabeth Barrett but also Charlotte Brontë,[23] fantasize about how their audience might perceive them, and at times reimagine themselves and their writing according to this fantasy. Because their seclusion nurtures delusions about how others might perceive them, their styles seem ill suited to the realities of their experience. Meynell extrapolates from the case of Barrett, who, when she became Barrett Browning,

> rose from her sofa, stood at her husband's side, received his friends, faced the fact of his fame with her own delicate physique, no longer lurking in that delusive bower which secluded writers—those who are women—are apt to build for themselves out of their fancies as to what they probably seem to be in the mind and thought of the world of their readers. Of all the bowers of women this is the least worthy, the least sweet, the least stable, and the least profitable. . . . A sham hiding-place, because the woman, despite her reason and her self-knowledge, can hardly resist the tempting peril of thinking of herself not as she is but as she thinks she may be conjectured to be by those who perceive her, or guess at her, from what she writes. It is an intricacy of guesses. And she, seeing a strange figure wearing her name and author of her words, feels a change enormously refreshing and relieving. She has known herself all too well for a certain

number of years, and here is a new self, and generally a flattered self, almost to believe in.[24]

Here, a "room of one's own" is destructive, for the imaginative freedom it affords clouds the secluded author's perceptions. Meynell pits freedom, guesses, conjecture, seclusion, and disjunction against truth, sincerity, certainty, sociability, and connection. It is far better, and more profitable, for women writers not to allow themselves the relief of conceiving of themselves as they might want others to see them. While Meynell criticizes the aggressive, secluded style as overbearing, she seems attracted to the "refreshing" quality of its flights of fancy. Yet because it is secluded, this writing risks becoming irrelevant. The style of writing that Meynell sees as overbearing comes from a lack of connection to oneself and to one's audience. The hiding place of the "secret sofa" allows women writers to develop confidence and assertiveness, but it is "sham" confidence based on an escape from self. For Meynell, that flight of fancy does not open new possibilities, a broadening of the self, but is a refusal of reason and knowledge. In contrast, Austen's "gentle self-denying practice" of pretending to be amused by her family's charades refuses only the expression of criticism, but remains aware and true to oneself in silence. To Meynell, the fantasies of self that she believes Barrett Browning's "strange courage" indicate are the far more self-denying practice.

Self-denial takes on a multitude of complex meanings here. At the most obvious level it refers to the refusal of pleasure, but it can also refer to the rejection of identity. To call the pretense of amusement self-denial prompts two interpretations. Meynell might suggest that there would be pleasure in airing the withheld criticism, or at least that its expression might put an end to the painful experience of watching the dull charades. In another interpretation, Meynell identifies the opinion with the self enough to call it a "self-denying practice." But for Meynell, Barrett Browning, in her aggressive letters and poems, does not pretend just to feel what she does not, but to be what she is not. In Barrett Browning's case, she must deny the pleasure of the relief she feels in imagining herself other than she is, in order to preserve the self. In this way, the denial of pleasure actually preserves the identity. Meynell insists on a self-acceptance that acknowledges the boundaries of the self and honors them, for without those boundaries, there can be no real interchange.

Meynell might seem to be anti-feminist in her assessment of Barrett Browning, for she rejects the idea that women's aggressive expression might empower them and give them a broader range of emotional possibilities in the public eye, allowing them to be truer to themselves. Yet for Meynell, playing at being powerful does not make one powerful. Her concern is for the "stability" and "profitability" of women's writing. By condemning the "delusive bower," Meynell hopes to guard women writers against another anti-feminist accusation: that they are hysterical. For Meynell, the best, and most feminist, stance for women is always to be fully in control. The loss of expressed emotional range is worth the gains of the power of discipline. Although Meynell does not say explicitly why the delusive bower is dangerous especially for women, other work of hers suggests that the danger results not from any inherently feminine characteristic, but rather from the social circumstances in which women were often forced to live. In an early diary entry, Meynell reflects on the ways in which work and exposure to the material world develops men's minds differently from women's, since women are forced to stay at home, and as a result can become lost in their own self-consciousness. She decries the "miserable selfishness that keeps women from work," writing that mental work, such as going to "college, or studying for the bar or for a civil service examination," would keep women from going "mad with her own soul over needlework."[25] A secluded condition in which women "ponder on them, seizing hold of the strong and feeble emotions of the inexplicable human heart and try to understand them, making a world for myself out of their shadows of which I ought to be wholly or almost unconscious" is a perilous one indeed, for it allows the boundaries of the self to lose their shape, and as a consequence women might lose reason and control.[26]

Meynell herself might be said to suffer from the tensions that she describes in her essays on other women writers.[27] Badeni writes, "Her passionate nature and the violence of her emotions frightened her, and she had no confident feelings of strength—only the realisation that somehow she must find a way to shape that nature to what she believed was its ultimate destiny."[28] Her criticisms of these other, earlier women writers justify her own style. Although her criticism of the Austen family charades is as sharp as anything in the work of Brontë or Barrett Browning, she never risked the accusations of "menacing" or "militant" tone that she levels at them. These essays ultimately defend the tempered quality of her own writing, which eventually came to seem too dispassionate for twentieth-century tastes.

Christina Rossetti presents the ideal balance of controlled passion and intense inwardness tempered by fellow feeling. Whereas seclusion might lead other writers to get lost in their own fantasies, Meynell understands Rossetti as solitary but nonetheless responsive to the outside world. Just as Meynell notes the social habits of Elizabeth Barrett Browning and Charlotte Brontë in their letters, she links Christina Rossetti's social habits to her literary practice. Whereas Brontë's and Barrett Browning's seclusion resulted in overly forceful styles, Rossetti's resulted in charity: "She lived sequestered by her own solemn choice, serving her mother. . . . To religious service and to the succor of the poor—in a word, to duty—she dedicated herself informally. . . . She refused to be tempted out of that solitude so full for her of spirituality; nevertheless, she did not deny herself to those who sought her. She was simply and frankly kind, rather talkative than silent, so as to make her visitor happier."[29] In this very short essay, attempting to characterize the nature of Rossetti's work as a whole, Meynell found it necessary to mention Rossetti's manner when entertaining guests. Amid her cherished solitude, she responded to her obligations to others, and that made all the difference to her poetic style.

For Meynell, Rossetti's brilliance as a poet lies in her ability to write profound emotion without being overly emphatic or forceful. Of "The Convent Threshold," Meynell writes, "It seems as though the lines were shaken by a force of feeling that never breaks into the relief of violence."[30] The difference for Meynell between Rossetti and Barrett Browning, and indeed, between Rossetti and Swinburne as well, lies in Rossetti's refusal to accept "relief." Whereas Barrett Browning and Brontë allowed themselves the relief of imagining themselves differently—and more powerfully—Rossetti maintains control, never releasing emotion into the chaos of "violence." Just as she is available to but not dominant with her guests, Rossetti makes feeling available to readers, presents it to them, so that the force of it belongs to the lines rather than to speaker or poet. Of "Amor Mundi" she writes, "There is terror, though the terror that is not instant, but that flies and sings, as ominous as a bird of warning—terror suggested but not suffered."[31] Meynell's description of Rossetti's writing echoes what I have already argued about her work in chapter 1: that it dissolves any notion of a speaking subject. In Meynell's description, there is no agent; the verbs are predominantly passive, and "terror" is the subject for the only active verbs, "flies and sings." It is unclear who suggests or suffers in "Amor Mundi." In Meynell's version of Rossetti, emotion is to be endured with patience and without revolt. Rossetti is distinguished, then, from Barrett Browning and from Brontë by a discipline she maintains in her emotional as well as in her poetic life. That discipline does not negate emotion, but rather gives it its own expression so that it "flies and sings." Meynell characterizes Rossetti's poetry as passionate: "In The Convent Threshold there is, I think, more passion than in any other poem written by a woman."[32] Her particular form of self-denial enables that poetic passion.

Because Rossetti does not deny herself to others in social life, she is able to deny a self in poetry.

Restraint and social connectedness emerge from these essays of literary criticism as paramount poetic values. These terms may seem to contradict one another, but that very contradiction is characteristic of Meynell's work. Although Meynell is quite clear about Barrett Browning and Brontë being very different authors from a poet like Swinburne, the fault that sometimes unites them is a failure to see and abide by their own boundaries. Meynell admires Rossetti most, and perhaps most identifies with her style because she maintains deliberateness and control. Paradoxically, that control relies not on tightening and force but on submission to natural and poetic law. Meynell connects these two types of law through meter in "The Rhythm of Life," where she writes, "If life is not always poetical, it is at least metrical."[33] Social restraint, silence, and absence allow for literary presence.

A View of "You": Imagining the Other at a Distance

In her essay "The Horizon," Meynell describes the changes in perspective while climbing up a mountain as a metaphor for the relation between subject and object. As the climber mounts, it seems as though the world itself moves upward and outward, expanding for the climber's vision, almost as though it responds to her: "As you climb the circle of the world goes up to face you."[34] The use of this particular metaphor emphasizes the point that relationships happen across distance and require separation and space within which to shift perspective. The distance allows subjects to see each other as separate and different and to respond to that difference. Indeed, this essay belongs to a genre of nature writing that, as Linda Peterson notes, Meynell "reinvented," where she "explored human relationships within the natural world by 'looking closely.'"[35] In this metaphor, relations between two masses in space become involved in a kind of intimate spatial repartee: "It is the law whereby the eye and the horizon answer one another that makes the way up a hill so full of universal movement."[36] By perspectival "laws," the movement of the person is transposed onto the entire landscape around her; from the point of view of the climber, the landscape moves in response to her movement. The horizon is "your chief companion on your way. It is to uplift the horizon to the equality of your sight that you go so high. You give it a distance worthy of the skies."[37] This is one of the few essays that Meynell addresses to a "you." This address calls attention to the relationship between reader and writer, in effect comparing the act of reading to mountain climbing. Just as the climber moves heaven and earth as his perspective shifts, so does the interpreting reader shift the text, making it answer her.

That "you" addressing the reader does perhaps less work than she would like it to, since, as we have seen in the introduction to this book, in "The Second Person Singular," Meynell laments the loss of the familiar "thou." Had she had the option to refer to her reader with the lost second person singular, she might have been able to specify what sort of relationship author and reader have in a prose essay, whether she means it to be familiar, intimate, and inviting, or a simple, formal address. The "you" would not be "merely pointing the rude forefinger of a pronoun."[38] The choice would reveal how well she feels she knows her readers, and they her. In "The Second Person Singular," Meynell writes that while industrial work becomes more and more specialized, the language becomes less so, with words being required to do a greater variety of linguistic tasks as the language simplifies. The dropping out of "thou" from everyday language has put too much pressure on "you," making it do the work of two pronouns rather than one. At least, she writes, the second person singular is still alive in the language of poetry and piety, able to convey its "single delight" and intimate inflexion. By addressing a "you," "The Horizon" avoids the sort of solipsism and narcissism that might seem inherent in a claim on the entire visible landscape as one's companion. (It is the sort of claim for which Meynell criticizes Swinburne.) By involving the reader, the tone becomes inclusive rather than boastful. Meynell may well have chosen to use the formal "you," for the very fact of distance in the figure of the horizon also keeps it from being solipsistic. It maintains a distance that is at once "enormous and minute," so that a scene of the sublime is also about dynamic relations between conceptions of scale.

The sonnet "Thoughts in Separation" uses the same imagery as "The Horizon," referring to the "hills of life" on which the "I" and "thee" meet one another, though they are never physically present to one another. This poem's vision of souls that meet in thought or prayer but not in person likewise risks presenting a one-sided relationship of the subject with her ideal of the object. Meynell acknowledges this danger, and yet avoids it by positing heavenly proxy spirits that rise above the desires and vicissitudes of human relationships.

> We never meet; yet we meet day by day
>   Upon those hills of life, dim and immense:
>   The good we love, and sleep—our innocence.
> O hills of life, high hills! And higher than they,
>
> Our guardian spirits meet at prayer and play.
>   Beyond pain, joy, and hope, and long suspense,

Above the summits of our souls, far hence,
An angel meets an angel on the way.

Beyond all good I ever believed of thee
    Or thou of me, these always love and live,
And though I fail of thy ideal of me,

My angel falls not short. They greet each other.
    Who knows, they may exchange the kiss we give,
Thou to thy crucifix, I to my mother.[39]

Several versions of the "I" and the "thee" appear in this poem. There are at least three versions of the "I": an earthly self, "thy ideal of me," and a guardian spirit or angel as its heavenly proxy. The poem acknowledges that both "I" and "thou" may sustain projected conceptions of one another, having internalized "all good I ever believed of thee / Or thou of me." Yet there is also a desire to get beyond an ideal version of the other. But because the "I" and the "thou" remain absent from each other, this "beyond" transcends even self. In this way the "angel" and the ideal self are different. The angel "proxies" are not defined here as products of human imagination, the way the "ideal of me" is. Rather, they "love and live" in an eternal realm, itself separated even from the knowledge of "I" and "thee." The "I" has to fragment herself in order to imagine intimacy. The poem begins and ends with the earthly "selves," but while they are united in the first word, the pronoun "we," they are separated in the last line into "Thou" and "I." Whereas most of the poem imagines their angel selves "above the summits of our souls" to be their substitutes, the poem finishes with material substitutes for objects of desire: a crucifix and a mother. This ending belies the confidence of the declaration of the guardian spirits, suggesting a fear that there is no alter-ego world to remedy their absence from one another.

The grammatical procession of the sonnet separates the two by beginning in the first stanza with the first person plural, switching in the second stanza to the third person, and moving into the intimate joy of the second person singular in the third stanza. The pronouns separate them in the third stanza, but that separation is precisely what allows for intimate address. That address allows the privacy of thought to emerge into the close space between two people (or figures of people). In "The Second Person Singular," Meynell writes that in French the second person singular is only a "single delight," since it can be used as a gesture of intimacy only once, the first time it is used for someone; after that, "the many thousands of 'toi' are insignificant."

Meynell claims the second person singular in English as the special province of poets, "our unique plot of disregarded language that the traffic of the world passes by."[40] Her use of the second person singular in "Thoughts in Separation" recalls both of these advantages, since it has the "single delight" of bursting onto the scene in the third stanza, but also conveys a particularly poetic intimacy.

Leighton has written that Meynell's sonnet "Renouncement" owes a debt to Christina Rossetti's "Echo," and "Thoughts in Separation" is also influenced by Rossetti's poem.[41] However, whereas Rossetti's poem can be read on the one hand as straightforward longing for an absent beloved—or, as I read it in chapter 1, as a refraction of the beloved object and speaking subject into emotions, ideals, images so that they can no longer be seen properly as "subjects"—"Thoughts in Separation" does not have this double meaning; it is pure refraction. It wears the fragmentation of the lyric subject on its poetic sleeve. There is not even a wish to be physically with the absent one, nor is there longing for a fleeting dream of him. Instead, Meynell's poem portrays perfect satisfaction with the absence; indeed, the two who love each other can, paradoxically, only be together in absence of the other, only by transcending anything that is identifiably them, such as pain, joy, hope, and suspense, "above the summits of our souls." Their separation makes possible the communion of their representative angels.

Textual Relations: Influence and Intersubjectivity between Readers and Poets

As for Rossetti, the transcendence of a "self" or "subjecthood" is the very condition of poetry for Meynell. Yet Meynell insists that there is an intimacy and companionship in reading. "Soeur Monique" is about reading poetry and about the process of looking for the other in poetry and finding the self. Yet that dynamic resists narcissism precisely because it involves a recognition of the differences between self and other, the ways in which someone imagines the other, and the ultimate unknowability of a person depicted in a poem. Although it is about a piece of music, it catalogs ways in which readers might respond to poems, how they imagine the "people" represented therein. It reflects upon the connection that readers and poets establish with the figures in poetry, in particular here with a figure that supposedly refers to a person but now exists only in the forms of music and poetry. The subtitle of the poem, "A Rondeau by Couperin," indicates that the poem is about a piece of music, an "impersonal" form, rather than a person. Meynell distinguishes her poem from that piece, however, by not writing it in the poetic form of a rondeau, one that was gaining in popularity in Britain at the time. By addressing "Soeur Monique," as "you," the poem both personifies the piece of music and formalizes any idea of a person:

> Quiet form of silent nun,
> What has given you to my inward eyes?
> What has marked you, unknown one,
> In throngs of centuries
> That mine ears do listen through?
> This old master's melody
> That expresses you;
> This admired simplicity,
> Tender, with a serious wit;
> And two words the name of it,
>   "Soeur Monique."[42]

"Nun" calls to mind a person, but here it is only a form of a nun, and a silent one at that. Because nun sounds like "none," the poem reminds the reader that there is no original person that it refers to. The poem is ambiguous about whether the silence, or in fact the nun, belongs to the poem, to the music, or entirely to the past. The nun exists both in the imagination of the speaker, on "my inward eyes," and on the page, "marked" and in sound "listened" to through "throngs of centuries." By the end of this stanza, "Soeur Monique" is the name not of a person, but of an indeterminate "it," for the pronoun might refer to the melody or to its simplicity.

The speaker acknowledges that the qualities she assigns to Soeur Monique are not her own. I use the term "speaker" here as a practical necessity, but it is an unstable term. In the third stanza the poem uses the pronoun "we," while an "I" appears later in the poem. A third-person pronoun, referring to still another poet, and "one / Pausing when young March is grey," further emphasizes the varied responses to both music and poem. Although there are numerous speculations about the nun here, the second stanza uses "we" to unify them. It presents the music as sad, but the third then revises that position, saying that the sadness comes not from the music but is a reflection of the listeners' own feeling:

> No, not sad; we are beguiled,
> Sad with living as we are;
> Ours the sorrow, outpouring
> Sad self on a selfless thing.

"Outpouring" might be translated as the psychological term "projection"; the listeners project their own sorrow onto the music they hear. As the poem continues, "Soeur Monique" rehearses all the possible incarnations of its title figure, considering all the ways in which the speaker(s), who is more a reader herself than a speaker, might impose a self or selves on the "two words" at the title of the poem. Those two words and the figure they signify form an empty repository for the readers' imaginations. In the process of reading, the figure becomes an imaginary other. The speaker speculates primarily about the nun's thoughts, and in doing so wonders how she might respond to being read: "Did it vex you, the surmise / Of this wind of words, this storm of cries?" The speaker/reader of "Soeur Monique" is like the figure she addresses, a "selfless thing," a disembodied response to the figure of a nun, embodied only in the forms of music and poetry.

The poem is itself an example of apostrophe but is also about apostrophes. It refers to other poets' experience of Couperin's music and the way they might imagine Soeur Monique. In doing so they speak to her:

> . . . but the poet, he
> In whose dream your face appears,
> He who ranges unknown years
> With your music in his heart,
> Speaks to you familiarly
> Where you keep apart,
> And invents you as you were.
> And your picture, O my nun!
> Is a strangely easy one.

This poet is a figure of a poet, for the poet "ranges unknown years" only through his poetry. As I will show below in my reading of the series of poems "A Poet's Fancies," for Meynell, poetry was a form of time travel, a way of responding to the past and speaking to the future. The primary function of poetry for Meynell is to speak to the absent. The "poet" in the above passage not only invents Soeur Monique, he invents a relationship with her, a familiarity. Yet that closeness across the distance of time and fabrication is not a falsehood because it is invented. Soeur Monique is a paradox, a "vague reality," a "mysterious certainty." Reading involves faith that one's guesses and inventions have some correspondence to the world outside the mind.

In the final stanza, the speaker calls on Soeur Monique to "remember" her, thereby granting imagined agency to the being that the previous stanzas acknowledge to be a mirage of figures:

> Soeur Monique, remember me.
> 'Tis not in the past alone

I am picturing you to be;
But my little friend, my own,
In my moment pray for me.

The speaker reverses their positions, situating herself in the past, to be re-membered, while Soeur Monique exists in "my moment" a point in time that is itself as indeterminate as the speaker. This ability to cross over past and present, to make what is irretrievably distant seem close, is the power of lyric. Soeur Monique is "pictured" and thereby a product of the poem, and of the reader's mind, but essential to that picture is the notion that she is separate, a friend, one who can have her own thoughts, inventions, pictures of the reader/speaker. The relationship between speaker and Soeur Monique is thereby imagined to be an intimate exchange, while at the same time the poem acknowledges that neither are "subjects" at all. "Soeur Monique" lays out the ways in which the process of interpretation reveals a self. In the fig-ure of the nun, the "speaker" observes herself imposing a "sad self" onto the figure but then continues to imagine the nun, aware that what she pictures can never be verified against some "truth" but becomes truth in itself. She rec-ognizes sadness as belonging to herself, the speaker/reader figure, and other properties as belonging to the "quiet form of silent nun." For Meynell, this differentiation allows a reader to discover a self.

"Soeur Monique" illuminates how difficult it can be to tell the difference between one's reading of a poem, and the poem itself, elaborating on ways in which figures are both the products of poems and the products of read-ers' minds. Meynell cautions against a reader's wholesale appropriation of a figure in a poem, or a poem itself. Such appropriation, and the failure to rec-ognize the difference between one's own feelings and language and another's, amounts to egregious insincerity. In her essay on Swinburne, titled simply "Swinburne," which appeared in *Hearts of Controversy,* Meynell denounces him as guilty of such insincerity. Meynell commends him for his breathtaking versification, but condemns what she sees as his lack of authenticity. Meynell is less interested in the truthful disclosure of private feelings than she is in consistency in the public eye, and fidelity of poetry to reality and of form to substance. Swinburne creates a sense both of utter detachment, in which the meaning and the form of his poems are dissociated, and of complete absorp-tion in which he appropriates the feelings, ideas, and language of his predeces-sors as his own. He never achieves, or even strives for, the carefully balanced distance that Meynell cultivates in her own work. What she calls his "insin-cerity" she sees as his failure to recognize that balance which she regards as natural and a refusal of the boundaries between himself and his predecessors.

Meynell criticizes Swinburne for having praised a poet and painter pub-
licly, and then, after he was offended by his posthumous autobiography, hav-
ing revised his opinion. Meynell distances herself from other critics of Swin-
burne by insisting that she interprets this incident "not as a sign of moral
fault, with which I have no business, but as a sign of a most significant literary
insensibility."[43] Swinburne's insincerity is a failure of consistency and sense.
In changing his opinion, his wounded pride dictates his words, rather than
a detached literary discernment, signaling an obligation to the personal and
the private over one to the reading public. Meynell writes that the primacy of
words over thought and image leads to images in his poetry that are virtually
meaningless. She cites a chorus in "Atalanta at Calydon" where the speaker
complains that "the pleasant streams flow into the sea." Meynell mocks the
lines, saying, "What would he have? The streams turned loose all over the
countryside?" For Meynell, the image is insincere because it does not corre-
spond to reality. She writes, "I am not censuring any insincerity of thought;
I am complaining of the insincerity of a paltry, shaky, and unvisionary im-
age."[44] According to this essay, the image has no possible, meaningful refer-
ent, realistic or fantastic, concrete or ideal. Where there are words without
referents, there is no possibility for sincerity.

Her definition of insincerity here is itself shaky, and a stronger objection
can be gleaned by comparing the lines from "Atalanta at Calydon" that she
dismisses with her essay "The Rhythm of Life." The lines Meynell complains
of appear in a long chorus that inveighs against God for ruining pleasure
with pain. Although elsewhere in his poetry Swinburne seems to revel in this
duality, as though one might not be distinguished from the other, this chorus
protests the coupling as cruel:

> Thou hast kissed us, and hast smitten; thou has laid
> Upon us with thy left hand life, and said,
> Live: and again thou has said, Yield up your breath,
> And with thy right hand laid upon us death.
> Thou hast sent us sleep, and stricken sleep with dreams,
>   Saying, Joy is not, but love of joy shall be;
> Thou has made sweet springs for all the pleasant streams,
>   In the end thou has made them bitter with the sea.[45]

As a metaphor for death as a bitter end to life, the corruption of fresh water
with brine makes sense. In her essay, Meynell finds it illogical because the
streams could not do otherwise, but that is exactly what Swinburne com-
plains about. While Meynell had plenty of illogical images to choose from
in Swinburne's work, she chose this passage, I argue, because it offended her

own sense of natural law. Whereas Swinburne shakes his fists at the injustice that suffering should exist at all, Meynell believes that suffering is necessary because happiness could not exist without it.

The dependence of opposites on one another is essential for Meynell's poetics. If opposites do not coexist, they follow with inevitability upon one another. In "The Rhythm of Life," Meynell argues that periodicity is one of the only reliable principles in life in general, but especially in cognition and emotion: "What the mind suffered last week, or last year, it does not suffer now; but it will suffer again next week or next year."[46] Meynell links this periodicity of the mind to natural events such as the change of the seasons, the tide, and the waxing and waning of the moon. Opposites are necessary to sustain one another, and this is especially true in human relationships, where "presence does not exist without absence."[47] To deny one axis of any pole means weakening another. In "The Rhythm of Life," Meynell criticizes the sentiment behind Swinburne's lines: "To live in constant efforts after an equal life, whether the equality be sought in mental production, or in spiritual sweetness, or in the joy of the senses, is to live without either rest or full activity."[48] Swinburne's complaint that the stream flows into the sea is not unrealistic so much as an image but as a concept.

Worse than Swinburne's alleged insincerity of image, however, are the "stolen" passions of his poetry. Meynell charges Swinburne with claiming that which is outside himself—the language itself and the literary tradition—as his own. The thoughts his poems express never belonged to him: "I believe the words to hold and use his meaning, rather than the meaning to compass and grasp and use the word. I believe that Swinburne's thoughts have their source, their home, their origin, their authority and mission in those two places—his own vocabulary and the passion of other men. This is a grave charge."[49] What others might call influence (or intertextuality) or imagination, Meynell calls, in the case of Swinburne, "promiscuity" and "license." Swinburne's work crosses the boundaries between these categories. For Meynell, what distinguishes mere literary influence from Swinburne's recourse to "Mazzini in Italy, Gautier and Baudelaire in France, Shelley in England" for a "base of passionate and intellectual supplies" is the lack of interchange between the poet and his influences. In other words, Swinburne uses old influences but does not generate new ones for the next generation of poets. Meynell uses a language of economics, referring to the "supply" of feeling and words, to the "booty" of vocabulary, to "goods" and "resources" to indicate that Swinburne is a consumer in this literary economy where he might have been an impressive producer, an influential source for future poets.[50] The ideal of influence that Meynell invokes is an example of the principle of periodicity she invokes in "The Rhythm of Life." Because Swinburne does not accept that periodicity, his writing is not generative.

Swinburne shuts down the interpretive potential of his poetry by using words without meaningful precision. The issue of liberty, for example, is a far more complicated one than Swinburne lets on. Meynell writes that he cries out for liberties already won, for the political battles of others, and uses "Liberty" as a "pocket-word," what we might now call a "buzzword," full of positive connotations and emotional resonance but without real significance. For Meynell, the very concept of liberty denies the fundamental interconnectedness of people: "Who, it has been asked by a citizen of a modern free country, is thoroughly free except a fish? Et encore—even the 'silent and footless herds' may have more inter-accomodation than we are aware."[51]

She does not accuse Swinburne of plagiarism, rather, she accuses him of absorbing the sentiments of other poems into his own obsession with poetic form. By pillaging literary resources without creating one, Swinburne leaves no room for others. For Meynell, his lack of restraint in his use of language and of literary sources makes him an antisocial poet. Swinburne's poetry does not allow for intimacy, because it does not allow for separate subjects, separate poets, with space between them. Because Meynell's vision of intimacy is so dependent on the space between subjects, on distance, detachment, and restraint, Swinburne's poetry comes across as disingenuous. There is no possibility for sincerity there, because there is nothing separate toward which to have fidelity. Sincerity, then, is a matter of restraint, rather than a matter of disclosure. Swinburne's offense, ultimately, is that he takes up too much room, attempting to absorb the literature of the past and the vocabulary of the present and future. Meynell likens his poetic practice to theft, saying that he "ransacks" the language.

Although Swinburne's poems are a triumph of sound, they are not a triumph of language. She charges that he uses words as a "booty," pulling them "out of his pocket" when he needs to indicate a particular emotion, so that "Hell" stands for hatred or "fire" for wrath or "foam" for sweetness, and he uses them so strongly and frequently that the terms lose all nuance. Because Swinburne does not possess a wealth of his own ideas, he has to make "economies of thought and feeling." In other words, he has to use them sparingly because he has limited resources. Similarly, Meynell casts words as a limited resource on which Swinburne draws more than his own share. Language, for Meynell, is a shared national (and international) resource. Those who use language imprecisely waste that which should be available to all. Despite his metrical precision, Swinburne lacks semantic precision and thereby damages the language for all. The loss of that precision in the language more broadly is precisely what Meynell laments in "The Second Person Singular." For Meynell, then, Swinburne contributes to the deterioration of the English language.

In writing about Swinburne, Meynell both presents a prescriptive argument for how poets should and should not respond to their predecessors, and answers a poet of the preceding generation. Her series "A Poet's Fancies" performs a similar function by creating models of poets responding to one another and to their worlds. This series often complicates and even contradicts the arguments she makes about Swinburne. For instance, a positive side of narcissism emerges in "The Love of Narcissus," the first poem in the series "A Poet's Fancies."[52] The poem opens with a simile that compares "the poet" to Narcissus. Here, the poet observes nature and recognizes himself:

> His dreams are far among the silent hills;
>   His vague voice calls him from the darkened plain
> With winds at night; strange recognition thrills
>   His lonely heart with piercing love and pain;
> He knows again his mirth in mountain rills,
>   His weary tears that touch him with the rain.[53]

These lines have none of the pejorative associations that come along with the term "narcissism."[54] Rather, a Romantic impression of emotion awakened through nature emerges here. This poem recalls Meynell's comparisons of human rhythms to natural ones in "The Rhythm of Life." The way in which nature helps the poet to recognize his own emotions contributes to his self-knowledge, and presumably makes him wiser. After all, Meynell criticized Elizabeth Barrett Browning and Charlotte Brontë for moments in which they seemed to lose sight of themselves.

Yet this poem might also be read as a parody of Romantic poetry, and also of Swinburne as an inheritor and perhaps corrupter of that tradition. The second poem in the series, "To Any Poet," responds to "The Love of Narcissus" by saying that poets who write about nature always leave something out because nature exceeds the grasp of any artist. The creatures of the earth flee the poet: "Dumbly they defy thee; / There is something they deny thee."[55] Nature shuns the poet "Though her flowers and wheat / Throng and press thy pausing feet." The movement of the "pausing feet" of poetry does not match the "thronging" rhythm of plant life. "To Any Poet" recalls Ruskin's pathetic fallacy, in which he decries poets who characterize nature as having emotion. These lines criticize the narcissistic poet who sees his own happiness in "mountain rills," for he cannot differentiate himself from nature:

> Sing thy sorrow, sing thy gladness,
> In thy songs must wind and tree
> Bear the fictions of thy sadness,
>   Thy humanity.
> For their truth is not for thee.

The poem carves out separate truths, one for nature, another for humanity. The emotions of the poet are fictions to the "wind and tree," not because the poet does not feel them but because the wind and tree do not.

After the fourth stanza, the poem shifts to say that the only way the poet can become a part of nature is in death:

> Thou shalt intimately lie
> In the roots of flowers that thrust
> Upwards from thee to the sky,
>   With no more distrust,
> When they blossom from thy dust.

Intimacy with the earth comes at the price of complete surrender. The poem represents art and nature as antagonists. While the poet is alive, the creatures and the plants of nature "fear" him; with the poet, dead Earth is "set free from thy fair fancies." In death, the secrets of the earth become available to the poet, but only because he has fully submitted to the will of God:

> Then the truth all creatures tell,
> And His will Whom thou entreatest
> Shall absorb thee; there shall dwell
>   Silence, the completest
> Of thy poems, last and sweetest.

This silence is not nothingness or pure absence but instead openness to the "other" that is nature and God. Whereas silence during a country-house game of charades is merely social tact, making room for the foibles of others, this silence is an expansive one, allowing for a sort of communication that could never take place in human speech. Silence is the place of intimacy, the completest poem because it is the only one that incorporates the secrets of nature that remain hidden to the living, writing poet. Paradoxically, because they can only be expressed in silence, they remain secrets. Meynell's vision of the afterlife, like Rossetti's, involves deep communion with God. The silence that Meynell imagines dominating the afterlife is her version of Rossetti's heavenly music, for the right sort of silence and submission are themselves art forms.

Two conceptions of poetry compete in this poem. On one hand poetry is limited, the secrets of nature just out of reach. On the other hand, the silent communication of the dead, God, and nature is itself a poem, if only in the abstract. Both of these conceptions go against the simplified Romantic vision of communion with nature in "The Love of Narcissus."[56] That poem is a sonnet with a strict rhyme scheme in strict iambic meter. "To Any Poet" is in trochaic meter, and thereby reverses poetic expectations, both thematic and metrical. In her essay on Swinburne, Meynell wrote that she favors iambic and trochaic feet in English: "I love to see English poetry move to many measures, to many numbers, but chiefly with the simple iambic and the simple trochaic foot."[57] Although Meynell casts the trochee as simple and common, her experiment with falling meter in "To Any Poet" is not. The syntax is labored in order to facilitate the unusual meter, as in "Pines thy fallen nature ever / For the unfallen Nature sweet." Just as the iambic feet are reversed, the subject and the verb and the noun and adjective are reversed. This meter requires an abundance of feminine rhymes, such as "flowers / bowers / showers" or "burden / garden / pardon," but Meynell also uses original feminine rhymes that depend not on paroxytonic words, but that take the stress off of a word that might ordinarily be stressed, as in these lines: "Though thou tame a bird to love thee, / Press thy face to grass and flowers, / All these things reserve above thee." In this case, the meter supports the meaning of the poem. By taking the emphasis off of "thee," and stressing "love" and "above," the poem indicates the importance of the relational over the individual.

Yet at the same time, the trochaic meter enacts disconnection. Often, an enjambed line ends on a stressed syllable, necessitating a pause before the stressed first syllable of the next line, as in "In thy songs must wind and tree / Bear the fictions of thy sadness." This meter makes a smooth enjambment nearly impossible so that the syntax works against the meter. While the meter is tightly controlled, this ambiguity, the meter that emphasizes at once connection and disconnection, implies that the poem, like the nature it attempts to represent, cannot be fully controlled. Indeed, in the third poem of the series, "To One Poem in a Silent Time," the speaker addresses one of her poems, wanting to know where it comes from. This poem is an extended metaphor that compares the mysteries of poetry to the mysteries of nature, representing the unexpected poem as a "mid-winter flower." The surprise and uncertainty of the speaker in "To One Poem" signal the poet's lack of control, her submission to the fleeting muse of inspiration. The address from the poet to the poem reverses apostrophe, for the thing addressed, the poem, may very well be the one that is present, the one that we read. It is rather the poet who is absent, and a measure of agency—or rather the agency of measure—is given over to the poem itself, which appears of its own accord.

"To One Poem" establishes a relationship between poet and poem, as does the last poem in the series, "Unlinked." In this poem, the speaker/poet asks what would happen to her art if she abandoned it, whether it would be consigned to the wind or to "mountain streams." She answers that even if she does not sing, she is still a singer, her art still her own. If she does not write them, however, she concludes that her poems will emerge on their own, that her poem could gather itself into being without her knowledge: "Through my indifferent words of every day, / scattered and all unlinked the rhymes shall ring / And make my poem; and I shall not know."[58] These lines indicate a notion of a poem that has a destiny and a purpose separate from its author. The poet imagines that the poem will coalesce from her ordinary speech, that all of the words are there even if they are not in the right order. This is a vision of an inherent order within chaos, an order that comes from outside the self but is somehow channeled through it.

The poet of "To One Poem in a Silent Time" does not know whether the poem is the last in a line of old poems or the beginning of a new period of productivity: "Where shall I look—backwards or to the morrow / For others of thy fragrance, secret child?" Indeed, the relationships between poets, between a poet and her poem, or between a poet and poetry happen across time, the distances of time separating one from another. In "The Day to the Night," these two entities, representative of poets of different generations, bemoan the fact that they can never coexist: "From dawn to dust, and from dusk to dawn / We two are sundered always, Sweet."[59] While in "To One Poem," the poet considers the development and the potential of her own oeuvre, the past and the future in the rest of the series "A Poet's Fancies" refers to intergenerational, intertextual influence. An intimacy of influence emerges in "The Moon to the Sun: The Poet Sings to Her Poet," where the sun represents the poets of the past while the moon represents the poets of the future. The moon reflects the light of the sun, changing its quality so that the light it gives belongs to both of them:

> Shine, Earth loves thee! And then shine
> And be loved through thoughts of mine.
> All thy secrets that I treasure
> I translate them at my pleasure.
> I am crowned with glory of thine,
>   Thine, not thine.[60]

What Meynell criticizes in Swinburne as intellectual and emotional theft, here she lauds as shared glory, the younger poet exalting the older. These poems construe poetry as inherently dialogic. The older poet is the source for the thoughts of the younger. Although the older poet cannot answer back, the future poets respond to the previous generation. In "The Spring to the Summer," the older poet addresses the younger poet, telling her that she must complete and fulfill ideas that began with the older poet: "O Poet of the time to be, / My conqueror, I began for thee / Enter into thy poet's pain."[61] Each poet renews the other. Meynell's models of intergenerational influence are strikingly similar to the ideals of parenthood and childhood that she discusses in essays and in poems. While ideas might be similar, the new poet, or the child, alters them by changing the rhythm. I turn, therefore, to Meynell's writing on mothers and children.

"Her Own Blood Moves Separately": The Poetic Rhythms of Mother and Child

While "Soeur Monique" and the poems in "A Poet's Fancies" speak to the literary relationships between poets and readers, present and past, and their inherent separateness, Meynell's poems and essays on motherhood and children establish the distance between mother and child as the constitutive feature of their intense but unequal intimacy. Critics have often addressed the political valence of these writings, noting their anti-sentimentality, but no one has addressed the quality of the intimacy described and its importance for Meynell's poetics. Leighton sees the ambivalence expressed in these works as modern and daring, upsetting conventional wisdom about the purity of a mother's love. She casts her as one of the first women poets to deal frankly with the complicated feelings of motherhood. Lee Behlman argues that Meynell's writing on children shows that it is possible to unite professional and personal life and that intellectual, professional life and affective, maternal life need not be mutually exclusive, as was commonly thought in the period.[62] Peterson asserts that misreadings of this body of work, even deliberate ones in the publicity for it, are in part responsible for Meynell's reputation as a domestic angel, a reputation that ushered her into literary obscurity for much of the twentieth century.[63] Yet the key to her unsentimentality, what Leighton calls "a troubling knowledge of separation and difference," is in fact a necessary part of intimacy.[64] Although Leighton criticizes the sentimentality of much previous poetry about motherhood as "treacly," she treats Meynell's poetry as confessional because her own criticisms retain the assumption that motherhood is "the love which should be primary and all engrossing."[65] Leighton thereby implies that Meynell is courageous in saying how difficult it is to live up to the ideal of the engrossed unambivalent mother, but she nonetheless upholds the ideal.

While Meynell's depiction of detachment within relations between mother and child certainly contains disappointments, she nonetheless re-shapes the ideal as one that incorporates distance. In the essay "Solitude," Meynell describes the intimacy between mother and child as one that con-stitutes a shared solitude, away from all the family and friends who wish to hold and kiss the baby. Yet even in such a profoundly shared moment, she recognizes separation:

> A woman is hardly alone long enough to become aware, in recollec-tion, how her own blood moves separately, beside her, with another rhythm and different pulses. All is commonplace until the doors are closed upon the two. This unique intimacy is a profound retreat, an absolute seclusion. It is more than single solitude; it is a redoubled isolation more remote than mountains, safer than valleys, deeper than forests, and further than mid-sea. . . . There is no innocent sleep so innocent as sleep shared between a woman and a child, the little breath hurrying beside the longer, as a child's foot runs.[66]

The baby is a paradigm of sameness and difference; the mother's "own blood" runs in its veins but with a separate rhythm. The intimacy and "innocence" that they share relies on their separation from others, on a retreat from the world, but there is also a distance between them that begins to form here. That difference in pulse, breath, and feet grows into a difference in desires, different kinds and levels of affection. It is a recognition that the child will become increasingly separate from the mother. The isolation is redoubled be-cause the mother and the child are both isolated from the world and separate from each other by virtue of their different rhythms.

While this passage from "Solitude" constitutes an ideal of intimacy and innocence, an ideal balance of mother and child, the relationship becomes more complicated in "The Modern Mother," which represents a matrix of pleasure and pain. It conceives of the relationship between mother and child as an exchange of affection, one that can never be fully balanced:

> Oh what a kiss
> With filial passion overcharged is this!
> To this misgiving breast
> This child runs, as a child ne'er ran to rest
> Upon the light heart and the unoppressed.
>
> Unhoped, unsought!
> A little tenderness, this mother thought
> The utmost of her meed.

She looked for gratitude; content indeed
With thus much that her nine years' love had bought.

    Nay, even with less.
This mother, giver of life, death, peace, distress,
    Desired ah! not so much
Thanks as forgiveness; and the passing touch
Expected, and the slight, the brief caress.

    O filial light
Strong in these childish eyes, these new, these bright
    Intelligible stars! their rays
Are near the constant earth, guides in the maze,
Natural, true, keen, in this dusk of days.[67]

This is not merely a poem about a mother drawing away from what she views as her child's excessive affection. Although it addresses exchange between the two, possessives hardly ever mark the feelings to show whether they belong to mother or daughter. Even "her meed" might belong to the mother or the daughter, whether the recompense of "a little tenderness" is what the mother owes her child or vice versa. The mother's feelings about what sort of emotions to expect from her child change. She vacillates between expecting gratitude and expecting forgiveness. Although this forgiveness might be for her misgivings, or her unreturned passion, she indicates that it is for bringing the child into a world of distress and eventual death. This desire for forgiveness speaks to the hopes the mother has for her child, not so much for the "overcharged passion" the child expresses for her, but for the child's own life. The mother asks forgiveness for the inevitable distress of life. In the last stanza of the poem, the filial kiss becomes filial light, directed not toward the mother but outward, guiding the child's path through "dusk of days." What began as love for the mother expands to become a light that links earth to sky. The distance that the mother of this poem feels allows the child to turn outward. The seeming disequilibrium of affection and her fears for the child trouble the mother here, but they also make room for the growth of the child.

    The shifting rhythms in this poem correspond to the different, separate rhythms of mother and child described in "Solitude." The distress of life manifests as metrical distress. In these stanzas, the number of stresses changes in a pattern of 2-5-3-5-5, while the meter rocks back and forth between iambic and trochaic. The inequality of affections in "The Modern Mother" may be not so much a result of ambivalence about motherhood, but an awareness of the differences between child and adult. In "The Child of Tumult," Meynell writes that "there is unequal force at work within a child, unequal growth and a jostling of powers and energies that are hurrying to their development and pressing of exercise and life."[68] Even in her assessment of childhood, Meynell is concerned with proportions. The affections in "The Modern Mother" are of different proportions and provide necessary but painful distance. Likewise, the rhythms of mother and child have different paces. In "Real Childhood," Meynell writes of the way time passes differently for a child; an hour for a six-year-old is a larger portion of his life than it is for an adult. Putting the reader in the child's position by addressing the essay to "you," Meynell explains that for a child, "Your hours when you were six were the enormous hours of the mind that has little experience and constant and quick forgetfulness."[69] Whereas blood is a figure of filial ties, rhythm marks a child's experience as separate from his parents'. By addressing the reader in this way, she figures herself as a mother and the reader as the child, establishing maternal influence as a paradigm for textual influence.

Although he is her elder, George Meredith figures Meynell as a kind of poetic progenitor when he writes to her about her collection *Later Poems*: "Of your little collection all passes into my blood except 'Parentage.'"[70] Meredith's image of poetry passing "into his blood" suggests that he identifies with it so profoundly that he feels as though it was a physical part of him. Yet even he, whose work takes relational ambivalence to new heights, cannot assimilate the troubling of the filial bond in "Parentage." In that poem, Meynell protests what her own "Rhythm of Life" might call natural law. The epigram to the poem refers to Augustus Caesar's declaration that unmarried citizens were "slayers of the people" because they did not reproduce. Meynell responds in her poem that it is not the childless but parents themselves who are responsible for death, for without the life they bring into the world, no one could bring "unnumbered man to the innumerable grave." Here is a darker side of Meynell's law of periodicity: "And she who slays is she who bears, who bears."[71] The bitter tone of the poem registers it as a complaint about this inevitable natural law, one that is reminiscent of Swinburne's complaint that sweet streams must be tainted by the bitter sea. For all her criticisms of him, Swinburne turns out to be in this poem a poetic parent. Although Meynell's rhythms are different, the substance, the "blood" in this poem, is the same. In this sign of influence, she proves her own conviction that distance eventually comes around to closeness, and Swinburne's "sweet streams throng into my breast."[72]

For Meynell, maternity is poetic and poetry should be maternal and generative, inspiring new poetry. Meynell closes "The Rhythm of Life" by asserting that the maternal dominates the rhythm of life: "Their [the young unfortunates'] joy is flying away from them on its way home; their life will wax and wane; and if they would be wise, they must wake and rest in its phases, knowing that they are ruled by the law that commands all things—a sun's revolutions and the rhythmic pangs of maternity."[73] Meynell allies maternal creation with poetic creation, their rhythms—their meters—dictating emotional and interpersonal dynamics despite any attempts at resistance. The "rhythmic pangs of maternity" also suggest the rhythms of intimacy that I have defined in this chapter, the dynamic of closeness and distance, of union and painful separation. Those who would give birth to poetry must observe the laws of such rhythm. Products of an attempt to be too close, such as Swinburne's, or of an environment that is too distanced, such as the "delusive bower" of women writers, ring false not because they are not true to the writers themselves, but because they are not true to the ruling rhythms. For Meynell, this comparison of the maternal and the poetic means that language and meter themselves can be generative and intimate, or sterile, as she claims Swinburne's is. The intimacy of poetry, the balance of distance from and closeness to other poets and poems, and between poetic figures of "I" and "thou," both preserves language and makes it new. Both the preservation and the renewal of language depend upon maintaining the precision of each word and distinctions between words. The distinctness of the second person singular, for instance, marks it as an intimate address, but one that is renewed only in poetry. Because the "thou" can only appear in "the phrase of poetry and piety," the most intimate address is only available in the distance of a poem.

5

"So I Can Wait and Sing"

DOLLIE RADFORD'S POETICS OF WAITING

In the preceding chapters, I have examined fin de siècle women poets' attempts to make lyric intimacy work, to represent as well as to enact a relational dynamic in their poems. In this final chapter, I explore how Dollie Radford questions the idea that poems construed as songs can establish intimacy. Radford frequently describes songs' failures to communicate in lines like these: "How I wished my love could hear," or "All the music would die," or "I have no voice now you have come."[1] She repeatedly calls attention to instances of songs' incompleteness, or even deception. Radford emphasizes that poems called "song" are often never heard at all. In response to the idea that songs often fail to deliver on a promise of a present voice, her poems insist on what this genre does offer in the fin de siècle: a space of waiting, a moment of attentiveness, and an acceptance of mere sufficiency. Radford's depiction of waiting, in song, for song, acknowledges, rather than trying to ban, the absence of the other. Reflecting on the presence of voice in a poem, in the past and in the future, as well as by experimenting with musical settings, Radford asks what counts as "song" in fin de siècle verse culture.

Because Radford is less well known than some of the other poets in this study, a brief introduction is called for. Radford was at the center of elite literary circles of the 1890s. On April 8, 1891, she and her husband, Ernest Radford, co-hosted a party with Arthur Symons in the Temple. In attendance were May Morris, Michael Field (Katharine Bradley and Edith Cooper), George Moore, Mathilde Blind, Havelock and Miss Ellis, John Lane and Graham Tomson. One week later, Radford notes in her diary that Michael Field paid them a visit at their home, and that her first volume of poems, *A Light Load,* had been sent to the *Academy* for review. The following week, she notes, "A very kind letter from Arthur Symons, telling me he has written a review of "A Light Load for the Academy + that he very much likes the small volume."[2] These diary entries surrounding Symons's review and the review itself attest to Radford's importance in the literary world of the 1890s. During the course of her career, Radford published five collections of verse, two works of fiction, and four children's books. She published her poetry with John Lane and Elkin Mathews at the Bodley Head, and her books were handsomely bound and printed in small runs. Although somewhat rare and nicely done, the books were inexpensive, 4 shillings, 6 pence for *Songs and Other Verses,* meant for a reader with discriminating tastes but not necessarily a wealthy one.[3] In addition to appearing at and sometimes hosting elite literary salons, she was also a member of the Hammersmith socialists and regularly attended their meetings. These socialist pursuits were a part of a robust and varied aestheticist culture, as Ruth Livesey attests.[4]

Radford's link between fin de siècle song and waiting takes on both political and aesthetic valence. By dedicating a poem to progressive novelist Olive Schreiner, she announces the necessity of patience for social progress. In Radford's view, patience is as important to progress as action, which risks turning in self-consuming circles. Welcoming new developments, she asserts, requires the openness and attentiveness of the wait. When Radford writes, "I can wait and sing," she suggests that singing fills the space in the absence of action. Turning to early musical settings of Radford's poems, I show how even musical performance cannot establish the presence that her poems often wish for.

By writing "songs" (a genre of the "small" by definition) that praise the advantages of waiting, an activity largely viewed as disempowering, she advocates for the virtues of minor poetry. I go on to show how Radford illuminates the importance of the "smallness" that also caused such anxiety. The position of the minor poet—with a small audience and a presumably limited impact—allowed her the freedom to be boldly unoriginal. She shows how songs that repeat tired tropes are extremely satisfying within the private relationship of mother and child. The presumed "unoriginality" of the woman poet limits her poetic possibilities, but that is precisely what allows intimacy with her child, the only context in which what Radford calls "tender measures" do successfully communicate. She makes no claims of finding or producing what is new or original. Ultimately, what she does defend is the small, the minor, the incomplete. As she elevates waiting to an important ethical and aesthetic status, she also looks not for the replacement of a lost original, but something that will be truly new, if always still incomplete. To find that new, she avers, one must have the capacity to reject old fantasies and to remain open and attentive. For Radford, singing and waiting demonstrate a profound acceptance of minority that asks readers to reconsider the standards of poetic value.

"If I, in Vain, Must Sit and Wait"

The concept of waiting is often gendered as feminine, leading one of Radford's contemporaries, Ella Hepworth Dixon, to ask in *The Story of a Modern Woman,* "I wonder if any man alive really knows how dreadful it is to be a woman, and to have to sit down, and fold your hands and wait?"[5] Yet the dynamics of waiting have an important resonance for the fin de siècle more generally, as a period that is often viewed as transitional. A number of recent scholars of the fin de siècle have recently resisted this marginalizing term, instead advancing the fin de siècle as intellectually rich in its own right, rather than as a way-station to modernism. Yet this view risks overlooking the positive qualities of waiting as important elements of the transitional. A paradox at the heart of Radford's poetics, and indeed of fin de siècle culture, the concept of waiting signifies at once endurance and rest, lassitude and effort, pause and preparation, procrastination and anticipation. Yet in most minds, waiting's negative connotations—boredom, emptiness, powerlessness—come to the forefront. The one who waits cannot make anything happen, must count on others for action. Waiting, it would seem, opposes progress, preserves the status quo. Radford presents waiting as an act of patient defiance, an attitude of attention and openness that she asserts is necessary for aesthetic and social progress. These inherent contradictions define her ideas about what poetry can do. Radford suggests that although songs often fail to communicate and therefore cannot form or strengthen intimate bonds, they can cultivate attention and patience.

In "A Novice," Radford presents waiting as inevitable and therefore advocates enjoyment of the unavoidable process. The title invites a comparison of the harried housewife who speaks the poem, complaining about spoilt broth, disaffected servants, and accounts of "varying amounts," with a nun. A cigarette, whose smoke forms a halo and inspires philosophical thoughts, enables the patient stance of this overburdened domestic wife, and transports her from practical to ethereal concerns. The poem thereby endows the figure of the smoking "New Woman" with the spiritual virtues of patience, which become evident in the final stanzas of the poem:

> In spite of those who, knocking, stay
> At sullen portals day by day,
> And weary at the long delay
>   To their demands.
>
> The promised epoch, like a star,
> Shines very bright and very far,

But nothing shall its luster mar,
　　Though distant yet.

If I, in vain, must sit and wait,
To realize our future state,
I shall not be disconsolate,
　　My cigarette![6]

Action and seeking, here figured as knocking on a closed door, are at least as useless as waiting patiently and more tiring. That the waiting may indeed be "in vain" nods to the gendered powerlessness that Hepworth Dixon alludes to. Yet although the "promised epoch" of full equality for women is distant, its light still shines brightly; waiting, rather than wearisome knocking will "realize" the future. While on the one hand the cigarette seems to represent capitulation, a mere pleasant consolation, on the other hand it is a very emblem of the progress women have already made. Although this "Novice" is merely waiting, she has encroached into previously male-dominated territory by philosophizing, smoking and rejecting domestic duties.

Radford often aligns song with waiting, a stance of watchful openness to the future, opposed to insistent and unproductive demands. In *A Light Load,* poems often celebrate the simple, if trite, joys of song, as in "Violets, sweet violets, / I can find the fairest."[7] One "Song" defends its genre on the grounds that singing is a form of preparation for intimacy, if not productive of intimacy itself:

Why seems the world so fair,
　　Why do I sing?
Why? In the meadow there
　　When it was Spring,
There when all fair things were
　　Clearer to see,
All the young dreams I'd lost
　　Came back to me.

I may not enter now,
　　But there's a Spring
Somewhere beyond the sun.
　　So I can sing,
So I can wait and sing,
　　While I prepare
My soul to welcome thine,
　　When we meet there.[8]

In the first stanza, "singing" seems only to look backwards; the singer sings because there *was* a time and a place that was better, which the songs idealize. Yet the "Spring" of the past was already a time of recurrence, when that which was lost returned. This pattern of loss and return allows the idealized past to merge with the idealized future in the following stanza. The patience of this wait acknowledges that what seems new will be *re*newed. The Spring will bring the clarity and intimacy of the past and of the future. The poem casts the present as a transitional moment. The singer cannot make the spring come, but can wait and prepare for it. With the addition of "wait" to the line "So I can sing," Radford indicates that singing at the fin de siècle is itself a form of waiting. By telling us that she "*can* wait and sing," the singer defers the song itself, emphasizing the potential that lies in her ability, rather than the satisfaction of fulfillment. Song fills the time until the new arrives and constitutes the preparation for it. Radford eschews a radically experimental style, embracing "song," which isn't a metaphor merely for poetry, but for short stanzaic lyrics. Radford justifies it as essential for the wait.

These poems do not reveal what the waiting is for. We often associate waiting with an object, as Roland Barthes does in his section entitled "Waiting" in *A Lover's Discourse*. The lover waits for the other to show up at the café or call on the phone; Barthes is interested in the experience of that lover and in the way he mentally fabricates the other for whom he waits. This relationship is an inherently unequal one, with a dynamic that Barthes characterizes this way: "*To make someone wait:* the constant prerogative of all power."[9] For Barthes, waiting signifies frustrating inaction, and the waiting lover is motionless of necessity. Those who wait in Radford's poems resemble more strongly Barthes's final example of the "mandarin" who is enamored of a courtesan who promises to be his if he will wait on a stool outside her window for 100 nights in a row. On the ninety-ninth night, the man leaves, without explanation.[10] Barthes offers no further commentary on this anecdote, but it opens up the possibility that the wait may be undertaken for its own sake, as an exercise in stamina or devotion, which makes it about the waiting subject rather than the anticipated object.[11]

Certainly, Radford's determination to "wait and sing" presents waiting as a good in itself. In "Why seems the world so fair?" the "singer" waits for the other, depending on the changing of the seasons so the lovers can meet. As Meynell does in her "Rhythm of Life," Radford extols the patience rewarded periodically by a renewal that she cannot control but that will inevitably come. Radford thus presents waiting as a potentially mutual activity. Someone who waits may well wait for something within himself, as Rossetti does in "Echo" for "dreams to come back." Because Radford's version of waiting does not depend specifically on the actions of some other empowered person, it can be a stance of strength, one that sees waiting as a good in itself as well as part of a progressive pattern.

Although Radford presents song as itself a form of waiting, she also goes further elsewhere in *A Light Load,* proposing the deferral of song itself. This "Song" from *A Light Load* marks both a desire for and a fear of singing. In it, Radford's lover leaves and then sadly waits to sing—if this waiting is for anything, it is for a set of unspecified conditions that will make singing possible. In "I am wanting to send you a song," the hesitation is a manifestation of the desire for that which one has already refused:

> I am wanting to send you a song, love,
>> From over the sea,
> But the way, Oh the way is so long, love,
>> Between you and me,
> All the music would die,
> In the waves and the sky,
>> Before it reached thee.
>
> I am wanting to tell you my love, love,
>> But you will forget
> How you lifted your sweet eyes above, love,
>> How their lashes were wet
> When you wished me good-bye,
> While the stars filled the sky,
>> And my sad sails were set.[12]

As a song about not singing, this poem performs a paradox familiar from Christina Rossetti's "Song," "When I am dead my dearest." Radford's poem indicts lyric for its failure to communicate, especially to express love. By insisting that the "you" the poem addresses could never receive a song, it emphasizes the emptiness of poetic address. Indeed, the poem extends and then revokes the address by calling to "you" but refusing to send the message. The poem expresses an anxiety about reading, for the speaker/singer knows that the song she would really like to sing cannot be heard or received at all. The poet is conscious of her own potential failure even as she performs her poetic success. That success lies in the charming performance of alternating anapestic tetrameters and dimeters and a rhyme scheme that effortlessly emphasizes the meter. Yet the poem also, ironically, successfully performs its own failure. The addition of "love" at the end of the first and third lines of each stanza undermines the meter with a stressed extrametrical syllable and reduces the rhymes of those lines to mere repetition without the balance of similarity and difference that characterizes even the most simple rhyme. This stressed extrametrical syllable addresses the beloved who can't hear the song anyway, reminding us that poetic address is a contrivance. Although the word "love" is meant ostensibly as a pet-name address, its intrusive presence suggests that there is no room for love here, no space for love within the prescribed meter of the poem. That extrametrical "love," especially in the first line of the second stanza, also functions as an echo. This word meant to address another does exactly the opposite. Not reaching the "you" of the poem at all, the address to "love" bounces back to the would-be singer. As she sings about wanting to sing, she waits for the echo of herself to respond, in the pause enforced by the adjacent stresses and the comma before "love."

The poem's contradictory logic also appears in the certain expectation of the song's failure. How can the singer know her song won't reach her beloved if she does not even try to sing it? The singer's intractable discouragement is as much an obstacle as the distance she professes cannot be traversed and as the memories that will not be recalled. The poem presents the desire to sing as a perpetual condition rather than an intermediate one; there is no sign that the distance between the lovers or the beloved's propensity to forget will change. In the final line we learn that the singer created these impossible conditions herself by setting sail; an act of will brought about this situation of powerlessness.

This departure is based on the expectations of Romanticism, articulated by Wordsworth in "Personal Talk," that "sweetest melodies / Are those that by distance are made more sweet."[13] Indeed, I argue in chapter 4 that distance is a necessity for other fin de siècle women poets such as Alice Meynell. Yet Radford suggests here that this romantic expectation can be easily disappointed when the distance becomes so great that the music is no longer audible. In "I am not One who much or oft delight," Wordsworth prizes the distance between reader and poet; in reading, the speaker finds all the communion that he needs, and solitary contemplation by his fireside is far more pleasing than the trivial gossip of "personal talk" in the same place. Written around the same time as Radford's, the poems that Alice Meynell groups into "A Poet's Fancies" confirm this belief in the intimate power of poetry and in the ability of its very distance to produce profound connection. Yet Radford questions this assumption that favors impersonal writing over "personal talk." For Wordsworth and Meynell, solitude—the absence of an addressee—makes intimacy possible. Radford declares this idea to be an illusion; she refuses to sing precisely because no one, or the addressed one, is not immediately present.

Despite the melancholy surface of "I am wanting to send you a song," Radford asserts that absence is in fact better than intimate distance. Songs cannot render an absent beloved present, but the beloved's absence is a hidden treasure. It creates not the poem that the singer wants, but the one that she has. Rather than reading the singer's departure from her beloved as a disappointing mistake, we might also read it as bringing about the desired state of active anticipation and desire—wanting is a form of waiting. Perhaps the song will not reach its intended audience, but it will preserve the tender moment of parting, the evidence of love. The potential song is not only better than the imagined love song, it *is* the love song. By refusing to sing the love song that she in fact is singing (or writing), Radford maintains a deep skepticism about the ideals embodied in the form of "song," while nonetheless celebrating its perseverance.

Radford's stance on waiting, deferral, and anticipation is distinguished from approaches exemplified by other fin de siècle poets, particularly male poets. Arthur Symons, her friend, reviewer, and member of the Rhymers' Club along with her husband, writes about waiting as a futile and thwarted hopelessness in "The Broken Tryst." In this poem a man waits until morning, long past the appointed hour, for his beloved to show up, and as the time passes he struggles with the realization that she will not come. In the initial stanzas, the lover's certainty makes the wait tolerable, even pleasant with his singing: "I felt so patient; I could wait, / Being certain. So the hours in song / Chimed out the minutes of my fate."[14] This lover sings to pass the time, but that song manifests his confidence and certainty, rather than the time passing itself. For Symons, patience requires certitude. In the schema of "The Broken Tryst," waiting for something not fully specified does not make sense. His disappointment renders him powerless not only to act but to think clearly:

> I had no hope, I had no power
>   To think—for thought was but despair.
>
> A thing had happened. What? My brain
>   Dared not so much as guess the thing.

The enjambment between "power" and "To think" underscores that this loss of mental capacity emasculates the lover; it is a complete loss of power. The form of waiting that Symons represents contrasts sharply with Radford's; Symons hollows out the hopefulness of waiting by suggesting that patience is only justified by certainty. Because we can never be truly certain in anticipation, he suggests, patience and hopeful waiting are futile at best and

emasculating at worst. Because the Rhymers position themselves so clearly in
a transitional literary historical moment, Symons's attitude is consistent with
their fear of poetic disinheritance.

Although Radford did not know Thomas Hardy, and could not have yet
known his poetry when she published *A Light Load,* a certain resemblance
between her attitude toward waiting and his suggests that Radford was not
alone among fin de siècle poets in resisting Symons's view that waiting disem-
powers. The opening poem of Hardy's 1899 *Wessex Poems,* "The Temporary
the All," declares like Symons that we cannot be certain of the future, but
unlike Symons, suggests that what we think is transitional is really all there
is. The man in this poem consistently expresses dissatisfaction with his cur-
rent state—with his friends, with the woman he courts, with his house—
accepting them for the present but all the while expecting that he will find
better versions. The man comes to see that his plans for his future have ruined
his present:

> "Then, high handiwork will I make my life-deed,
> Truth and Light outshow; but the ripe time pending,
> Intermissive aim at the thing sufficeth."
>   Thus I . . . But lo, me![15]

The man's mistake is not his "intermissive aim" but the "high handiwork"
he thinks will be his "life-deed." His mistake is in thinking of his thoughts
and actions as "intermissive" and the ripe time as "pending" at all. Formally,
this poem imitates that intermissive state, with tongue-tying alliteration and
antiquated diction that slow its forward movement and give it a musty air.
Even the ellipsis in the last line of the stanza above forces the reader to wait
for the next words and leaves the disappointment outlined but not filled out.
But while Hardy's point seems to be that when we think we are waiting, we
are actually living, Radford tries to strike a delicate balance where someone
can actively wait for the future and engage with the present at the same time.
It is a posture of satisfaction without complaisance.

I go on to show how Radford figures waiting as a political stance in her
tribute to the activist experimental prose of Olive Schreiner, but first I want
to understand the politics of waiting in the comments from her diary on
William Morris's utopian novel *News from Nowhere.* This novel presents
an idealistic society in which the ugliness and inequalities of industrializa-
tion have been stripped away, and everyone shares equally, voluntarily, and
pleasurably in a variety of work that satisfies workers' needs to exercise both
their bodies and their creativity. As it continues, it develops a critique of late

Victorian society that savages not only industrial capitalism but also literary culture and education. Radford makes these notes about the novel: "It is a beautiful book & endears Morris to his reader; but it makes present life *too* hopeless and miserable I think & ignores all the beauty there is *now* in our lives & our world. Morris forgets that it is, after all, in this age that *he* has been born & grown to love the beautiful world so much."[16] While Radford agrees with Morris's socialist aims, she declares that his idealism fails to find necessary satisfaction in the present. More important, he fails to acknowledge the elements of present life that have inspired his idealized future. Excessively idealizing the future risks giving the present, as well as the transition from the present, short shrift. (Morris's account of a thoroughgoing revolution brought about entirely by nonviolent resistance, though the revolutionaries suffer violence, is not particularly plausible.) A politics of waiting exemplifies the nonviolence that Morris advocates, but allows a realistic embrace of necessarily generations-long transitions.

Radford's use of style anticipates aesthetic innovation and carves out a socially and politically progressive stance. As LeeAnn Richardson and Ruth Livesey have noted, although Radford was socially and politically radical, she was stylistically rather conservative.[17] Livesey accounts for this conjunction by showing how the lyrical exploration of subjectivity and affect advance a "secular ethical agenda." I offer a different, two-pronged explanation: Radford uses conventions of late nineteenth-century song to show precisely how it is not useful anymore as a communicative tool. Within the space of that critique, however, she offers song as a place of attentiveness that welcomes change. Radford alludes to the progressivism of waiting in a tribute to South African writer Olive Schreiner, who, like Radford, circulated in the socialist organizations of the 1880s and was a close friend of Eleanor Marx, daughter of Karl. Radford was personally acquainted with Schreiner and enormously admired her intellect. In her 1893 diary, she noted, "Yesterday week May 27th I went to see Olive Schreiner . . . One feels Olive Schreiner's genius in her conversation. She has a box of M.S. in her room. I wonder if her great novel is finished."[18] Radford closes *A Light Load* with "A Dream of 'Dreams'" dedicated to Schreiner, whose collection of allegorical tales, *Dreams,* came out only a year before *A Light Load.* In these brief tales, Schreiner dramatizes waiting for better social conditions to come along, depicting the wait as necessary for progress. In "Three Dreams in a Desert," the figure of woman is a beast buried in the sand with a burden tied to her back. "Mechanical Invention" cuts the band of "Inevitable Necessity" that tied the burden to her. The dreamer then watches the woman struggle to get up. The story emphasizes that up to this point the woman has the "terrible patience of the centuries," a patience necessary while she waits for the event that will allow her struggle towards freedom.

Dreams opens with an image of waiting in "The Lost Joy," where Life is a young woman who lounges along the seashore.[19] It is worth quoting at some length because Radford not only develops the concept of waiting in parallel with and in response to Schreiner, but also imitates her style in the tribute poem.

> All day, where the sunlight played on the sea-shore, Life sat.
> All day the soft wind played with her hair, and the young, young face looked out across the water. She was waiting—she was waiting; but she could not tell for what.
> All day the waves ran up and up on the sand, and ran back again, and the pink shells rolled. Life sat waiting; all day, with the sunlight in her eyes, she sat there, till, grown weary, she laid her head upon her knee and fell asleep, waiting still.[20]

The style here appropriates the anaphora, simplicity, and repetition of religious language to endow its lessons with the weight of religious dicta. Although the waves, wind, and sunlight are all active, and Life falls asleep, waiting is not a passive enterprise. Looking is essential for it; Life must confront the boredom, the ignorance, and the exhaustion of waiting in order to remain steadfastly open to Love, who arrives on the beach in the next paragraph. Life and Love proceed to have a child, Joy, who is lost, but who then returns, unrecognizable, but matured into Sympathy.

For Radford, and for Schreiner, waiting is precisely what allows them to endure change that comes only slowly. The dedication to Schreiner's feminist, activist writing also signifies that waiting is not only an abstract virtue of patience, but part and parcel of the evolution of social progress. Radford's "A Dream of 'Dreams'" begins with the speaker falling asleep, dreaming, and then waking up to a world much like the ones in Schreiner's stories. Radford borrows Schreiner's style, with its archetypal natural features and deliberately vague religious tones:

> The great World-Spirit watching still
> Broods over all with folded wings,
> And ever down-cast eyes until
>   The first bird wakes and sings,
>
> And through the eastern clouds the sun
> Breaks with a new unnumbered day

> And now His watching is all done—
>> The night has passed away.
>
> He turns toward the dawn, and I
> Wait as he breathes the sweet fresh air,
> Then with a new-born joy I cry
>> To see His face so fair.[21]

This final poem of *A Light Load* establishes a hopeful sense that the new is arriving with the dawn. Here, the mantle of watching passes from the "World-Spirit" to the speaker, who, at break of day, must take over the waiting. The reward for that waiting is the vision of the World-Spirit's face, which brings a cry of "new-born joy." Yet if this poem alludes to Schreiner's story "The Lost Joy," in which Joy is a newborn baby, we know that this moment of fulfillment concludes a lyric poem but not a narrative. Radford cannily enacts the process of waiting in her use of enjambment: in the final stanza, readers must wait for the next line even to get from the subject "I" to the verb "wait." The enjambed separation of subject and verb happens repeatedly, in "World-Spirit still / Broods," "sun / Breaks," so that being and action are separated by a gap. This poetic tribute to Schreiner thus ends the collection with a note of triumph but also of anticipation, for the joy that must turn into sympathy, as in Schreiner's story. By closing with this allusion, Radford signals her allegiance with Schreiner's feminist, socialist stance, with her experimental style, and joins her in asserting that patience is part of the effort required to welcome the new. By ending her first collection with a reference to Schreiner, Radford carves out a similar status to hers, at the center of fin de siècle culture, and yet taking advantage of the outsider status of the minor. Radford can critique the genre she writes in from the outside, but write as fluently in it as a major player. As the final poem of *A Light Load,* "A Dream of Dreams" speaks for the collection, asserting that for all of its failings, fin de siècle song cultivates the attention and openness of waiting, preparing poets and readers for the dawning of some transcendental truth.

Perfect Songs

When Radford writes the line "So I can wait and sing," she implies that singing is itself a form of waiting. As this section will show, Radford did not take for granted the commonplace that lyric poems *are* songs, though many admirers of her work did. In his review of *A Light Load,* Arthur Symons dubs Radford's poems "perfect songs," emphasizing this musical term: "It is a book of songs, and the songs are full of instinctive music, which soars naturally."[22] Others made similar comparisons. According to Radford's diary, John

Lane quoted George Meredith's response when he wrote in his own copy of *A Light Load,* "How different this is—it is really songfull."[23] The *Musical Times* singled out the volume as especially appropriate for musical settings: "Many of the verses, though forming their own music, will tempt composers to try the effect which may be gained by the addition of such melodies and harmonies which may help to find further admirers for the words here given."[24] (The author of this notice may not have known that several of the poems had already been set to music.) Radford invites this focus on her poetry as "song"; a number of the poems in *A Light Load* are entitled simply "Song," paradoxically so, since many are about the inability to sing. Yet the charm of her style often dominated characterizations of her verse. Radford's frequent use of "Song" as a title, as well as Symons's, Meredith's and Lane's enthusiastic responses evoke questions about what "song" means to Radford and to fin de siècle poetic culture.

These were questions that Radford actively struggled with early in her career, as her pursuit of musical settings attests. In 1884 she discussed musical settings of her work with George Bernard Shaw, and 1888 saw the publication of the sheet music for "Six Songs" with words by Caroline Radford and music by Erskine Allon. Allon died a young promising composer in 1897 and these songs have long been lost to public view. Yet they are an important key to understanding Radford's work and the way in which she conceptualizes poetry. While to title a poem "Song" might seem like a lyric commonplace, it is precisely this commonplace, as well as modern lyric's relationship with its musical origins, which Radford's use of the title calls into question. By having her poems set to music, Radford may initially have sought to bring the presence of a singer and a pianist to the absence of voice that defines silent reading. When the songs are performed in a drawing room, not to mention a small concert hall, the presence of music and voice might establish a sense of intimate presence between singer and audience. Ultimately, however, careful readings of the poems Radford chose to set to music underscore the detachment that many of her poems describe. I suggest that for Radford these songs were an experiment in solving the problem of lyric absence, and one that proves that whether sung or recited or read silently from a printed page, songs remind us that something or someone is missing. By the Victorian period, the relationship between music and lyric poetry is largely figurative. Using "song" as a title reinforces the presence of voice as a fantasy. Radford's ventures into the musical setting of her works render literal the lyric metaphor of song. Yet, as I will show, even when her songs are actually performed, the presence of a singing voice alludes to the absence of another more ideal music. Of the poems in Erskine Allon's "Six Songs" of 1888, all of which reappear in *A Light Load,* two stand out for the way in which they contain multiple voices and sounds, which include birds, bells, wind: sounds that a human voice or a piano can only imitate. The effect of this imitation in music is to emphasize the absence of those elements in the same way that the poems do. The musical settings can only offer a replacement or an echo of a sound that in fact is not even an original sound to be imitated, but an artistic and poetic convention. Thus, if a musical setting of a poem tries to create the sound of birdsong, it imitates the convention of birds as a metaphor for poetry, rather than actual birds.

One poem in Allon's set of "Six Songs" produces an effect of inaccessible music. Published in a periodical, set to music, and appearing in *A Light Load*, "Westleigh Bells" is central to Radford's oeuvre and to her approach to song. In "Westleigh Bells," a young man sings about birdsong and bells, hoping to meld his voice with them. In outline, the poem creates a picture of a young man who parks his boat on a spot on the river where he can see the light shining in the window of the woman he loves. He tells us that he does so because to "send her blessings across from here, / When they ring the Westleigh chimes, / Makes my summer glad."[25] In this sketched scenario, this young man may also seem like a fool for performing this desperate row-by, but to think of him this way ignores the way in which the poem sets the scene around him, and the way he describes it, which is more important than his longing for the woman in the window:

> How gently this evening the ripples break
>   On the pebbles beneath the trees,
> With a music as low as the full leaves make,
>   When they stir in some soft sea-breeze,
> And as day-light dies, if I rest my boat
>   'Neath this bough where the blossoms fall,
> I shall hear the curlew's last good-night note,
>   As he answers the sea-gull's call.[26]

Even set to music and sung aloud, these words gesture toward a music and singing that we cannot hear. The real music, the poem suggests, is in the movement of the water and the wind, and is so "low" as to be barely perceptible, even in the imagination. And the effective singing here comes from the birds, who, importantly, answer each other in reciprocal singing. The poem's alternating anapestic tetrameters and trimeters and plentiful alliteration create a sound that mimics not the voice of the man, but the sounds of the scene he describes. The lush description of the setting along with the luxuriant verse suggest that pleasure lies in waiting for the beloved, rather than having her. Melding his own song with the bells makes the man "glad"; he does not emphasize any wish for a response from her to the "blessings" he sings out, which she is too far away to hear anyway. If this is a poem that signals the failure of lyric intimacy, offering its possibility among only the birds, who call and fly to one another, then it also celebrates the delights of music. Moreover, these delights come to one who waits and sings. Hearing this poem sung in a drawing room, listeners are invited to consider the music that is inaccessible to them, while they enjoy what they hear in the moment.

In Allon's setting of "Westleigh Bells," the piano accompaniment echoes the sound of bells, and the rocking rhythms and tones of the vocal line might be said to mimic the rippling waves of the scene. In contrast with the meditative scene, the rhythm of the music might be described as almost frenetic, with abundant sixteenth notes that crowd several syllables into the jaunty 4/8 measure, emphasizing "ripples break" over the adverb "gently" or the "soft sea breeze." Yet however much we seek a mimetic understanding of the music, certainly on a first or even second hearing the words of this song rush by, enveloped by the pace of the music.[27] The poem enacts what the musical setting performs: it privileges sound over voice and meaning in a way that suggests that even when a voice is present and singing, it is ephemeral. When a rush of notes leads into a more sustained phrase, as on the words "trees" and "breeze," whose vowels slide from one note to another, or even on the word "call," which is held longer, the movement of the music reminds the audience that singing and listening are themselves forms of waiting. These sustained notes and phrases make the listener wait for one to end and the next to begin. The contradiction implied in the simultaneous ephemerality of the singing voice and suspension of a waiting note epitomizes the poem's dual temporality: meant to preserve and over too soon.

"Westleigh Bells" importantly links Radford's aesthetic experimentation with her political progressivism. Before the musical setting appeared, Radford published nine poems, including "Westleigh Bells," in the radical secularist journal *Progress* in the years 1883 and 1884, under her maiden name or initials, Caroline Maitland. There are two ways of reading the poem's scenario within the secularist context of *Progress*. First, we can read the young man as having a naive faith in what will never come to him. He refers to the woman in the window as his "love" even though she is not. After referring to her as "my love," he goes on to say, "If she were my love she would come to me / This evening, I long for her so." In these lines, the young man seems to believe that simply by wanting something, he can make it happen. On the other hand, we might read him as a secularist hero, who replaces his faith in God with a trust in his own desires, and a pleasure in desire rather than in attainment. Indeed, he appropriates the bells of a rural church to send blessings of his own, as though the sound of those bells could carry his message to his beloved. He is also someone who waits: he stays his boat, he rests. He is heroic simply in his ability to wait and to take pleasure in that wait. As such, he embodies a political stance that combines hope with an awareness of limits. If this political stance coincides with the secularist goals of progress, we might read the beloved as a figure for God, and his deferral of action as a rejection of God. Ultimately, it does not matter whether she exists or returns his feelings, so long as the man can be fully alive in the present moment. Livesey has argued that *Progress* published lyric poems like Radford's in order to offer a secular model of subjectivity in place of the religious models it rejected.[28] If the absence of God is indeed a background to this poem, it offers an aesthetic experience in its place that relies on absence: of God, of the beloved, even of the music itself.

Some insight into the way in which the Radfords may have thought about song comes from a poem that Ernest published in *Progress* around the same time that Dollie was first publishing her poems there, including "Westleigh Bells." One titled "Verses" has the subtitle "Containing a very grave reflexion on the Essence and Decadence of Song." It suggests a deep skepticism about whether we can have faith not only in God, but in song:

> Had "Robbie" Burns espied thy lips
>   He'd have kissed them, that I know:
> We modern bards dare no such quips,
>   But slowlier go;
> And wind about with ill grimace
> For tardier shows of scantier grace.
>
> Could "Robbie" see the "sonsie" eyes
>   That glint from out their lashes so,
> They'd have no time for shy surprise,
>   ('Twixt Robbie's kisses, don't you know!)
> With laughter slow he'd kiss, and kiss, and whisper low
> A song no living bard can show.[29]

Here "Decadence" refers not to the Radfords and other writers of the fin de siècle, but to Robert Burns, the Scottish poet who often wrote in dialect, wrote many songs, and had a reputation as quite the séducteur. Although another poem in the very same issue of *Progress* signed "E.R." is entitled "Song," this poem is very deliberately only "Verses," indicating that it reflects modern reluctance rather than swift passionate advances. Ernest Radford represents Burns as a man of action and fulfillment before song, but he suggests that invigorating song becomes both the result of and impetus to action. This poem describes song as an outmoded, impossible ideal, sincere and decisive. In contrast, modern "singers" or poets, with their dissipated energy and sense of dispossession—indicated by the "ill grimace," cannot summon such a seductive and full-throated expression of pleasure. By using Robert Burns as an example, rather than any Elizabethan poets, the poem also idealizes the perceived authenticity of song, an authenticity that it declares is gone in the fin de siècle.

Ernest Radford may have associated Burns's songs with action, immediacy, and authenticity because Burns himself did. Kirsten McCue writes that Burns himself connects his early flirtation with Nelly Kilpatrick and the honesty of his love with his first song, "O Once I Loved a Bonny Lass."[30] McCue notes that Burns the songmaker was both a writer and a collector, and that upon choosing a tune he would write new lyrics, printing the title of the tune along with the new lyric, leaving the reader/singer to combine the two into a new song.[31] In this early Romantic ideal, the orality of these songs was a testament to their cultural authenticity, if not to sincerity of feeling. In fact, the early Romantic era song, identified especially with Scottish and Irish culture in the songs of Burns, Sir Walter Scott's *Minstrelsy of the Scottish Border,* and Thomas Moore's *Irish Melodies,* existed primarily in the medium of print, while seeking the perceived authenticity of orality. Maureen McLane argues that this intersection of print and oral culture made minstrelsy a figure for poetry in general in the Romantic period. McLane writes that the culture of minstrelsy, which blurred boundaries not only between orality and print, but between the literary and the rural, between poet, ethnographer, and collector, gave "the lie to the romantic fetish of originality."[32] McLane discusses the intersection of orality and print in a context almost entirely of print circulation, suggesting that even as poets such as Burns collected tunes to which he could write new lyrics, for his audience, the songs were seen before they were heard, and any hearing was a reconstruction of song rather than an original apprehension of one. Terence Hoagwood argues that music falls out of Romantic song culture, using Moore's *Irish Melodies* as an example. Whereas in 1810 these poems were published with scores, by the 1822 republication, only the words appeared.[33] I would argue that although a score might accompany a poem, that in any kind of print medium, the music is already gone, and must be reimagined with any performance. Ernest Radford's "Verses" invokes the Romantic ideal of presence, orality, and action in order to shed light on the presumably sophisticated dissipation of the fin de siècle song, but both Radfords may indeed have understood that even in the Romantic period, and for the collectors and writers of songs such as Burns, Scott, and Moore, the music of a poetic "song" could only be imagined or reconstructed.

Dollie Radford's lyrics also address a later Romantic concept of song, which recognizes that presence and performance are unavailable. The inaccessible music of "Westleigh Bells" echoes Keats's famous phrase "Heard melodies are sweet, but those unheard / Are sweeter."[34] Keats prizes the poetry we imagine in an intense ekphrastic experience because it remains full of possibility; for him those unheard melodies are sweeter because they relate to the spirit rather than to the "sensual ear."[35] Similarly, Radford prizes the sense of potential in an unheard melody. As "Westleigh Bells" shows, even music played and sung aloud can gesture toward an unheard melody. In another of her poems set to music by Allon, the unheard music is a conclusion to a story that the song begins but does not finish. Whereas the shorter musical setting of this song allows for pleasant possibilities, the longer version in the poem forecloses on them. For Radford, heard songs often are not so sweet. In two poems discussed below, poems present songs as occasions for misinterpretation and deceit that fundamentally mar a listener's experience. Radford presents the dangers of listening too carefully to, and believing in, lyric song.

In the long version of the poem in Allon's song "Sweetheart," songbirds lead a young woman into heartbreak by telling her that her lover waits for her, which turns out not to be true. If these birds, a metaphor for "song," itself a metaphor for poetry, are lying, then might not this poem suggest that lyric itself is false, that the tropes and rhythms that Radford herself performs so beautifully are ultimately empty? This version appears in 1891 in *A Light Load:*

> The birds sang from the tree,
>   "Sweetheart
> Go forth across the silent hills,
> For in the vale their shadow fills
> Thy love awaiteth thee
>   With lonely heart."
>
> She wound a wreath of flowers
>   So Sweet,
> And, while the birds still sang their song,
> Across the hills she passed along
> In the fair sunrise hours,
>   Her love to meet.
>
> But when the sun, asleep
>   At eve,
> Lay hid behind a purple cloud,

> Each little bird in leafy shroud
> Saw her return and weep,
>   "And dost thou grieve."
>
> Ah no, I am not sad,
>   She said,
> He did not know me when I came,
> But I have crowned him all the same,
> And how can I be sad,
>   My heart is glad.[36]

Had this young woman continued to wait, she might have forestalled disappointment, to remain in the matrix of pleasure and pain that the birds' song created for her. Indeed, because it begins with the birds' song, the poem suggests that lyric poems create, rather than express, desire. In the final lines, in return for the birds' lies, she lies to them, and perhaps to herself. Although she returns home weeping, she declares that she is not sad because her heart is glad. The victim of lyric, she has divided herself, separating her "heart" from her "I." As a victim of lyric, she must also perform its tropes, crowning her beloved with the wreath she made. She is a lyric antiheroine, uselessly performing its rituals and attempting to shape her own feelings by its lies rather than by the truths she witnesses.

Radford penned a shorter version of this poem in 1884 in a diary, with a note following that reads "music by Erskine Allon," and that version appears in "Six Songs" in 1888. Both the diary version and the version set to music end after the birds send the woman across the hills, leaving the audience with a sense of anticipation but without the rejection in the longer version. A note inside the first pages of the diary in which the poem appears labels these compositions "curtailed verses!"[37] This cryptic note cannot tell us whether Radford wrote the longer version someplace else first or not, nor do we know when she wrote this label in the notebook, but it draws attention to the ambiguity of an ending without a conclusion in this poem. It also suggests that Radford may have had the second two stanzas in mind but that she, perhaps alone or perhaps in collaboration with Allon, decided that this dark conclusion did not suit an art song destined most likely for amateur, bourgeois, drawing room entertainment. Radford and Allon title the musical version of "Song" ("The birds sang from the tree") "Sweetheart," and in its shorter version, without the final two stanzas that appear in *A Light Load,* the pet name is all endearment, free from irony. Yet the shorter version also leaves open the question, what happens when the lovers meet? It poises the moment in possibility, without fulfillment, but also without disappointment. As we have already seen, in Radford's poetics of waiting, this position of anticipation is an important one, not simply a poetic imperfection or an avoidance of disappointment. Allon's musical setting provides a series of chords that indicate that the song is over, but that do not answer the questions that stem from the poem's open-endedness.

Radford must have had an especially keen interest in musical collaboration in 1884, for in the same year that she collaborated with Allon, she asked George Bernard Shaw to set some lyrics to music. Radford may even have labeled her poems as "curtailed verses" after receiving this comment from Shaw:

> You will find, on examining the song as it stands, that it is inconclusive—leaves a "Is that all?" feeling behind it. You seem to have an extraordinary kaleidoscopic talent for stringing all manner of beautiful images and associations harmoniously together, and these, when combined with the pithiness and conclusiveness of an epigram, form perfect songs. But you are neither pithy nor conclusive. For instance, put a good epigram in verse beside the verses I have set, and you will have two opposite extremes in poetry.[38]

Although Shaw refers to a song called "How She Comes," rather than to "Sweetheart," he recognizes the unfinished quality that the "Sweetheart" song also exhibits. It is reasonable to conclude that in the time between this letter and the publication of *A Light Load* in 1891, Radford's style had matured, and she may have written with the intention of creating the pithiness that Shaw claimed she lacked. This development in style may account for the dark turn Radford's poems often take, as in the full version of "The birds sang from the tree."[39] However, the feeling of incompleteness that Shaw notes may not have been accidental, may, in fact, have been the point. The conclusion of the *poem* "The birds sang in the tree" is too complete. Although the song leaves the story before the climax, it holds in suspension the excitement of a meeting between lovers. The poem, on the other hand, finishes the story with utter disappointment, in the lover certainly, but more importantly in the birds' song and its falsehoods. In the early days of her career, Radford faced the challenge of writing a poem about incompleteness that still did not feel stylistically incomplete.

Shaw's letter to Radford does not elaborate on the effect his music has on her words, but he does imply that the music does not complete, but rather changes the poem somehow: "I send you a setting of one of your songs for a tenor voice. It goes high enough to keep most amateur tenors at a distance; but the song would not be bright enough in a lower key. . . . The music is

trumpery enough; but I am not a composer, and only profess to be tremen-
dous in the third volume of a novel, so do not be too hard on my common-
places. They will suffice to shew you the extent to which music alters the
aspect of a poem."[40] Shaw does not say how the music changes the poem, he
only mentions the "extent" to which it does. His use of this word suggests a
view that music does not "add" to a poem, but rather unmakes it, or remakes
it. Shaw's apology for the quality of the music (or lack thereof) indicates
that the music itself is not as important as the experiment that he and Rad-
ford undertook together: to see what effect music would have on the poem.
Shaw's letter makes clear that the original intention was not for the song to
be professionally performed, but to be sung in a drawing room by an amateur.
That amateur, though, as Shaw notes, must have a special talent for high notes
or the song will not be "bright enough." This letter elucidates the ambiguous
ground of Radford's musical settings, and by extension of her idea of "song."
Her songs require refined talent and taste but are nonetheless for amateurs
to sing. It is important to note that in order to consider Shaw's comments on
his setting, Radford must either engage someone to sing it for her (since she
is not herself a tenor) or imagine what it would sound like, based on a reading
of the manuscript notation that Shaw sent to her. This imaginative exercise
would be even more complicated than imagining someone reading the poem,
and therefore hardly a more "immediate" experience than reading a poem in
print. As Radford herself notes in a poem I discuss below, "If you will sing the
songs I play," an actual performance of a song requires singer and musician
to come together, an event much to be anticipated and entirely fleeting. The
experience of song, therefore, is not only of the singing itself, but also of the
expectation that precedes it. It is defined both before and during as a kind of
waiting, both for it to begin and for it to be over.

In seeking out musical settings to her work, Radford may have been at-
tempting to unravel her own text by means of another art form. Writing about
the interaction of music and poetry in the nineteenth and twentieth centu-
ries, musicologist Lawrence Kramer claims that in musical settings of text,
rather than complementing the words, the music undoes them. He writes,
"Song, we seem forced to conclude, is not a refined way to throw language
into high relief. It is a refined form of erasure."[41] In a musical setting of text,
he argues, the music takes over the words. In this sense, the musical settings
of Radford's songs may perform exactly what her songs do to themselves. The
ending of the later version of "The birds sang from the tree" does "erase" the
first section, the birds' encouraging song. The song/poem undoes itself.

While Radford's songs, in print and performed, wryly wink at the im-
possibility of lyric presence, the musical settings also have ambitions toward

bourgeois amusement. Letters and diary entries suggest that Radford would have imagined her songs performed in private social gatherings, some of which were sometimes quite large, but were nonetheless not public performances. These amateur performances were part of a social world that was also at the center of leading literary conversations. Radford's diaries reflect a genuine pleasure at the prospect of hearing her own words, as well as Ernest's, set to music. Radford notes in her diary, "On Sunday 17th we went to the Elkin Mathews' At Home, taking Clara who sang Ernest's 'London Song' very sweetly. Bedford park friends very kind + welcoming. Willie Yeats looking much older + worn."[42] That the Radfords' songs were (or aspired to be) art songs, exchanged in elite artistic circles, although performed by amateurs, testifies to the importance of the musical performance of poetry at private literary events. The songs had a hybrid class status—part of elite cultural coteries, not necessarily meant for broad consumption. They increased the circulation of Radford's poetry, while also keeping it carefully delineated from popular culture. In this sense the performances of the Radfords' songs were much like their books, circulated in small numbers presumably among a literary upper class.

In having her songs set to music, Radford entered Britain's musical culture at the fin de siècle, in which composers were building an art-song tradition, while popular ballads had a strong foothold in bourgeois culture. The status of art song in England in the late nineteenth century, as Stephen Banfield illustrates, was in the ascendancy. He writes that although the production of Victorian songs was vast as well as popular throughout the century, the quality of these works was not as distinguished as those from the Continent, especially German lieder and French melodies.[43] From the 1870s on, the drawing-room ballad became "loftier, artier" and this bourgeois ballad culture gave rise to the culture of the art song.[44] The emergent Victorian art song aimed at the sophistication of music from the Continent, while also striving to establish a specifically English tradition, particularly by setting English poems to music.[45] The rise of art song in England coincided with the rise in prestige of music in England more generally. Although cultural arbiters such as Carlyle, Arnold, and Ruskin did not give music the intellectual or cultural importance of painting or literature, an English music renaissance began in the midcentury and continued into the twentieth. While the midcentury popularity of Mendelssohn defined much English musical taste well into the 1880s, when conservative critics like Joseph Bennett (who coined the term "renaissance" for the state of English music around that time) rejected the influence of Wagner on English music, new generations of composers and critics incorporated Wagnerian romanticism into their style and preferences.[46] Among these critics was George Bernard Shaw, a member of the Radfords' inner circle. By participating in this culture, the young poet Radford would have been able to increase the distribution of her work, to participate in collaborative exchange with the composer, and to exploit and explore the social relations of performer and audience. The place of musical settings in the Victorian drawing room attests to song's function, as identified by Elizabeth Helsinger, to facilitate social relations. She argues that "performances, whether at home or in concert, real or fictional, are for Victorian poets largely experienced and imagined as social occasions."[47] Set to music, Radford's songs can both participate in these practical social dynamics and express skepticism about the extent of intimate possibilities that music provides.

Yet Helsinger's formulation is too quick to collapse the experience and imagination of song. In contrast to Romantic ballad culture, and despite the use of British poems to elevate musical culture, Victorian poetic culture often prized the imagination over the experience, building on Keats's dictum that unheard melodies are sweeter. By the Victorian period, the use of "song" to refer to a poem is a metaphor, as Yopie Prins has argued.[48] When Victorian poetry reflected on music and song, it did not necessarily aim to embody performativity. Considering embedded songs in the longer works of Tennyson and Swinburne, arguing that they are "presented as sung," Helsinger has rightly called these songs "fictions." But the distinction between imagined and experienced song is crucial because Victorians privileged the unsung songs, and the use of song as a figure, metaphor and fiction. The merely "singable" song collapsed this figure. For this reason, Radford emphasizes, especially in the songs she selects for musical settings, songs that cannot be sung and songs that disappoint, failing in their aim to communicate, and, as we shall see, to soothe.

Alice Meynell, whom Radford admired, asserted the "song" as a genre to be completely outmoded. Of the challenges of reading Browning, and the "difficulty of thought" at the "heart of poetry," Meynell writes:

> Those who complain of it would restrict poetry to literal narrative for its epics, to unanalyzed—and therefore ultimately to unrealized and conventional—passion for its drama, and to songs for its lyrics. Doubtless narrative, dramas of primary passion, and singable songs are all excellent things; masterpieces have been done in these ways—but in the past—in a fresher, broader, and simpler time than ours. Those masterpieces bring their own age with them, as it were, into our hearts; we ourselves assume a singleness of mind as we read them; they are neither too obvious nor too unthoughtful to interest

us; but it is far otherwise with modern work which is laid upon the same lines.[49]

Meynell dismisses the genre of "song" as inappropriate for the complexity of the era. Clearly for Meynell, the term "song" is not synonymous with lyric, and she is anxious to establish a modern lyric that exceeds singabilty. Modern lyric, Meynell implies, can do no more with old forms—modern songs are "too obvious or unthoughtful." I argue here that Radford's poetry does indeed embody the "importance of thought" that Meynell prizes. But it does so precisely by paradoxically querying its own "beauty of manner" and "charm of form," as Meynell puts it. Radford sent a copy of *A Light Load* to Meynell, and her diary indicates that she received a prompt and polite reply. The entry for 4 May 1891 reads simply, "A nice letter from Alice Thompson thanking me for my book."[50] Broadly speaking, Radford agrees with Meynell's assessment of "song" as an outmoded literary form, but wants to see what it means to do it anyway, and whether it's possible to do it with modern skepticism. Ironically, Radford's songs question the boundary between singable and unsingable. In Allon's musical settings, they clearly are singable, but not, with their crowding of words, unusual rhythms, and sustained notes, melodically catching. Even in the songs set to music, as I have shown, Radford is invested in how to embody songs that are not sung and not heard.

Aestheticist culture also tended to think of songs and music in the abstract rather than in terms of performativity. Walter Pater's iconic declaration that "all art aspires to the condition of music" inspired poets, authors, and painters for decades to come, but is rarely mentioned in histories of nineteenth-century English music.[51] For Radford, "Song" is importantly not synonymous with "music," a concept that alluded to abstract form and was at the apex of aestheticist ideals invoked by Symons, by way of the French poet Verlaine, and Pater. It is important to distinguish between this idealization of music as pure artistic form and the concept of song. The voice, and words, so essential for song, do not play a part in the aestheticist vision of pure form. In his characterization of "The Decadent Movement in Literature," Symons takes his ideal from Verlaine's "Art Poétique," which privileges "music first of all and before all": "To fix the last fine shade, the quintessence of things; to fix it fleetingly; to be a disembodied voice, and yet the voice of a human soul: that is the ideal of Decadence, and it is what Paul Verlaine has achieved."[52] In this list of paradoxes, Symons wants it both ways, the fixed and the fleeting, the trace of a body without the body itself. In other words, if the poets of the 1880s long for exuberant action, as described by Ernest Radford's "Verses," they also establish the fashionable decadence in the 1890s that relies on immateriality. In her relationship to music, then, Radford also relies on paradox: she positions her poems as singable songs, aspiring to connect and to please, while at the same time bemoaning, as her husband's ineffectual bards do, her inability to make them do so. Radford emphasizes the disappointment intrinsic to song, which the idealization of music as abstract form ignores. By reflecting on her poetry as musical, and making her poems into music, Radford exposes the emptiness of the aestheticist aspiration to the abstract form of music. Songs may be pleasantly satisfying, but they do not forge connections in the way her poems themselves fantasize that they might.

The ineffectuality of song appears in another poem from *A Light Load* that uses the moniker "sweetheart" ironically. "My Sweetheart" depicts a lover who cannot hear his beloved's songs in the way that she wants him to, displaying an anxiety about poetic reception and the failure of communication. This poem confirms fears that a song will not reach its intended auditor:

> My sweetheart lays her hand in mine
>   When she would have me glad,
> She sings and sings, she never knows
>   What music makes me sad.
>
> My sweetheart holds my heart to hers
>   When she would have me rest,
> She never hears the heavy sigh
>   Which breaks within my breast.
>
> Her sweet lips press my tired lids
>   When she would have me sleep;
> Alas, they have no power to stay
>   The burning tears I weep.[53]

In flawless ballad meter, this metrically confident performance is about listening to another's song, and knowing that it is impossible to receive it as intended. Here, the singer/sweetheart wants to allay her lover's sadness but cannot. She sings effusively, without knowing what effect her songs have on her auditor. Her fundamental misunderstanding of her audience comes from her failure to read his sighs. Radford presents listening to song—a metaphor for reading poetry—as intensely heartbreaking because it can never fulfill the singer's or the auditor's desire for comfort. She presents lyric here as stunningly insufficient, holding out the promise of comfort and failing to deliver. The pet name "sweetheart" appears as a brutal irony in the context of the sorrowful distance the lover in the poem feels. "The birds sang in the tree," and its alternate song-version "Sweetheart," act as counterparts to the poem

"My Sweetheart." Perhaps the girl who, at the behest of the birds, travels to find her lover is as uncomprehending as the young woman who cannot read her lover's sighs or looks. The comparison of these songs—musical and metaphorical—reminds us of the myriad ways in which a song might fail and tells us that a song that fails by virtue of incompleteness is far better than one that misses its mark or maliciously misinforms. In Radford's poetics, the unraveling of these poems signifies her disappointment in their potential to establish intimacy.

Recently, however, Kramer has suggested that song generates intimacy by virtue of music's immediate appeal to the senses. Because musical setting alters the rhythmic and tonal patterns of speech, it "defamiliarize[s] utterance." He describes the effect this way: "The most immediate impact of song is to convert this dissociated speech-image into an occasion of expressive intimacy. By replacing the phonetic/syntactic integrity of the text with the gestural continuity of a melodic line, song reconnects the impulse to speak with its basis in physical sensation and the felt continuity of the ego. . . . Song is in essence a stylization of the sound and feel of the self in its openness."[54] This version of intimacy focuses much on the self and its presumed readiness for relation with another, but not much on how a relation happens. Read this way, Kramer's understanding of the "intimacy" of music is not intimate at all, for there is nothing reciprocal, nothing communicated. What he really seems to be implying is that music is more "embodied"—it is "physical" and "felt"—than poetry is. His equation between physicality and intimacy is too easy. For Kramer, because music has a "physical origin" in vocalization, "the primary use of song in social life is to create intimacy."[55] Taking a psychoanalytic approach, Kramer notes that song helps to establish an infant's bonds to others and to himself and "to relax inhibitions, and often to release erotic feeling." Yet in practical terms, these are very different scenarios. With an infant, someone is usually singing, but in our own time, when music is used to "relax inhibitions or release erotic feeling," someone has put on a recording.

It is ironic that Kramer, in an age of easily reproducible music, both in sheet music and in sound recordings, would attribute such immediacy to the art form. As Christina Rossetti's unsettling experience of hearing a recorded voice attests in chapter 1, music, particularly recorded music, is no more resonant of an idealized "physical origin" than is a poem in print. It might seem that a live performance of a poem set to music would establish the sense of immediacy and presence that is presumably lost in a poem in print. However, Radford's choice of songs to set to music is telling. In "The birds sang from the tree," an omniscient voice sings about the birds, and then directly quotes the birds. (Had the last two stanzas in the poem been set to

music, there would be three voices that the singer would have to imperson-
ate.) This quotation within a song tells even the audience of a performance
that there is another song, the birds' song, that is inaccessible, that must be
imitated or performed. Setting poems to music does not solve the problem
of those poems' absent voices; rather, it makes those absences, paradoxically,
more startlingly clear. Moreover, for aestheticist and decadent culture, music
did not signify embodiment or physicality. On the contrary, as I have shown,
Symons, who praised Radford's "perfect songs" in his review, also idealized
music as a "disembodied voice."

For Radford, the act of creation is more likely to create a sense of connec-
tion than an act of reception. Although she does not suggest that song estab-
lishes intimacy, she does say that it can be a balm for isolation and bring about
an awakening to the world. Radford was attentive to questions of class, writ-
ing in her diary about song as a democratic art form and writing occasionally
about working-class singers in her poetry, as Livesey has shown.[56] One of
Radford's diary entries casts "song" and art in general as profoundly demo-
cratic: "I do know many people—sad and hopeless—creeping through their
lives in a shell—shut up and withered. If they could have painted one picture,
made one song, or done one little thing of their very own, I think they would
have awakened. It is all in 'Towards Democracy.' Edward Carpenter under-
stands well."[57] Here, "song," like a "picture," is a stand-in for art itself. In this
entry, art also encompasses crafts, since Radford is writing after visiting Wil-
liam Morris, and discusses the vibrant center of arts and crafts at Hammer-
smith, including Mary (Morris) Sparling's embroidery and Charles Spooner's
furniture. Ruth Livesey has written persuasively about the overlap of Rad-
ford's socialism and aestheticism, and it is not my purpose here to pursue that
further. This diary entry is important, however, for considering Radford's ap-
proach to song because it reveals her emphasis on production and sheds light
on the way in which she conceptualizes the place of intimacy in song and, by
extension, in poetry. Her reference to Edward Carpenter helps her to define
the intimacy of poetic creation. Carpenter's poetry in *Towards Democracy*,
as has been well documented, resembles Whitman's in *Song of Myself.*[58] Its
intimacy is not so much about a relation between two people or even an ab-
stracted poetic "I" and "you," but rather about finding the place of the poet
in the universe. This comment also reveals how very important the small is
for Radford. She presents "one little thing" here as utterly transformative. In
this idealized view, an act of creation, no matter how small, rescues a person
from sadness and hopelessness and engages her with the rest of the world.

In a poem from her second collection, *Songs and Other Verses,* she represents this act of creation as collaborative in a way that is particular to song, and which she must have had in mind as she requested musical settings to her verses. Here, musical collaboration establishes intimacy between musician and singer:

> If you will sing the songs I play,
>   Then you shall be my dear,
> And I will cherish you alway,
>   And love you far and near;
> If you will, in sweet singing, say
> The songs I play.⁵⁹

This poem at once presents and withholds the possibilities of artistic pleni-tude and intimacy. Radford suggests that without voice and words, a song's music is incomplete. Conversely, without performance, any lyric song in print represents its own absence. Rather than merely bemoaning it, Radford was committed to representing and exploring this absence, or incompleteness. The contrast between a poem in print and a poem in musical performance only cemented the version of lyric she presents in her books. With its use of the verbs "play," "sing," and "say," the poem evokes the condition of song, an instrumental accompaniment together with a voice. Significantly, the "I" of the poem is not the voice but the musician. The poem thereby calls at-tention to its status as incomplete. The equation of singing and saying here suggests that the completed "song" is more than a metaphor for a poem; it represents an ideal of harmony embedded within the genre. This poem holds out great hope for the intimate possibilities of lyric, but perhaps the most important word in the poem is "If," its conditional mode reminding readers that the poem's communicative potential is not a foregone conclusion. This mode indicates that the love the poem seems to promise so sweetly is itself conditional on the repetition of song. The "If" allows Radford simultane-ously to put forward this ideal and to withhold it. The incompleteness of the proposed song partakes of the open-endedness of waiting. Because so many songs are desired in her work, Radford asks us to redefine song as a work proposed rather than a work achieved.

Another "conditional" poem undermines the ideal of the redemptive power of making even one song that Radford articulates in her diary. Whereas the past conditional of the diary's "If they could have painted" and the future of "If you will sing" imply a past failure and potential future success, the pres-ent conditional of this poem suggests that success is impossible. It forecloses more readily on the possibilities that they present:

> If my poor words were colours,
>   A magic brush my pen,
> Ah me, what radiant pages
>   My songs would make you then.[60]

The conditional tells us that we indeed are reading a poem, not a song, and that these are only poor words, not an ideal synesthetic merger of the visual and the musical. With the use of the conditional, Radford defines lyric song as always at once promising intimacy and denying it. This inherent contradiction coincides with the other contradictions in her view of "song": she presents her work as unachieved songs but asks for them to be set to music; she wrote fluently in a genre she simultaneously declared to be exhausted. Although the poems I have investigated so far question songs as a viable modern lyric form, the poems I examine in the last part of this chapter assert that songs can nonetheless be satisfying and cultivate intimacy when they eschew an ambition to be original and successful in a modern literary context.

Tender Measures

Alice Meynell's indictment of the singable song implies a kind of smallness, by which I mean not so much that songs are short (though that is part of their charm) as that they are unimportant. To use Meynell's terms, they lack complexity and thought, risk being too obvious. Meynell's critique burdens the modern form of this compact genre, whether we call it song or lyric, with expansive expectations. I begin this section with a poem that considers just how small a song can be, observing that songs contract within a person, within a moment, unrepeatable and therefore a dead end. But I go on to show how Radford presents songs between a mother and child, for instance, as both entirely trite and perfectly pleasing. To admit the value of the banal, then, is also to question the significance of the original and the ambitious. Radford shows that what seems small, sentimental, and trite, including the tender measures of motherhood, are part of a common experience that in its universality is quite large.

With *A Light Load,* Radford both expressed major literary ambition and embraced a minor status. On the surface, the volume hides well her aim to critique lyric's failures. It is a small white volume, a mere sixty-eight pages. Upon its release, Radford wrote in her diary, "A very nice little book. I think I should be quite pleased with it if I met it unawares. I wish it was not *so* small. What shall I hear about it? It is no matter."[61] An anxiety about size reveals itself here, as her view of "little" swerves from an accompaniment of "nice" to an excessive smallness, one that presumably takes the book too far away from public view. Radford's dismissal of the question about how the reading public will respond reveals that the book's "smallness" was a point of concern as well as pride, something she embraces as well as retreats from. In the illustration on the title page, a mother holds a baby while an older girl looks out of an open window into the starry night. The scene juxtaposes the intimacy of its domestic setting with the grandeur of the cosmos, suggesting that the mother's load extends beyond the care of her children. Most important, the illustration in conjunction with the title asserts that both the burdens of caring for children and of contemplating the universe are bearable. At the same time, the domesticity of the scene embraces the small size of the book, and seems to declare that its sphere of influence is limited. The title of Radford's first volume proclaims that it is both large and small. *A Light Load* suggests a paradox: a load can only be a burden, and yet it does not encumber. The verse itself seems light: Radford's poems are short in the length and number of lines, with lilting, regular iambic tetrameters and trimeters and easy rhymes. She draws on standard—and feminine—lyric tropes of songbirds, flowers, woods, ocean waves. The delicacy of her verse draws readers in, but once in they discover a poetry that advertises its own impotence and its inability to communicate. To be a fin de siècle poet was also to be a minor poet in the sense that many poets of the period were self-conscious about living in an age identified with "degeneration," and viewed, during the time itself as well as afterward, as transitional rather than great. Like her male counterparts, the Rhymers, Radford writes formal, metrical verse that displays anxiousness about what can be considered poetically original when every trick of form seems already to have been tried.

This feeling helps to explain why the "minor poet" was such a major concept in the period.[62] Indeed, Radford's title, *A Light Load,* responds to her good friend Amy Levy's suicidal "Minor Poet," who declares, "I only crave for rest / Too heavy is the load. I fling it down."[63] Levy's minor poet bears the burdens of poverty, of his inability to find "sound's completeness" and of the "jarring discord" of his life. His load is too heavy because he fails to live up to his only companions: the canonical authors who occupy his bookshelf. For both Levy's minor poet and Dollie Radford, the "load" refers to the labor and burden of writing lyric at the fin de siècle, when formal experiments spawned by the Rossettis, Swinburne, and others seem to be fully exhausted. Levy's minor poet rages against his minor status, but Radford embraces it, freed, largely, from its insistent demands. Paradoxically, that freedom gives her room to comment from a distance on the genre as a whole. Whereas Levy's minor poet fails to write, we have seen that poetry itself fails the poet of *A Light Load.* In the fin de siècle atmosphere of lyric failure that Levy's dramatic monologue evokes, the only solution, Radford suggests, is to embrace the small, the minor, the merely acceptable, and to wait with patience for the new. While acknowledging the limits of a "tender measure," Radford also frankly asserts its pleasures, especially in the context of motherhood.

This embrace of the "light," Radford tells us, is, however, not so easy. In a poem that treasures "tender measures" and "little songs," proudly proclaiming their satisfying smallness, those measures and songs are still incommunicable. Modernity, as Meynell testifies, wants originality and complexity, and thus the literary ground is not very receptive to the small and simple. Lamenting the irremediable privacy of a poem / song, this poem depicts, in songlike lyric, of course, the unsuccessful attempt to transmit a song:

> The little songs which come and go,
> In tender measures, to and fro,
> Whene'er the day brings you to me,
> Keep my heart full of melody.
>
> But on my lute I strive in vain
> To play the music o'er again,
> And you, dear love, will never know
> The little songs which come and go.[64]

Radford emphasizes the smallness of the songs here, using the word "tender" in order to unite the definition connoting fineness and delicacy with its meaning connoting affection and sweetness. Their unrepeatability signals their ephemerality—these imagined songs are as fleeting as any performance, and subject to even less control by the silent would-be singer. The songs and the day have more agency here than the people do, bringing the beloved and coming and going. These songs belong to no one and have no origin—even though they are heard internally, and "keep my heart full of melody." The would-be singer cannot control how or when they "come and go" nor can she "play the music o'er again." She wishes to share the "fullness" they bring to her, but, tragically, she can't. Ironically, she can sing about her fruitless striving to sing. The first stanza represents an ideal in which smallness or "tenderness" enlarges to the "fullness" of the heart. But in the second stanza, when the plenitude of one person's heart cannot become the fullness of another's, that presumed abundance shrinks. In the contrast between the two stanzas, the poem does not make an argument but rather asks a question about why the tender measures fail, or rather, why the would-be singer cannot reproduce them. One answer that it posits, especially in the context of fin de siècle lyric culture, is that these verses are too tender, too sentimental. In an era in which every lyric possibility seems to have been explored already, these tender measures, which expand outward, are no longer possible.

Angela Leighton has criticized Radford's poetry along these lines. She refers to it as "minor" women's poetry in the "sentimentalist model." By "minor" she clearly hopes to distinguish it from "major" or important, high-quality women's poetry. She refers to "The little songs which come and go" as a "furtive, miniaturist passion, blandly addressed to the observing reader."[65] Leighton also suggests that Radford's poems on motherhood imitate too much the "jingle" and "babbling" of baby speech. In contrast, I argue that Radford identifies the profound ways in which the daily routines of motherhood hamper her creativity yet at the same time she celebrates the joy of motherhood's intimacy. If these poems imitate childish rhymes, it is because those are the rhythms that take root in a mother's mind. A critic of the early 1990s, like Leighton, trying to gain critical attention for long-ignored women writers, must cast her subjects in the language of seriousness, hence the argument within her title *Writing Against the Heart:* these women writers do not embrace the fussy sentimentality assumed of women poets. Radford becomes a foil in Leighton's argument to show that while certain middlebrow poets might have given the stereotype some currency, women poets as worthy of our regard as Tennyson did exist. Yet Radford's importance lies precisely in the ways in which she seriously considers the significance of the small—the genre of song, the short poem, the unshareable song, the unoriginal poem or song, the children's song.

When Radford writes about motherhood, she still laments the inability to sing, but also tells us what the mother can sing: children's rhymes. She turns the disappointment of the unsingable song into the satisfaction of the singable one. This poem from *A Light Load* represents the mother/poet as incapable of singing more sophisticated songs than nursery rhymes, but as, for the moment, perfectly content:

> What song shall I sing to you
>   Now the wee ones are in bed,
> What books shall I bring to you
>   Now each little sleepy head
> Is tucked away on pillow white,
> All snug and cosy for the night.
>
> Many many singers now,
>   Sing their new songs in the land,
> Many writers bring us now
>   Many books to understand,

> But I can sing, these evening times,
> Only the children's songs and rhymes.
>
> All the day they play with me,
>   My heart grows full of their looks,
> All their prattle stays with me,
>   And I have no mind for books,
> Nor care for any other tune
>   Than they have sung this golden June.[66]

The desire to sing a song presumably to the husband, followed by the inability to do so, reminds readers of the failure to sing in other poems as well. This poem displays both ambition and resignation. It presents an ideal in which a mother can flower intellectually after the children go to sleep, engaging with new thought, producing original songs. But the poem reverts to the realism of an exhausting day and acknowledges the persistence of the styles of verse that dominate the day. Head and heart are full of children's songs and looks; the children's personal gestures here merge with their "songs and rhymes" so that the personal and the poetic seem united. In this poem, poetry fails, or at least originality fails, but intimacy succeeds. Taken with others in which a desire for lyric intimacy is thwarted, this poem seems to suggest that song, particularly modern, experimental, original lyric, is perhaps the last mode in which to attempt to establish intersubjective connection.

Radford writes about singing to children in *Songs and Other Verses*, contending still that her song will be unoriginal:

> Shall I make a song for you
>   Children dear,
> Not too hard or long for you,
>   Just as clear
> As your lives which opened so,
>   A while ago?
>
> How shall I find any word
>   Old or new,
> That the wise earth has not heard
>   Ages through,
> Ever since her ways grew sweet
>   With little feet?[67]

Its unoriginality makes the song suitable for children; it must be short, easy, and simple. Radford asserts that there was perhaps never a time when such a song was new. Here, originality is not even a possibility and so the poem replaces its presumed virtue with an ideal of identification. The poem presents the children themselves as a stunning combination of new and old: their lives have only just opened, yet they themselves continue to make the earth's ways sweet with "little feet" that mimic every pair of little feet in the history of the human race. Just as children's feet are the same across generations, the metrical feet of these poems, little by virtue of their seeming insignificance, are also the same across generations. The reliable sameness of the songs and children is precisely what makes the ways of the earth "sweet."

The palimpsest of historical children and the children addressed mirrors the way in which the mother/singer layers herself into mother earth:

> How I love you, she repeats,
>   How rejoice,
> All my singing she completes,
>   For my voice,
> Of the song in her great heart,
>   Is but a part.[68]

The mother/singer's authority comes not from her originality but from her identification with the ur-mother earth. That ur-mother voice is made up of the voices of many mothers, of which the present singer is only one. Radford includes these poems about the experience of the mother/poet in order to argue for the viability of song within the mother-child relationship. The burden of writing lyric is a "light load" in this context because these songs make no claims for originality or intellectual power. In these poems about children's songs, Radford experiences and then thwarts what Sandra Gilbert and Susan Gubar called "the anxiety of authorship," or a woman's "radical fear that she cannot create."[69] Her response to that anxiety declares that even if children's songs are not original, they can establish feelings of intimacy and connection in ways that highbrow poetry often claims to but does not. In fact, it is their very familiarity that makes them satisfying.

Alice Meynell, as chapter 4 attests, approaches motherhood by proclaiming a necessary distance between mother and child. This stance is also a defense that keeps the mother from becoming wholly absorbed in her child's life. For Radford, that absorption—"My heart grows full of their looks"—is also certainly a source of anxiety because it keeps her from composing original songs. However, it is also importantly a source of deep satisfaction. Her children's songs and rhythms provide intimacy with her children, but also a profound sense of being connected in the world. With this embrace of domesticity, Radford claims for motherhood and femininity a power that she declares that modern lyric poetry, whether profoundly new or repeating tired forms and tropes, lacks. By acknowledging the problems of the mother/poet, the ways in which life with children can occupy one's mind as well as one's time, Radford makes space for an ambivalence that renders what Leighton has called her sentimentality multidimensional. By accepting the insufficiency of her poetic output along with the satisfactions of her children's songs, Radford claims an importance for devalued concepts that are often associated with femininity: song, tenderness, unoriginality, and waiting.

The most positive review of *A Light Load* came from Arthur Symons, who praised the volume on rather different grounds than I have sketched out here. Although he noted the smallness of both the volume and the poems within it, Symons sought to align Radford's volume with the standard terms of aestheticist success: an appeal to a small audience with exquisitely refined tastes. Symons concluded, "So small a volume can scarcely be expected to conquer the attention of a public which takes its poetry unwillingly, but in big doses. It will win its way, however, I am sure, to the grateful regard of that select public within the public which really cares for poetry, and would give most epics for a perfect song."[70] Here, Symons derides the audience for poetry at the fin de siècle, casting them as an ignorant bourgeoisie who cannot gauge quality and so must insist on quantity instead. Viewing poetry as a kind of necessary cultural medicine, these readers, Symons suggests, wrongly believe only a large dose can cure them of their cretinism. Symons thereby elevates the genre of lyric over epic. Only a "select" public with a genuine concern for poetry understands the superiority of "song" to "epic." What Jackson calls "the lyricization of poetry" is at work here, for Symons tosses aside epic so that lyric may carry the mantle of true poetry.[71] In Symons's formulation, the lyric offers greater potential for intimacy than epic does because it cultivates a "select" group that "really cares." Indeed, the perfection of song derives from the narrowness of its scope. If those who "really care for poetry" prefer lyric, then lyric becomes the ur-genre of poetry.

Other reviewers were less kind than Symons; although Symons transforms that smallness into the virtue of the rare gem, the *National Observer* brands the volume as "excessively trivial," and the *Athenaeum* insists on its diminutiveness, "with themes so slight and vague that oftenest they are nearly nothing—no more than the trill and twitter of a song-bird."[71] These critiques—even Symons's—miss the way that Radford deliberately pushes the genre of lyric to its limits. Symons's review nonetheless emblematizes the central concerns not only of *A Light Load* but also of Radford's poetics throughout her career. She embraced the lyric subgenre of "song" all the while exposing all of its fault lines—in particular, and against prevalent assumptions made by Symons, its failure to establish intimacy. Many of her songs are about songs that long to communicate, but cannot. These songs seldom reach the ears they are meant for, and when they do the meaning turns out to be false or misunderstood. Radford's poems expose the failure of lyric intimacy, except in circumstances that are as trite as her reviewers suggest. Radford's songs about song confront generic conventions that compare lyric to music, which often assume for it a physical and emotional immediacy to which the reader has ready access.

Radford punctures the fantasy of a song as a form of fullness within a small gem, a fantasy that Symons extols in his review. Instead, she elevates the very incompleteness of a song, or its unorginality. For Radford, these traits are not signs of failure; instead, the song must satisfy in the same way that waiting does, in an acceptance of what one has and in anticipation of what may come. Radford declares, "I can wait and sing," aligning these actions because they embody attentiveness and openness rather than plenitude. At the dawn of the twentieth century, Radford asks readers to temper their expectations of lyric, to problematize its musical origins, while at the same time asking us to value its limitations, its smallness, its confinement within a moment of time that puts readers in a position of waiting. For Radford, the song, like waiting, and as a function of waiting, succeeds where it seems to fail.

Conclusion

MARY E. COLERIDGE AND THE SECOND PERSON PLURAL

The previous chapters have explored the role that the concept of intimacy plays in the poetics of women writing in the fin de siècle. These poets have constructed a paradoxically impersonal intimacy, in which readers can see a dynamics of interaction at work, without positioning that dynamics within the specific circumstances of the lives of people or characters. I have argued that in their use of short lyric forms, primarily songs and sonnets, these poets have questioned the nature of poetic voice, whether and how it is heard, and what kinds of presence and absence it might signify. These poets claim the silence and even passivity of the conventionally feminine muse position as engaged in a dynamic of mutuality and exchange. Alice Meynell, for instance, shows solitude to be the other side of sociability, silence to be the necessary outline of sound. I have drawn out the intersection of these poets' approach with some cultural questions of the day, as when Augusta Webster's sonnet sequence *Mother and Daughter* challenges the idea that a mother's love is infinite and when A. Mary F. Robinson's collection *The New Arcadia* questions the assumptions of aesthetic philanthropy. *Second Person Singular* has discussed how women poets in the late Victorian period drew upon the patience, reserve, and restraint evident in Christina Rossetti's poetry in order to write poems that established a dynamic of mutual recognition. Rossetti's poetics created new ways of thinking about how subjects and objects relate in songs and sonnets, ways that moved beyond the idea that a woman's poem must spontaneously express personal feelings.

In conclusion, I look to a poet who writes within the same expectations about the dynamics of subject and object in women's poetry, but whose poems often reject intimacy: Mary E. Coleridge. Coleridge wrote outside the literary and social world of urban aestheticism that the other women in this study occupied.[1] The connections between these women—their attendance at the same salons, their reviews of each other's work, their letters and presentation copies of their books—all suggest that whatever their differences, they were a part of the same literary conversation. Coleridge participated in that conversation from a distance and from the context of her own social and literary circles. Lifelong friends with a group of five women who called themselves the "Quintette," she established an even more exclusive club when her friend Margaret Duckworth married the poet Henry Newbolt. Coleridge, along with Duckworth, Newbolt, and Ella Coltman, established the "Settee," which came together frequently primarily to discuss Newbolt's and Coleridge's works-in-progress. Another friend showed Coleridge's poems to Robert Bridges, who immediately took an interest and offered to mentor her.[2] Coleridge participated in a literary context that has recently received new attention in Meredith Martin's *The Rise and Fall of Meter,* which describes how both Bridges and Newbolt debated the virtues of accentual, syllabic, foot-based, or classical approaches to meter.

With the encouragement of Robert Bridges, Coleridge published a small volume of poems with the Daniel Press entitled *Fancy's Following.* She reissued a very similar collection entitled *Fancy's Guerdon* with Elkin Mathews's series "The Shilling Garland," with which Newbolt published his extraordinarily popular *Admirals All.*[3] Mary E. Coleridge was the niece of Samuel Taylor Coleridge, but because she never wanted to capitalize on the family connection or on her name, she published her poetry under a pseudonym, "Anodos." Coleridge takes this name from the protagonist of George Macdonald's *Phantastes,* but the name means "wanderer," and most important for her poetry, it signals her intention to write an impersonal poetics, what Alison Chapman calls contextlessness. Coleridge wrote in a diary that she took the name "lest this *I* should grow troublesome and importunate."[4] To which "I" did she refer here? To the niece of S. T. Coleridge? To the "I" of the woman poet? To the lyric speaker that a reader might assume incarnates the poet? Her statement here contends that the impersonality of her poetry is its defining feature.

Friends and critics who wrote about Coleridge's poetry after her death found ways to incorporate this impersonality with the warmth they perceived in Coleridge as a person and the intimacy they subsequently wanted to ascribe to her work. Theresa Whistler, the editor of the *Collected Poems of Mary Coleridge,* describes her poems this way: "When she came to make her own comment on life, in verse, it is as one would expect to find it on a Greek tomb or wayside shrine—brief, charged with intimate emotion, and yet aware of a larger relevance than the particular occasion. For poetry so personal in impulse, hers is curiously bare of particular circumstance."[5] Whistler assumes that the poetry is "personal" and therefore needs to use the metaphor of the "Greek tomb or wayside shrine" in order to square the "intimate emotion," presumed to be Coleridge's own, with the sense of distance in her verses. Whistler's use of the word "intimate" follows earlier writing about Coleridge's poetry. When these critics used this term, they typically meant that poetry reveals secrets to the reader. Their descriptions of her work consistently place her within the expressive conventions of women's poetry, almost in spite of themselves. Upon her death in 1907, Coleridge's mentor, Robert Bridges, remembered her poems in *Cornhill Magazine* this way: "It is their intimacy and spontaneity that gives them so great a value. They will be her portrait, an absolutely truthful picture of a wondrously beautiful and gifted spirit . . . not in conventional attitude nor with fixed features, nor lightly to be interpreted, nor even always to be understood, but mysterious rather an enigmatical: a poetic effigy, the only likeness of worth: a music self-born of her contact with the wisdom and passion of the world, and which all the folly and misery of man could provoke only to gentle and loving strains."[6] Although Bridges compares Coleridge's poetry with the work of men—Heine, Blake, R. W. Dixon—in this concluding paragraph of his memorial essay his characterization relies on decades of received wisdom about women's poetry.

Although Coleridge initially published under the androgynous pseudonym "Anodos," most of her readers knew the identity of the poet. *Fancy's Following* was, as Bridges's obituary tells us, mostly circulated among Coleridge's family and friends.[7] Coleridge received a wider readership after her death in 1907 when Henry Newbolt published a collection under her name, entitled simply *Poems,* that ran to multiple editions until 1918. Most of her readers would have been familiar with the rhetoric about women poets that Bridges draws on. He equates the woman poet with her poem, a move typical in contemporary reviews of women's poetry. In doing so, he labels her poetry as remarkable for its "intimacy" and its "truth," when in fact her poetry is repeatedly at pains to entertain and finally reject both of these terms. To account for the "rare and beautiful nature" of Coleridge's poetry, Newbolt cites Maurice Baring, who also uses the term "intimate" in asserting that her work contains "the confidences and confessions of what is too intimate save for Poetry."[8] Baring's and Whistler's comments especially rely on assumptions that however disconnected from the original speaker or writer, lyric poetry reveals intense, secret emotion, functioning as a confession that pretends not to be publicly made.[9] These very assumptions blind Baring, Newbolt, and Whistler to Coleridge's emphasis on failures of intimacy. Her poems consistently approach interpersonal interaction with wariness and skepticism. Mary E. Coleridge is in fact a limit case of intimacy in a fin de siècle woman poet.

Rather than struggling to overcome the inaccessibility of the other, Coleridge's poems invite it. Taking the distance that Meynell and others prize to an extreme, Coleridge's "On the Arrival of a Visitor" recoils at the presence of another person. Opening with this apostrophe, "Farewell, my Loneliness!," the poem presents solitude, rather than the visitor as "beloved." The voices of the living mar the music of silence. Like Michael Field, Coleridge suggests that one might share a more profound intimacy with the dead than with the living. Yet for Coleridge, her communion with the dead does not replace or continue relationships with the living but rejects them:

> Lo, when the house is empty come the dead,
> And once again they say the words they said,
> Breaking the charmèd silence of the grave!
> I have sat lonely with my closest friend
> As in the throng. Ah, wherefore, to what end?
> The dead have power to give more than the living gave.
>
> Lo, when the house is empty, live the dreams
> Of the old poets—and my chamber seems
> A palace for the women long ago
> That, whilst the living shadows round me move,
> Are shadows also, dumb, remote from love,
> Vain figures, vainly mouthing at a show![10]

Even the presence of a close friend forecloses on the intimacy that this poem suggests is possible with the dead. Yet this idea really is only a suggestion; the dead are present when the house is empty, but there is no conversation, no mutuality. They have the "power" to give, but the poem only hints at that gift by encouraging us to imagine the opposite of what the dead are when their presence is attenuated by the living: "remote from love" and "vainly mouthing." The speaker feels so profoundly disconnected from others that the living are merely "shadows" whose presence renders the more vivid dead shadows as well. At their most vivid, these dead can only repeat words from the past, but these words are a foundation for an intimacy more profound than is possible with a living person. Coleridge builds the space and emptiness of the house into the poem with a dash-enforced caesura that creates the distance she seeks: "Of the old poets—and my chamber seems." The living are too close: "Among the crowd of those too near and dear / Too often have I known disgust and fear." In contrast with Meynell's appreciation of solitude, which she understands as a resting-place from which one can return to others with renewed energy, Coleridge anticipates Sartre's famous dictum that "hell is other people." Mary Coleridge's distance is so far away that it is not a vantage point from which to appreciate difference but a collapse into an internalized world.

"On the Arrival of a Visitor" is an ironic title for a poem that in fact celebrates the visitor's departure. The dead are not so much visitors as constant presences that come out of the background when living people leave. The poem presents the dead as analogous to figures from the pages of old poets; both are "women long ago." Coleridge wrote about these women of the past in her private writings, reprinted after her death by her friend Edith Sichel in *Gathered Leaves*. Describing an exhibit of Venetian artwork at the New Gallery, she writes, "They are dead, dead, dead as dead as the dodo . . . we have lost those ladies forever. We never could be so broad as that, however hard we tried, nor so brown-eyed and red- and golden-haired. They couldn't be revived, not if we wore their clothes at twenty masquerades. . . . It's the strangest, most dream-like feeling, to be in the midst of these silent and secret lives, these faces that are so many sealed books."[11] Although "On the Arrival of a Visitor" elevates the presence of the dead over the living, those dead are still inaccessible. Coleridge presents attempts at imitation as a mode of knowing another that is always bound to fail. Wearing ancient costumes gives us no access to the minds of the past (nor to their hair or eyes). It is precisely the silence and secrecy of these long-dead figures that are appealing to Coleridge.

With an awareness of Coleridge herself as such a long-dead and inaccessible figure, recent scholars have nonetheless drawn on biographical information in reading her work. Alison Chapman accounts for the place of her close group of friends in Coleridge's poetry, arguing that the "contextlessness" of Coleridge's poetry emerges from these social, romantic, and literary friendships, so that her poems perform "the ghosting of an illicit desire." This desire is not "an interpretive key" but "the condition of their production."[12] Kasey Bass Baker also draws on a biographical reading of Coleridge's work, citing from unpublished letters, in order to argue that Coleridge's poetry focuses on the "point of contact between self and other," representing it as "possibly horrific, but always exhilarating."[13] Baker notes that Coleridge frequently signed her letters to her friends "Anodos," blurring her authorial persona with her personal life. In that vein, it is easy to read the poem "Gone" as a representation of a life dominated by friendships whose nature necessarily modulated as some members of the group that called themselves the Quintette married:

> About the little chambers of my heart
>   Friends have been coming—going—many a year.

> The doors stand open there.
> Some, lightly stepping, enter; some depart.
>
> Freely they come and freely go, at will.
> The walls give back their laughter; all day long
> They fill the house with song.
> One door alone is shut, one chamber still.[14]

The final lines, in which one "chamber" of the heart is closed off to others, resonates with a letter that Coleridge wrote to her friend Violet Hodgkin about her friend Helen Duckworth, Margaret's sister, in which she complained about Helen's attempts to take care of her: "The worst of it is, it's a new thing; she never took care of me before, & I do *wish* she wouldn't. And yet it's lovely of her. 'There's something of the child & something of the mother in my love for you' she said afterwards. . . . Somehow I couldn't tell her what I always feel, that her love for me is the love of the bird for the bough in 'Misconceptions.'"[15] Although Baker offers two opposite and plausible readings of this allusion to Robert Browning's poem, in which a bird thrills a "spray" that he lands on before moving on to a more suitable treetop to build his nest, I cite this letter in order to draw attention to Coleridge's internal rejection of her friend's attempts at closeness and affection, and to her inability to communicate that rejection directly. The poems "Gone" and "On the Arrival of a Visitor" as well as the letter emphasize insuperable interpersonal barriers. Together, they suggest that Coleridge believed that a person can never fully know another, and that attempts to know another as well as to give and elicit affection can violate the privacy of the individual heart and mind.

Yet "Gone" also functions in the larger framework of a tradition of women's poetry in the late Victorian period. Like the other women poets in this study, Coleridge responded to Christina Rossetti. "Gone" recapitulates the dynamic of Rossetti's "Echo," where the poem likens itself, as well as the psyche it represents, to a purgatorial room admitting souls. At first, "Gone" evinces a freedom missing in Rossetti's "Echo," where "the slow door / That opening lets in, lets out no more." It takes for granted the "echo" that Rossetti's poem cries out for, understanding that the repetition that assures presence also requires absence. In this way, it is reminiscent of Alice Meynell's ideas from "The Rhythm of Life." At the same time, the notion of a soul's mobility in and out of the hearts and minds of friends resembles the idea of "sycamine keys" around the relic laid in the "heart's tomb" in Michael Field's "There is a fair white relic." Although it is safe to assume that Coleridge would not have been familiar with Michael Field's *Underneath the Bough* when she wrote "Gone," nor with Meynell's essay, these similarities argue for the trend I have identified in fin de siècle women's poetry toward depicting relationships that leave space for separateness.[16] "Gone" takes a blithe attitude toward the mutability of friendships; even when friends depart, they leave traces—"The walls give back their laughter"—that compensate for their departure.

The devastating turn of the final line depicts an impassable barrier that provides the self with the ultimate privacy of inaccessibility, but also protects her from full attachment to her friends, with their whimsical departures. The difference between the present tense of the poem and the past participle of the title is striking. In light of the final line, that difference suggests that the "speaker" of the poem herself is gone, shut behind the door in a still chamber, while her cheerful friends are blithely unaware. Alternately, it could imply that the friends who come and go will ultimately all go for good. Either way, it disallows the balance of distance and intimacy that so many of the poets in this study are at pains to construct in their lyrics. Without the discordance of the final line, the space afforded by the shorter third line in each stanza might be seen to exemplify the principle of intimate distance, as in Meynell's poems. With it, those short lines create empty space that points to real vacancy, rather than a restful pause. Adela Pinch's deft interpretation of Coleridge's short lines, which she argues are organized around end-rhyme rather than meter, asserts that Coleridge used a variety of line lengths in order to "tell the story of ends and of resistances to ends."[17] The rhyme of "there" with "year" disappoints not only as a slant rhyme, but because it comes too soon in a trimeter line following pentameters. It doubly confounds aural expectations, in lines whose content conveys both steadfast predictability and openness. This short line introduces a formal indication of limits, anticipating the closed door in lines that suggest spatial and temporal extension in the slant rhyme of "there" and "year." Whistler relays that Coleridge reworked "Gone" under the tutelage of Bridges, though she does not convey how she changed the poem to respond to his advice. It is possible to speculate, however, that the pauses that come mid-foot in this otherwise regular poem owe something to Bridges's openness to multiple prosodic systems, in opposition to prosodies that relied steadfastly on classical foot scansion.[18] The semicolons in lines 4 and 6 appear mid-foot, disturbing the logic and timing of foot scansion. The words "all day long" thus aurally have a discrete rhythmic effect, preceded by a pause that interrupts the continuity implied by the words. This poem's reversals, both formal and figurative, in what initially appears to sketch an ideal of openness within intimate friendships, signal what Coleridge writes about more explicitly in her letter to Violet Hodgkin: the impossibility of full emotional openness in intimate relationships.

Christina Rossetti's poems echo elsewhere in Coleridge's oeuvre as well.

Several poems answer Rossetti's foundational "Song (When I am dead my dearest)," in which the dead or dying soul anticipates the absence of her own capacity to remember or perceive: "I shall not hear the nightingale / Sing on, as if in pain." Rossetti's poem asserts that the dead soul will not be able to see or feel the consequences of a beloved's forgetting, nor will the beloved know or feel whether he is remembered in the afterlife. The female "speaker" tells him, "Haply I may remember, / And haply may forget." Coleridge's poems take forgetting, of both the living and the dead as the presupposition, and ask what happens afterward for the living:

> I SHALL forget you, O my dead,
>   I shall forget you!
> You will not care.
> Less visible than air,
>   You are where no forgetfulness may fret you.
> But I, how shall I bear
>   Visible earth, my dead, when I forget you?[19]

Coleridge revises the scenario in Rossetti's "Song" by using the second person plural, challenging the presumed dyad in the earlier poem and emphasizing the intimacy of group dynamics. While this plural "you" might refer back to the importance for Coleridge of group friendships that scholars have noted, these poems are not traceable to a specific experience, since Coleridge was the first of her friends to die, succumbing suddenly in her forties to appendicitis. Rather, this poem, along with the one I discuss below, "Only a little shall we speak of thee," writes the possibility of coterie intimacy into the conventions of late Victorian women's poetry. The playfulness of Rossetti's "Song" both gives voice to the woman that might be mourned in a man's poem and tells that man that his gestures of sorrow will not matter to her. "I shall forget you" revises Rossetti's poem by bringing back the tragedy that Rossetti disavows but situating it in the forgetting subject rather than in the forgotten object. Coleridge emphasizes the androgyny of her pseudonym in the multiplicity of the address to "O my dead." The addressed dead, as well as the mourning, forgetting "I," could easily be gendered masculine or feminine. The openness of gender here situates Coleridge well beyond the gendered dynamics of Mermin's problem of the "damsel and the knight," the "poet-muse" dynamic to which I referred in the introduction. By sweeping away the power dynamics of the dyad, often gendered even in a same-sex erotics, Coleridge can get to the heart of the matter: the inability of the mind and the memory to compensate for the absence of the dead. This poem contradicts "On the Arrival of a Visitor," for this very solitary soul cannot help but forget her beloved dead. For Coleridge, actual absence does not matter as much as mental absence. Coleridge writes the disappearance of the dead by de-emphasizing the "you" metrically, allowing the word to trail off in the extrametrical syllable of a feminine rhyme.

Even as it reinforces the barriers to intimacy that Coleridge describes elsewhere, "Only a little shall we speak of thee" reverses the dynamic of "I shall forget you," in two ways. It describes a group response to the loss of a singular "thee," and it depicts the other side of the vision of mourning in Rossetti's "Song" so that the group "haply may remember."

> Only a little shall we speak of thee,
>   And not the thoughts we think;
> There, where thou art—and art not—words would be
>   As stones that sink.
>
> We shall not see each other for thy face,
>   Nor know the silly things we talk upon.
> Only the heart says, "She was in this place,
>   And she is gone."[20]

Here, the imperfect memory of the absent beloved interferes with the intimacy of those who are still present. They cannot "bond" over shared feelings of loss. Rather, their words are so insufficient to their feelings that they can only talk about "silly things." As in "I shall forget you," a vivid memory of the other is painfully inaccessible. The insufficient memory nonetheless exerts its influence, keeping the group's thoughts separately on their friend who is gone. Their independent thoughts of her keep them from interacting with each other: the absent beloved's fact keeps intruding. Whereas for Christina Rossetti at times the failure of intimacy functions as a badge of honor, a refusal to participate in gendered norms, Coleridge has done away with those norms far enough to be able to express the pain of that failure. These poems proclaim the impossibility of presenting credible versions of other people to ourselves, whether they are present or absent; others are always mediated by thoughts and memories.

In the late nineteenth century, "song" was a powerful form mediating ideas about how people love. Like other women poets of the fin de siècle, Coleridge writes, and writes about, songs. I close with a poem that might be interpreted to promote a different version of the story I tell about late nineteenth-century women's verse:

TWO SONGS

The blossoming of love I sang.
  The streams adown the mountain sprang,
And all the world with music rang.

A cloud has darkened Heaven above,
I only hear a moaning dove.
I sing the withering of love.[21]

On the surface, "Two Songs" offers a simplified comparison of the optimistic poetry of the mid-century and pessimism in the poetry of the late century. "Two Songs" recapitulates in brief Christina Rossetti's response in "Monna Innominata" to Elizabeth Barrett Browning's *Sonnets from the Portugeuese,* sequences that describe the "withering" and the "blossoming" of love, respectively. The second sonnet of Barrett Browning's sequence declares that the lovers will overcome obstacles, even death, to meet in heaven: "Our hands would touch for all the mountain-bars: / And, heaven being rolled between us at the end, / We should but vow the faster for the stars."[22] Whether "heaven" in Barrett Browning's poem refers to the sky or the afterlife (the lowercase "h" blurs that boundary), Coleridge's poem casts a cloud over it. Both of Coleridge's predecessors refer to the female lover as a "dove": Barrett Browning's sequence depicts the female lover as a dove folded in the heart of the beloved, while in Rossetti's the dove produces "friendly cooings."[23] But in Coleridge's poem the dove is only moaning, and the cloud she casts over Heaven, which Rossetti sincerely proposes is full of music, seems to suggest that fin de siècle women's poetry itself is further withered in the shadow of these two nineteenth-century greats. In this way, "Two Songs" not only implies a shift from blossoming to withered love, but also presents the dove's moaning as the diminished poetry of the end of the century.

"Two Songs" contains a fundamental assumption about what "song" is expected to do at the end of the nineteenth century: to convey something about love, whether its development or its demise. Like Dollie Radford's songs, the poem both sings and refuses to sing. As much about hearing music as making it, the first stanza of "Two Songs" emphasizes how the love the singer presumably feels produces her song, which in turn allows her to hear the mountain springs and the music with which the world rings. Yet the second stanza reverses this order, so that a perception of the sky alters what her ear can pick up, which in turn seems to wither her love. By altering the order between feeling, singing, and hearing in these two stanzas, "Two Songs" questions how these actions influence each other. Does one feel because one sings or sing because one feels? Does one sing or hear a song first? Does hearing create feelings? The triplet rhymes of each stanza signal a compulsion to repeat, or to end with a sense of predictability and finality over and over again, as though singing, hearing, and feeling were only slightly different versions of the same thing. Whereas Pinch reads Coleridge's varied line lengths as attempts to forestall or hasten endings, the scrupulously regular meter with its end-stopped lines emphasizes the transformation of love as well as music.

Reading "Two Songs" in light of Coleridge's clear skepticism about the possibilities of intimacy, it would seem like the song of withering would always follow the song of blossoming. But by focusing on the title's attention to the genre of "song," it becomes clear that for Coleridge as well as for other fin de siècle poets, the genre is inextricable from ideas about how relationships happen. Recently, scholars have argued that the genre of the novel not only represented but also created ideas about sympathy.[21] Far too little attention has gone to poetry's role in shaping ideas about how people relate—not only in its content but also in its form. It would take a very different kind of book to show that people put into practice ideas they gleaned from poetry, but, as I hope I have shown here, late Victorian women poets used poetic form to circulate ideas about intimacy that challenged the received wisdom both about "song" and about the experience of a wide variety of relationships. They demonstrated how a woman's love poem can consider a host of deeply affecting relationships, with friends, family members, readers, and God and present those in the relationship as mutually regarding. These poets offer alternatives for renegotiating the power dynamics implied in the poet/muse dyad. At the heart of fin de siècle women's poetry are the multiple ways that women sing the bonds of verse.

Notes

Introduction

1. Meynell, *Second Person Singular,* 136.
2. Patmore, *English Metrical Law,* 8.
3. Thain, "Poetry," 224.
4. "Intimacy" as I define it here is sharply distinct from studies of sympathy in the Victorian novel. Audrey Jaffe's study of sympathy in the novel, *Scenes of Sympathy,* focuses on identification, or imagining oneself in the position of another. Rachel Ablow in *The Marriage of Minds* argues that sympathy plays a role in identity and subjectivity and thereby deemphasizes relational dynamics. Both of these studies correlate sympathy with modes of representation and narrative inherent in the novel form. My approach also departs from a concept of the intimacy of poetry that defines it only as a subject's innermost thoughts and feelings. Helen Vendler's version of "lyric intimacy" in *Invisible Listeners* falls back on the significance of the subject, as well as the biography of the poet, in her argument that poets' works invoke "invisible listeners" to compensate for relationships that were missing in their lives. William Waters's *Poetry's Touch: On Lyric Address* considers various kinds of addresses to "you"—contemporaries, friends, imagined others—and discusses the way in which all of these implicate the reader. Waters's account, which attempts to look at the lyric "you" in all of its range, often tends to culminate in a reader that identifies with the "you." Both Elizabeth Helsinger ("Song's Fictions," 158) and Anne-Lise François (*Open Secrets,* 155) helpfully argue against a model of poetic intimacy in which a reader imaginatively identifies with a single speaker.
5. The relational dynamics of these short subgenres, as I read them, are explicitly different from those of the dramatic monologue. They do not embody characters or speakers, and their "I"s and "thou"s stand apart from the kinds of contextualized situations that constitute the speakers and interlocutors of dramatic monologues. E. Warwick Slinn identifies some key features of the Victorian dramatic monologue as "self-interested eloquence, verbal immediacy, mimetic detail, interlocutory intrusion" ("Dramatic Monologue," 82). Innovations in the dramatic monologue also occupy an impersonal poetics. Herbert Tucker has argued persuasively for ways in which Victorian dramatic monologue destabilizes rather than reinforces the metaphysically comforting ideas of "voice," "speaker," and "persona" ("Dramatic Monologue and the Overhearing of Lyric"). Isobel Armstrong discusses women poets' use of the dramatic monologue as a mask in *Victorian Poetry* (325). For further discussion of

Victorian women poets' dramatic monologues, see Glennis Byron, "Rethinking the Dramatic Monologue."

6. Rossetti, *Complete Poems*, 1:58.

7. Hassett, *Christina Rossetti*, 31.

8. Rowlinson, "Lyric," 73.

9. Hassett, *Christina Rossetti*, 1.

10. For more on women poets and the trope of silence, see Billone, *Little Songs;* Lootens, *Lost Saints;* and Prins and Jackson, "Lyrical Studies." In "What Kind of Critical Category Is Women's Poetry?" Thain argues for a variety of gender-based genres, acknowledging the numerous attitudes that women poets had, especially in the fin de siècle, toward the category of women's poetry.

11. Meynell, *Collected Poems*, 94.

12. Webster, *Portraits and Other Poems*, 344.

13. Robinson, *New Arcadia*, 4.

14. Radford, *A Light Load*, 11.

15. Wilde, "English Poetesses," 105.

16. LeGallienne, "Woman Poets of the Day," 650.

17. These works include Schaffer and Psomiades, *Women and British Aestheticism;* Schaffer, *Forgotten Female Aesthetes;* and Vadillo, *Women Poets and Urban Aestheticism.*

18. Vadillo, *Women Poets and Urban Aestheticism*, 9.

19. Thain and Vadillo, "Introduction: Fin-de-siècle Renaissance."

20. See, for example, Sharp, *Women's Voices*; Robertson, *English Poetesses;* and Stedman, "Some London Poets."

21. Dollie Radford Diary, 8 June 1894, Dollie Radford Papers.

22. "Earlier Poems of Elizabeth Barrett Browning," 766.

23. Prins, "Poetess."

24. Armstrong, *Victorian Poetry*, 333.

25. Brown, "Victorian Poetess," 194, 196.

26. Le Gallienne, "Women Poets of the Day," 650–51.

27. Armstrong, *Victorian Poetry*, 339–40.

28. Mermin, "Damsel," 69.

29. Peterson, *Becoming a Woman of Letters*; Feldman, "Poet and the Profits."

30. Marion Thain notes that Michael Field's dual authorship avoids the conflict women poets faced in being both poet and muse. Thain also describes how A. Mary F. Robinson and May Probyn sought to work around the poet/muse conflict by establishing what Margaret Reynolds calls a "sister/muse" device in which singer and muse are on equal footing (*Michael Field*, 104–5).

1   "I, for Thou Callest Such"

1. Rossetti, *Complete Poems*, ed. Rebecca Crump, 2:122. All subsequent citations of Rossetti's poetry will be from Crump's edition, hereafter abbreviated as *CP.*

2. Culler, "Apostrophe."

3. The most influential proponent of the biographical approach has been Lona Mosk Packer, in *Christina Rossetti.*

4. McGann, *Beauty of Inflections*, 220.

5. Harrison, *Rossetti in Context*, x; Lootens, *Lost Saints*, 159.

6. Hassett, *Patience of Style*, 64–116.

7. Griffiths, "Disappointment," 123.

8. *CP,* 1:124–25.

9. *CP,* 1:125.

10. Ibid.

11. Ibid.

12. Ibid.

13. *CP,* 1:126.

14. Roe, *Rossetti's Faithful Imagination,* 8–29.

15. Palazzo, *Rossetti's Feminist Theology.*

16. D'Amico, *Rossetti: Faith, Gender, Time,* 157.

17. A number of critics have commented on the ways in which "Monna Innominata" adapts the Petrarchan tradition. William Whitla argues that Rossetti writes both in and against the Petrarchan form. He notes where the rhyme scheme follows and departs from Petrarchan form and maps how the content of the "macrosonnet" forms Petrarchan thematic "rhymes" ("Questioning the Convention," 111, 112). Considering what it means to have a woman articulate Petrarchan sonnets, Antony Harrison asserts that "Monna Innominata "exposes the inadequacies of the tradition itself and of her own historical moment" (*Rossetti in Context,* 155). Citing Heather Dubrow's definition of Petrarchism, Hassett notes the sequence's "commitment to the paradox at the core of Petrarchism," which is that the success of the poem relies on the failure of the erotic relationship (*Patience of Style,* 165). Hassett also provides a detailed discussion of the epigraphs. Marjorie Stone considers the relationship between "Monna Innominata" and *Sonnets from the Portuguese,* citing the way in which both subvert a masculine sonnet tradition but have "diametrically opposed spiritual trajectories" ("Sonnet Traditions," 47).

18. *CP,* 2:88–89.

19. Hassett argues that in love Rossetti "rejects the whole business of assayable worth," but that in poetic achievement she introduces an element of rivalry between lover and beloved (*Patience of Style,* 177). In contrast, I suggest that the second "quatrain" of sonnets demonstrates the inevitability of measuring love.

20. Cynthia Scheinberg reads this sonnet as expressing the gender inequality of Christianity: "[The speaker's] position as a Christian woman guarantees none of the same privileges as for the man." Scheinberg understands the term "helpmeet" to signal that the female lover of the sonnets "accept[s] the role assigned to her in Genesis" (*Women's Poetry and Religion,* 138). Billone resists taking seriously Rossetti's commitment to a principal of submissiveness, reading these lines as a satire of Barrett Browning's sonnets: "It seems nothing can be done with these lines except to read them as painful self-caricatures" (*Little Songs,* 105).

21. *CP,* 2:89.

22. Krista Lysack reads "Monna Innominata" as representing a "spiritual economy" in which "bodies labor in order to produce desire between them." For Lysack, the interchangeability of the lover, beloved, and God in the second quatrain of the "macrosonnet" stems from their identification with each other because they all lack something ("Economics of Ecstasy," 402, 410). Lysack identifies the exchange between these three as one of autoeroticism, identification, and sameness. In contrast, I read these relationships as depending on difference, as disrupting the ideal of "happy equals." Antony Harrison views the conflict between the beloved and God in intertextual terms, viewing the lover as "torn between love of God in purist Dantean tradition, on the one hand; and eros and corrupt Petrarchism on the other" (*Rossetti in Context,* 179).

23. *CP,* 2:90.

24. Scheinberg, *Women's Poetry and Religion,* 142–44.

25. *CP,* 2:90.

26. Ibid.

27. *CP,* 2:91–92.

28. Hassett reads the word "breath" as indicating the poetic medium, and these lines as a request to "repair the tradition's founding neglect of women's love and women's song" (*Patience of Style,* 184).

29. *CP,* 2:92.

30. Billone, in *Little Songs,* notes a similar fluidity, arguing that the "I" and "you" in "Monna Innominata" can be read interchangeably as the speaker-poet and the unnamed poetess, or as a pair of lovers.

31. Pinch, *Thinking about Other People,* 105.

32. *CP,* 2:93.

33. Chapman, *Afterlife,* 15.

34. McGann, *Beauty of Inflections,* 244–47.

35. Harrison, *Rossetti in Context,* 4; Hassett, *Patience of Style,* 38.

36. *CP,* 1:46.

37. Ibid.

38. Vendler, *Invisible Listeners,* 4–6.

39. *CP,* 1:46.

40. Conley, "Rossetti's Cold Women," 278–80; Hassett, *Patience of Style,* 36. Both critics also refer to the longer manuscript version, Conley using it to affirm that the poem is articulated from Hell, Hassett in order to register the longer poem's echoes of other poems, especially Tennyson's "Tears, Idle Tears."

41. Griffiths, "Disappointment," 111–12.

42. Leighton, "On Some Sonnets," 510.

43. Griffiths, *Printed Voice,* 66.

44. Rossetti, *Selected Prose,* 301.

45. Chapman, *Afterlife,* 44.

46. Rossetti, *Selected Prose,* 301.

47. Indeed, John Picker argues in *Victorian Soundscapes* that the Victorians seized on the advent of the phonograph not as an opportunity for passive listening, as we use it most frequently now and as Picker claims modernists viewed it, but as a way to record their own voices at home and to repeat them as often as they liked. They even imagined it as a method for delivering audio messages (110–46).

48. Sterne, *Audible Past,* 290.

49. Prins, "Voice Inverse," 44.

50. Lootens, *Lost Saints,* 163.

51. *CP,* 2:127.

52. Rossetti, *Selected Prose,* 321.

53. Armstrong, *Radical Aesthetic,* 253.

54. Reynolds, "Speaking Unlikenesses"; Conley, "Rossetti's Cold Women."

55. Hassett discusses this phenomenon in "At Home" (*Patience of Style,* 33).

56. *CP,* 1:38.

57. Reynolds, "Speaking Unlikenesses," 11.

58. Conley, "Rossetti's Cold Women," 265–66.

59. *CP,* 2:181.

60. Rossetti, *Face of the Deep,* 286.

61. Lootens, *Lost Saints,* 170.

62. Armstrong, "Era of the New Woman," 23.

63. Michael Field, "To Christina Rossetti."

64. Conley, "Poet's Right," 367. Conley also reads this sonnet as a critique of Rossetti's religious devotion. This critique, in Conley's view, short-circuits the poem's fantasy wherein the female poet is both writer and muse. Conley also reads Barrett Browning's "A Musical Instrument" as a dramatization of Syrinx from a woman poet's point of view (369–72).

65. Maitland (pseudonym for Buchanan), "Fleshly School of Poetry," 339.

66. D. G. Rossetti, "Stealthy School of Criticism."

2 "Appraise Love and Divide"

1. D. G. Rossetti, *House of Life,* 86.

2. Ibid., 95–96.

3. Margaret Reynolds addresses the question of measuring love in "Love's Measurement in Elizabeth Barrett Browning's *Sonnets from the Portuguese.*"

4. W. M. Rossetti, "Introductory Note," 336.

5. Rigg, *Julia Augusta Webster,* 256–65.

6. Webster, *Portraits and Other Poems,* 349.

7. Ibid., 350.

8. Badeni, *Slender Tree,* 75.

9. Webster, *Portraits and Other Poems,* 350

10. Meynell, *Second Person Singular,* 134.

11. Although family size was declining in the latter half of the nineteenth century, only children were unusual. Robert Woods shows that "for those married aged 20–24 the number of children ever born fell from 7.4 for the pre-1851 marriage cohort to 5.1 for the 1891–96 cohort, and for those married aged 25–29 the decline was from 5.9 to 3.3 between the same marriage cohorts" (*Demography,* 116). Woods suggests that "appliance" methods of contraception were available but not in widespread use in the latter half of the nineteenth century (122–24). It is unknown what, if any, method of birth control Webster might have practiced. Leonore Davidoff and Catherine Hall show that in the late eighteenth and early nineteenth centuries, large families were the norm, with a typical mother spending twenty years of her adult life pregnant or breastfeeding 85 to 95 percent of the time (*Family Fortunes,* 338).

12. Holmes, *Dante Gabriel Rossetti,* 112.

13. Webster may also have been critiquing the common practice of favoritism in mothers of siblings. M. Jeanne Peterson suggests that mothers in the nineteenth century were often open about their preferences for one child over another. Peterson also contends that motherhood was not idealized until the interwar period, as evidenced by the frequent use of nannies and governesses to raise children (*Family, Love, and Work,* 103–7).

14. Rigg, *Julia Augusta Webster,* 263–65.

15. In addition to being a poet, Webster was a journalist whose columns were collected in a book called *A Housewife's Opinions,* a social activist, a suffragist, and an elected member of London's school board. She was engaged in important activist and literary circles of the

day and corresponded with Christina Rossetti, though none of her letters from this correspondence remain. Webster's translations of the Greek dramas *Prometheus* and *Medea,* as well as her original verse dramas, received much acclaim in the period. In the 1880s and until her death in 1894, she served as the primary poetry critic for the *Athenaeum.* Of her tenure in this role, her colleague Theodore Watts wrote, "I know that she never wrote a line that was not inspired by honesty and good feeling, while as a conscientious and painstaking critic . . . she had no superior, scarcely an equal" ("Mrs. Augusta Webster"). Webster was married and had one daughter, who went on to become an actress. For more on Webster's life, see Rigg, *Julia Augusta Webster.*

16. Webster, "Poets and Personal Pronouns," in *Portraits and Other Poems,* 379.

17. Shelley, "Defence of Poetry," 501.

18. Ibid., 483.

19. Ibid., 484.

20. Anne-Lise François also complicates Shelley's binary. She notes that the term "count" implies a connection, because it signals inclusion within a group: "Originally meaning to consider, count in both its transitive and intransitive meanings—to assign numerical value to and include within a set of similar objects: to matter, make a difference of the future by having an impact on other events—implies a mode of having reference to others." François's wide-ranging study suggests that a critique of an overly rational attitude preceded Shelley (*Open Secrets,* 150).

21. Leighton, *Victorian Women Poets,* 257.

22. Ibid., 259.

23. Shuttleworth, "Demonic Mothers."

24. Ellis, *Mothers of England,* 36–37.

25. Ibid., 40.

26. Cobbe, *Duties of Women,* 88.

27. Wigley, *Thoughts for Mothers,* 48.

28. Ibid., 53.

29. Regaignon, "Infant Doping," and Thaden, *Maternal Voice.*

30. In her essay "Vocations and Avocations," Webster addresses the way in which other interests compete with the work life of someone who does "brain work," such as "scientific research or literary production." Webster complains that people often think that these brain workers are constantly available because the work can be pursued "at one time as well as another." Women in particular, she writes, are considered as "being[s] whose time is reckoned needless to the owner and free to whoever takes it, like blackberries on a hedge." As a result, social obligations to entertain unexpected callers and to return their calls, for instance, whenever they appear, often detract not only from literary production but from "duties to husband, children, or household" (*Housewife's Opinions,* 158–61).

31. Patricia Rigg prefers the term "monodrama" to "dramatic monologue" for these poems, and "The Happiest Girl" in particular, because it accounts for the speaker's awareness of her fluctuating emotional states and her attempts at emotional self-manipulation ("Augusta Webster").

32. Webster, *Portraits and Other Poems,* 189.

33. Ibid., 191–92.

34. Ibid., 180–81.

35. Sutphin, "Representation," 383.

36. Webster, *Portraits and Other Poems,* 343.

37. It is not clear whether Webster ordered the sequence or whether her husband ordered it after her death, so I assume that regardless of order each of the sonnets can be read in the context of the others.

38. Webster, *Portraits and Other Poems,* 350.

39. Behlman, "'Loving Stranger-Wise,'" paragraph 14.

40. Critics are divided on whether we ought to consider separate female and male traditions in the sonnet. Jennifer Wagner considers the male meditative sonnet tradition to be separate from a female sentimental one, in *A Moment's Monument.* Natalie Houston, on the other hand, challenges the idea that there are different sonnet traditions according to gender and identifies a strain of sonnets about perception in "Towards a New History."

41. Curran, *Poetic Form and British Romanticism,* 30–31. Amy Billone argues for a women's tradition of sonnets in the nineteenth century, looking particularly at the way it problematizes the relationship between gender and silence in *Little Songs.*

42. Laura Linker reads the child of the sequence as a muse in the model of Schiller's elegiac mode, the child signifying an irrecoverable naiveté (*"Mother and Daughter,"* 55).

43. Van Remoortel, "Metaphor and Maternity," 476.

44. Gregory, "Augusta Webster Writing Motherhood," 41–42.

45. Behlman, "Loving Stranger-Wise," paragraph 16.

46. Chapman, "Sonnet and Sonnet Sequence."

47. Van Remoortel also argues that *Mother and Daughter* "promot[es] presence and unity, rather than otherness and ambivalence," which she sees as the hallmark of Rossetti's *The House of Life* ("Metaphor and Maternity," 476).

48. In her discussion of Webster's "English Rispetti," Rigg makes an argument similar to Chapman's about *Mother and Daughter,* that these poems cite the renewal of natural cycles as a way to express the infinitude of human love ("Webster and the Lyric Muse").

49. Nicole Fluhr explores the way in which Webster distinguishes maternal love from married love—that the former is born while the latter is made—but also notes that Webster uses the very conventions of romantic love to describe a mother's love ("'Telling what's o'er'").

50. Reynolds, "Love's Measurement," 53–67.

51. Ibid., 62.

52. Gray, "Sonnet Kisses."

53. Barrett Browning, *Sonnets from the Portuguese,* 418.

54. Rossetti, *Complete Poems,* 59.

55. Ibid., 86.

56. Webster, *Portraits and Other Poems,* 344.

57. Ibid., 344.

58. Shakespeare, *Shakespeare's Sonnets,* 115.

59. Gregory suggests that "perhaps a collapse of aesthetic distance may be exactly what writing motherhood requires," and that the sonnet sequence offers opportunities for a shared voice unavailable in the dramatic monologue ("Webster Writing Motherhood," 36–37).

60. Fluhr makes a different kind of distinction between voices in this sequence, noting the contrast between the analytic and the personal tones of the poem. She also compellingly discusses the sequence's interest in intersubjectivity, noting how the mother/daughter relationship constructs the mother's subjectivity ("'Telling what's o'er'").

61. Webster, *Portraits and Other Poems,* 370.

62. Ibid., 366.

63. Ibid., 367–68.

64. Ibid., 338.

65. John Holmes notes that Webster's use of the image of birdsong, music, and seasonal change in this sonnet recalls both Dante Gabriel Rossetti's *The House of Life* and Christina Rossetti's *Later Life* (*Dante Gabriel Rossetti,* 108).

66. Watts, review of *Mother and Daughter.*

67. Webster, *Portraits and Other Poems,* 345.

68. Ibid., 327.

69. Rigg, "Webster and the Lyric Muse."

70. Kirstie Blair, in *Victorian Poetry and the Culture of the Heart,* has shown how in mid-century the boundary was blurred between metaphoric heartbreak and literal cardiac disease. She investigates the ways in which poetic and medical discourses around the heart influenced each other and brings to light the belief that heart disease was related to emotional disorders.

71. Webster, *Portraits and Other Poems,* 329–30.

72. Ibid., 333.

73. Ibid., 331.

74. Leighton, *Victorian Women Poets,* 259.

75. Webster, *Portraits and Other Poems,* 333.

76. Ibid., 335.

77. Ibid., 335.

78. Ibid., 346.

79. On the heart as a consistent figure for, if not a cliché of, poetic rhythm during the Victorian period, see Blair, *Victorian Poetry.*

80. Van Remoortel, "Metaphor and Maternity," 482–83.

81. Webster, *Portraits and Other Poems,* 341–42.

82. Watts, review of *Mother and Daughter.*

3 The Strain of Sympathy

1. Robinson, *New Arcadia,* 4.

2. Robinson, *Handful of Honeysuckle,* 31.

3. *Academy,* review of *Handful of Honeysuckle,* 20 July 1878.

4. Stedman, "Some London Poets," 874–92.

5. Ablow, *Marriage of Minds,* 1.

6. This salon, among others, is described in Vadillo, "New Woman Poets."

7. This democratizing impulse of aestheticism has appeared in studies of its relationship to commodity culture by Jonathan Freedman, who defines aestheticism as a "a process by which a zone was defined in the rapidly enlarging cultural marketplace where artists and writers could connect with an expanding audience eager to purchase high-cultural artifacts and the prestige that went along with them," and Regenia Gagnier, who suggests that it was "an engaged protest against . . . the whole middle-class drive to conform" (Freedman, *Professions of Taste,* xxiv; Gagnier, *Idylls of the Marketplace,* 3).

8. Dellamora, *Victorian Sexual Dissidence.*

9. Fletcher, "Some Aspects of Aestheticism," 25; Maltz, *Beauty for the People.*

10. Pater, *Renaissance*, 189.

11. Seth Koven and Linda Dowling both define the distinction between Ruskinian and Paterian aestheticism. See Koven, *Slumming*, 211; and Dowling, *Vulgarization of Art*, 75–76.

12. Wilde, "Soul of Man under Socialism," 232.

13. Maltz, "Wilde's *The Woman's World*," 185–90.

14. A. Mary F. Robinson, letter to John Addington Symonds, 4 March 1879, Bibliothèque Nationale de France (hereafter BN), Fonds Anglais 248, folio 37. Although some of Symonds's letters to Robinson are published, her letters to him remain available only in manuscript at the BN.

15. Vernon Lee, letter to A. Mary F. Robinson, 20 November 1881, BN, Fonds Anglais 244, folio 34. While most of Lee's letters to Robinson remain in this collection, almost none of Robinson's letters to Lee remain, Lee having burned them at Robinson's request.

16. Lee, letter to Robinson, 31 January 1881, BN, Fonds Anglais 244, folio 88.

17. I focus here on the artistic collaboration between Robinson and Lee, but do not consider the precise nature of their personal relationship. Critics disagree about it, debating whether it might be classified as a platonic friendship, a romantic friendship, or a lesbian partnership. For more on this question, see Colby, *Vernon Lee*, 58 (Colby insists that their relationship was "nonsexual in the physical sense"), and Gardner, *Lesbian Imagination* (Gardner maintains that they were sexually intimate, but the work is dated in its treatment of lesbianism as a pathology). See also Vicinus, "Legion of Ghosts." Evidence that they were physically involved can be found in their letters. Lee wrote to Robinson that she felt Robinson belonged to her "not as a mere matter of silly girlish kissing and hugging" but because "I am continually holding you in my thoughts." See Lee, letter to Robinson, 27 February 1881, BN, Fonds Anglais 244, Folio 113.

18. Robinson, "In Casa Paget," 936.

19. Lee, *Belcaro*, 1–2.

20. Lee, letter to Robinson, BN, Fonds Anglais 244, folio 116.

21. Lee, *Belcaro*, 7.

22. Ibid., 8.

23. Ibid., 245.

24. Ibid., 234.

25. Ibid., 256.

26. Christa Zorn reads Lee's anxiety about the modern as one of "the threats of mass manipulation and the triumph of vulgarity and self-indulgent pleasures that society denied ordinary individuals in real life" (*Vernon Lee*, 128).

27. Lee, *Miss Brown*, 2:307–9.

28. Koven, *Slumming*.

29. Psomiades, "'Still Burning.'"

30. My use of the term "influence" here bears no relation to Harold Bloom's theory in *The Anxiety of Influence*. When I say that Robinson and Lee influenced one another, I mean simply that in the course of their exchanges, they each adopted and adapted ideas that originated with the other.

31. Psomiades, "'Still Burning,'" 21–42.

32. Lee, *Belcaro*, 246.

33. Ibid., 240.

34. Zorn, *Vernon Lee*, 128.

35. Lee, *Belcaro,* 274.

36. Spacks, "Poetry of Sensibility," 267.

37. Toker, "Vocation and Sympathy," 267.

38. Glennis Byron has argued that this aim for readers' sympathy distinguishes women's dramatic monologues from men's in the period ("Rethinking the Dramatic Monologue," 79–98).

39. Robinson, *New Arcadia,* 3 (italics in original).

40. Ibid., 4.

41. Symonds, *Letters,* 2:910.

42. Ben Glaser argues that Robinson developed dissonant meters in earlier works as well, especially in her experiments with translating classical verse. Her cultivated discordance was formal as well as thematic, he suggests: "Robinson's first two volumes consistently develop as a theme the uncertainty of meter, often tying that uncertainty to the uncertainty of the soul, divinity, and their relation" ("Polymetrical Dissonance," 209).

43. Of course, not all poetry that might be called pastoral is naively idealizing or supportive of an aristocratic status quo. As Terry Gifford points out, some pastorals, such as Pope's "An Epistle to Bathhurst," maintained "oppositional potential" by positing a future ideal, and many pastoral poems are satirical or political in nature. *The New Arcadia* also follows in a long tradition of anti-pastoral poetry, especially from the eighteenth century, which includes Stephen Duck's "The Threshers' Labour," Oliver Goldsmith's "The Deserted Village," George Crabbe's "The Village," as well as work by working-class woman poets, such as Mary Collier and Ann Yearsley. See Gifford, *Pastoral: The New Critical Idiom.*

44. Robinson, *New Arcadia,* 6.

45. See Ely, "Not a Song to Sell," 99–100, and Vadillo, "Immaterial Poetics," 28. For references from Robinson's contemporaries, see reviews of *The New Arcadia* in the *Spectator,* the *Athenaeum,* and the *Saturday Review.* See also Sylvanie Marandon, *L'oeuvre poetique de Mary Robinson.*

46. Robinson, preface to *Collected Poems,* x.

47. Robinson, *New Arcadia,* 13.

48. Ibid., 14.

49. Ibid.

50. "The Hand-Bell Ringers" was one of Vernon Lee's favorite poems in the volume. She wrote to Robinson, "The descriptions are new subtle, modern; especially delicate the description e.g. of the way in which the Bell Ringers appear in front of the railing" (Lee, letter to Robinson, 25 April 1884, BN, Fond Anglais 245, folio 215).

51. Robinson, *New Arcadia,* 26.

52. The poem makes it clear that, according to the Thorns, Miss May was alive when they put her into the cart and that they killed her not in outright malice but by neglect.

53. Robinson, *New Arcadia,* 45.

54. Ibid., 53.

55. Robinson's biography of Emily Brontë similarly describes Brontë's passionate love for a stark landscape: "Beyond this the moors, the wild, barren, treeless moors, that stretch away for miles and miles, feeding a few herds of mountain sheep, harboring some wild conies and hares, giving a nesting-place to the birds of heaven, and, for the use of man, neither grain nor pasturage, but quarries of stone and piles of peat luridly smouldering up there on autumn nights" (*Emily Brontë,* 55).

56. Robinson, *New Arcadia,* 79.

57. Ibid., 81.

58. Lee, letter to Robinson, 29 October 1883, BN, Fonds Anglais 245, folio 100.

59. Colby, *Vernon Lee,* 80, 101.

60. Lee, letter to Robinson, 1 April 1884, BN, Fonds Anglais 245, folio 215.

61. Edmund Gosse (1849–1928) was a prominent critic, essayist, biographer, and poet who was a part of the same aestheticist circles in which the Robinson family participated. He dedicated a poem entitled "A Ballade of Poetesses" to Mary Robinson (see Lee, letter to Robinson, 1 April 1884).

62. *Saturday Review,* review of *New Arcadia,* 9 August 1884.

63. *Spectator,* review of *New Arcadia,* 4 October 1884.

64. Symonds, *Letters,* 2:926.

65. Robinson, *Italian Garden,* 68.

66. Ely, "Not a Song to Sell," 103.

67. Robinson, *Italian Garden,* 81, 61.

68. Although he refers primarily to French literature, some of Arthur Symons's characterizations of decadence in his 1893 essay "The Decadent Movement in Literature" might just as well describe Robinson's efforts; she turns to "the very essence of truth . . . the truth of spiritual things to the spiritual vision" (136). Symons also cites Verlaine's "ideal of poetic art" as "Car nous voulons la Nuance encor. / Pas la Couleur, rien que la Nuance!"

69. Robinson, *Italian Garden,* 17.

70. Vadillo, "Immaterial Poetics."

71. Ely, "Not a Song to Sell."

72. Robinson, *Italian Garden,* 97.

73. Lynch, "A. Mary F. Robinson," 275. Reviewers of *A Handful of Honeysuckle* wrote, "The simplicity and grace of the whole, the genuine pathos which makes itself felt under a somewhat conventional form, and the skill with which a somewhat difficult metre is handled, are worthy of high praise" (*Spectator,* 1878), and "Miss Robinson has a considerable mastery of verse, she has style. . . . Her collection is infinitely superior to most handfuls of lyrical honeysuckles. . . . One may hope that Miss Robinson will write more lyrics" (*Academy,* 1878). One reviewer of her second volume, *The Crowned Hippolytus,* praised the "considerable merits" of her translation and wrote of the "sense of style, which she, almost alone among contemporaries of her own sex, undeniably possesses" (*Athenaeum,* 1881). E. C. Stedman refers to her as "the young songstress who of all seemed to be most hopefully and gallantly regarded by her fellow poets and the surest among new aspirants to fulfill the predictions made for her" ("Some London Poets," 886). See also Symons, "A. Mary F. Darmesteter"; Lynch, "A. Mary F. Robinson"; Warner *Library of World's Best Literature.*

74. Dellamora, "Productive Decadence."

75. Maltz, "Engaging 'Delicate Brains.'"

4   "Be Loved through Thoughts of Mine"

1. Jackson, "Tides of the Mind," 444; Leighton, *Writing Against the Heart,* 247; Burdett, "Poems of Alice Meynell," 106; Chesterton, "Alice Meynell," 2–3.

2. Leighton, *Writing Against the Heart,* 247, italics hers.

3. Maria Frawley in "Tides of the Mind" productively reads the silence and solitude prevalent in Meynell's work as a way of thinking about mental processes and perception.

4. Cited in Badeni, *Slender Tree*, 143.

5. Meynell, *Poems* (1893), 9. Because two different collections are entitled *Poems*, I will cite title and year for these volumes.

6. Meynell, *Spirit of Place*, 16.

7. Ibid., 18.

8. Vanessa Furse Jackson writes, "To understand her work, we have to understand that restraint and renunciation play integral roles within it, that she used intellect as a shield not simply against personal revelation but also against personal distress" ("Tides of the Mind," 461). Leighton quotes a letter of Meynell's from her daughter's biography stating that she feared she had not made her love apparent enough to family and friends (*Writing Against the Heart*, 248). Leighton then uses this letter to connect Meynell's distance in her personal life and to that in her writing. Kathleen Anderson assumes that the "poetic identity" she investigates in the poem is the same as Meynell's own, "'I make the whole world.'"

9. Meynell, *Prose and Poetry*, 15.

10. Vadillo, *Women Poets and Urban Aestheticism*, 78–116.

11. Quoted in Viola Meynell, *Alice Meynell*, 117.

12. Quoted in Badeni, *Slender Tree*, 97.

13. Schaffer, *Forgotten Female Aesthetes*, 163.

14. Ibid., 176.

15. In *The Powers of Distance*, Amanda Anderson explores the complex ways in which Victorian authors understood critical distance to allow both greater clarity and distorted vision. Anderson's chapter on Oscar Wilde notes that unlike the earlier authors she discusses, "the Aesthetic Movement directly and flagrantly espoused the cultivation of radical detachment" (147). The emotional and psychological distance that Meynell establishes in her work emerges in the context of a discourse about the virtues and drawbacks of detachment.

16. Schaffer argues that *A Room of One's Own* represses Meynell, as well as other fin de siècle women authors, by excluding them as examples of literary mothers. This exclusion emphasizes the break between Modernism and the Victorian period, and saves Woolf the difficulty of identifying with an experimental, feminist author who also epitomized, in her public persona, Victorian "Angel in the House" womanhood (*Forgotten Female Aesthetes*, 191–96).

17. Meynell, *Wares*, 1.

18. Meynell, introduction to *Art of Scansion*, vii.

19. Meynell, *Wares*, 163.

20. This does not mean that Meynell disapproved of political poetry in general. In fact, she wrote her own poetry to further the cause of women's suffrage. See especially "A Father of Women," in *Prose and Poetry*, 380–81.

21. Meynell, *Wares*, 163–64.

22. Ibid., 164.

23. In *A Room of One's Own*, Woolf, too, criticizes Brontë's writing for being too angry: "She will write in a rage where she should write calmly. She will write foolishly where she should write wisely" (69). Woolf may well have been influenced by Meynell's writing, for at this point she notes how damaging the Brontës' isolation was and emphasizes the importance of travel-enabling money as well as that of the secluded room.

24. Meynell, *Wares*, 164–65.

25. Quoted in Badeni, *Slender Tree*, 28.

26. Ibid., 27.

27. As Schaffer has shown, Meynell deftly manages her audience, appealing on the one hand to Aestheticists with her Paterian effusions on singular moments and objects (rain, waterfalls, walls) and on the other to those who expected the epitome of Victorian femininity (*Forgotten Female Aesthetes*, 159–96). If, as Schaffer argues, Meynell's reputation was one of her greatest works, then it is ironic that in her criticism of other women writers she condemns their fantasies of their reputations. According to my argument, their fault was not in trying to understand how their audience pictured them, but in not controlling audience perception more tightly.

28. Badeni, Slender Tree, 36.

29. Meynell, *Prose and Poetry*, 147.

30. Ibid., 146.

31. Ibid.

32. Ibid.

33. Meynell, *Essays*, 78.

34. Ibid., 177.

35. Peterson, *Becoming a Woman of Letters*, 193.

36. Meynell, *Essays*, 177.

37. Ibid.

38. Meynell, *Second Person Singular*, 134.

39. Meynell, *Poems* (1893), 2.

40. Meynell, *Second Person Singular*, 137.

41. Leighton, *Victorian Women Poets*, 248.

42. Meynell, *Preludes*, 28.

43. Meynell, *Prose and Poetry*, 150.

44. Ibid., 158.

45. Swinburne, *Major Poems*, 34.

46. Meynell, *Essays*, 78.

47. Ibid., 79.

48. Ibid., 80.

49. Meynell, *Prose and Poetry*, 154.

50. That Swinburne *was* an important influence for later poets is not part of Meynell's vision of him.

51. Meynell, *Hearts of Controversy*, 159.

52. The poems are published for the first time as a series in the 1913 *Poems*. The first seven poems in the series of ten appear in the 1893 *Poems*, while the last three are published for the first time with the series in 1913.

53. Meynell, *Poems* (1913), 54.

54. The term "narcissism" as a pathological term did not come into use until later with the publication of Havelock Ellis's *Alienist and Neurologist* (1898).

55. Meynell, *Poems* (1913), 55. The poem appears in *Poems* (1893) as "To a Poet," 4.

56. Peterson registers Meynell's uneasiness with the Romantic ideal of nature, in *Becoming a Woman of Letters*, 187–95.

57. Meynell, *Prose and Poetry*, 152.

58. Meynell, *Poems* (1913), 65.

59. Ibid., 60.

60. Ibid., 58.

61. Ibid., 59.

62. Behlman, "'Pencilling Mama.'"

63. Peterson, *Becoming a Woman of Letters*, 201–6. Schaffer also notes the detrimental effects of Meynell's angelic reputation in *Forgotten Female Aesthetes*.

64. Leighton, *Writing Against the Heart*, 259.

65. Ibid., 261.

66. Meynell, *Spirit of Place*, 19–20.

67. Meynell, *Poems* (1913), 87.

68. Meynell, *Prose and Poetry*, 296.

69. Ibid., 290.

70. Quoted in Badeni, *Slender Tree*, 135.

71. Meynell, *Poems* (1913), 86.

72. Ibid., 62.

73. Meynell, *Essays*, 81.

5 "So I Can Wait and Sing"

1. Radford, *Light Load*, 9, 11, 44.

2. Dollie Radford Diary, 8, 14, 21 April 1891, Radford Papers.

3. The Bodley Head printed 310 copies of *A Light Load* in 1891, and a letter from Elkin Mathews notes that by the first of December that year, 46 remained unsold. See letter from Elkin Mathews to Dollie Radford, 1 December 1891, Radford Papers. A subsequent letter from John Lane in 1896 notes that 400 copies of *Songs and Other Verses* were printed, of which 200 were sold to an American distributor. See letter from John Lane to Dollie Radford, 31 December 1896, Radford Papers.

4. Livesey, *Socialism*, 132–60.

5. Dixon, *Story of a Modern Woman*, 119.

6. Radford, *Songs and Other Verses*, 81.

7. Radford, *Light Load*, 16.

8. Ibid., 20.

9. Barthes, "Waiting," 40.

10. I acknowledge, but do not have time to discuss here, the problematic cultural assumptions about the Chinese inherent in this character's nationality.

11. Anne-Lise François uses Barthes's anecdote of the "mandarin" as an example of "a temporal sequence set loose from the ordering energies of the quest for possession and freed from the pendulum of anticipation and (non)fulfillment" This freedom itself, François suggests, is the fulfillment. François's theory of "recessive action" and identification of the genre of "lyric inconsequence" can help us to understand the passivity in Radford's poems—her refusal to pretend that music compensates for lyric absence, an association of lyric singing with waiting—as a stance that she owns proudly, rather than something that is imposed upon her, by the limitations either of gender or genre (*Open Secrets*, xxii).

12. Radford, *Light Load*, 11.

13. Wordsworth, "I am not One who much or oft delight" (1807), 269–70. "Personal Talk" is a later title for the poem. In these lines, Wordsworth cites William Collins's "The Passions: An Ode for Music," in which the allegorized Passions make different kinds of music. In Collins's poem, Melancholy's music comes "In notes by distance made more sweet."

14. Symons, "Broken Tryst," 19–20.

15. Hardy, "The Temporary the All," 1–3.

16. Radford Diary, 1 May 1891, Radford Papers.

17. Richardson, "Naturally Radical"; Livesey, "Radford and the Ethical Aesthetics."

18. Radford Diary, 4 June 1893, Radford Papers.

19. Although Schreiner declares in a prefatory footnote that the stories are printed in the order in which they were written, it is certainly no accident that in this highly wrought aesthetic volume the word "waiting" appears three times in the brief opening paragraphs.

20. Schreiner, *Dreams*, 13.

21. Radford, *Light Load*, 63–64.

22. Symons, review of *Light Load*.

23. The diary goes on to say that "Lewis Morris was the one different" (24 May 1891, Radford Papers). Lewis Morris, the now forgotten poet, was a candidate for poet laureate after the death of Tennyson and published a collection entitled *Unsung Songs* in 1884 by Kegan Paul, Trench and Co.

24. *Musical Times,* review of *Light Load*, 1 June 1891.

25. Radford, *Light Load,* 29.

26. Ibid.

27. No commercial recording exists of this music. For the opportunity to hear it, I am grateful to Kate Scally, soprano, and Wenny Chandra, piano, from the Penn State School of Music and to Bob Klotz of Klotz Audio, who took the trouble to learn the songs and record them for me.

28. Livesey, "Radford and the Ethical Aesthetics," 141–42.

29. Ernest Radford, "Verses," 76.

30. McCue, "Burns' Songs," 75.

31. For instance, "O, Once I Loved a Bonny Lass" was to be sung to the tune of "I Am a Man Unmarried" (McCue, "Burns' Songs," 75).

32. McLane, *Balladry, Minstrelsy,* 15.

33. Hoagwood, *From Song to Print,* 73.

34. Keats, "Ode on a Grecian Urn," 344.

35. Marshall Brown argues that in "Ode on a Grecian Urn," Keats defends the importance of abstract form, and above all privileges the thought of the poet and reader. In Brown's reading of Keats, unheard melodies are perceived, but indirectly ("Unheard Melodies," 467). Brown goes on to compare Keats's understanding of "unheard melodies" with a musical example from Schumann of a melody written *not* to be performed, but to be kept in mind by the performer. Brown argues that unheard melodies are perceived in other ways than in direct hearing.

36. Radford, *Light Load,* 13–14.

37. Radford Diary, undated, 1884, Radford Papers.

38. Shaw, *Collected Letters,* 80.

39. All of the "Six Songs" set to music by Allon and published in 1888 appear in *A Light Load* with exactly the same words, with the exception of "Sweetheart" / "The birds sang from the tree."

40. Shaw, *Collected Letters,* 80.

41. Kramer, *Music and Poetry,* 129.

42. Radford Diary, 22 April 1894, Radford Papers.

43. The performance of ballads in the home was intertwined with their performance in concert halls via the sale of sheet music: in the royalty ballad system, publishers paid celebrity singers to perform their songs in order to increase sales (Banfield, *Sensibility and English Song,* 3).

44. Scott, *Songs of the Victorian Drawing Room,* 141. See also Banfield, *Sensibility and English Song.*

45. For instance, despite writing numerous "songs," Tennyson was not always pleased for his own poems to be set to music and performed. His poems frequently reflect on the function of song and his verse was often considered "musical," but he did not court actual music. When Arthur Sullivan sought out him out to collaborate on a work that ultimately became "The Window: or The Loves of the Wrens," Tennyson was reluctant because he thought the work would be too slight and might damage his reputation. Sullivan aimed to convince him by arguing that poetry written for music was held to a different, and lower, standard (Copely, "Tennyson and the Composers," 507).

46. Hughes and Stradling, *English Musical Renaissance;* see also Hughes, *English Musical Renaissance.*

47. Helsinger, "Song's Fictions," 153.

48. Prins, "Sappho Recomposed," 231.

49. Meynell, "Robert Browning," in *Prose and Poetry,* 94.

50. The use of Meynell's maiden name suggests that Radford knew her work primarily, if not exclusively, from the 1875 *Preludes.* Her next collection, *Poems,* would not emerge until 1893.

51. Pater, *Renaissance,* 106.

52. Symons, "Decadent Movement in Literature," 139–41.

53. Radford, *A Light Load,* 3.

54. Kramer, *Music and Poetry,* 131.

55. Ibid., 130.

56. Livesey, "Radford and the Ethical Aesthetics," 132–60.

57. Radford Diary, 23 March 1893, Radford Papers.

58. Elfenbein, "Whitman, Democracy and the English Clerisy."

59. Radford, *Songs and Other Verses,* 34.

60. Ibid., 19.

61. Radford Diary, 15 April 1891, Radford Papers.

62. Herbert Tucker suggests that in the Victorian fin de siècle, "poets bred on the aestheticism Morris had heralded became too exquisitely tired to aspire to more than minority" ("Over Worked, Worked Over," 124). Tucker goes on to argue that the fatigue of literary Decadence partakes of Tennysonian romanticism.

63. Levy, "Minor Poet," 20. Linda Hunt Beckman discusses the friendship between Radford and Levy, and the nameless, mixed-gender "club" they both belonged to, which met frequently in the early 1880s to listen to and discuss literary presentations, music, and culture (*Amy Levy,* 80–86).

64. Radford, *Songs and Other Verses,* 20.

65. Leighton, *Victorian Women Poets,* 227–28.

66. Radford, *Light Load,* 23–24.

67. Radford, *Songs and Other Verses,* 37.

68. Ibid., 38.

69. Gilbert and Gubar, *Madwoman in the Attic,* 49.

70. Symons, review of *Light Load.*

71. Jackson, *Dickinson's Misery,* 8.

72. "Second-Hand Verse," *National Observer,* 6 June 1891; "Recent Verse," *Athenaeum,* 8 August 1891.

Conclusion

1. Although Angela Leighton identifies a critique of women's place in aestheticism in Coleridge's short story "The Devil at the Guildhall" ("Women Poets," 3–4), and Katharine McGowran finds her "self-reflexive" critique similar to much aesthetic writing ("Rereading Women's Poetry," 487), Alison Chapman argues that whatever "debt" she may owe "to late nineteenth-century aestheticism, her literary career and intellectual interests were removed from aesthetic culture" ("Mary Elizabeth Coleridge," 146).

2. Chapman, "Mary Elizabeth Coleridge," 152–54.

3. Chapman asserts that publishing with the private Daniel Press offered Coleridge both the limited circulation she wanted and association with eminent poets like Bridges and Richard Watson Dixon ("Mary Elizabeth Coleridge," 150).

4. Cited in Sichel, *Gathered Leaves,* 23.

5. Whistler, introduction to *Collected Poems of Mary Coleridge,* 53.

6. Bridges, "Poems of Mary Coleridge," 605.

7. Ibid., 594.

8. Newbolt, *Later Life and Letters,* 92.

9. These assumptions inherit John Stuart Mill's influential and controversial position that poetry is the "overheard" utterance of a self to itself in solitude ("What is Poetry?," 12).

10. Coleridge, *Collected Poems,* 222.

11. Sichel, *Gathered Leaves,* 252–53.

12. Chapman, "Mary Elizabeth Coleridge," 158, 155.

13. Baker, "'Oh lift me over the threshold,'" 213.

14. Coleridge, *Collected Poems,* 120.

15. Cited in Baker, "'Oh lift me over the threshold,'" 205. (See letter in Eton College Library, MEC 87, f1d–2a.)

16. "Gone" was first published in *Fancy's Following* in 1896, but Theresa Whistler, editor of *The Collected Poems of Mary Coleridge,* dates it to 1888, while admitting in her introduction that much of her dating of Coleridge's poems is speculative.

17. Pinch, "Rhyme's End," 486.

18. Martin, *Rise and Fall of Meter,* 94.

19. Coleridge, *Collected Poems,* 223.

20. Ibid., 221.

21. Ibid., 141.

22. Barrett Browning, *Sonnets from the Portuguese,* 2.12–14.

23. Barrett Browning, *Sonnets from the Portuguese,* 25.14; Rossetti, "Monna Innominata," 4.3.

24. Harrison, "Narrative Relationships" and "Paradox of Fiction"; Greiner, *Sympathetic Realism.*

Bibliography

Ablow, Rachel. *The Marriage of Minds: Reading Sympathy in the Victorian Marriage Plot.* Stanford, CA: Stanford University Press, 2007.

Academy. Unsigned review of *A Handful of Honeysuckle,* by A. Mary F. Robinson. 20 July 1878, 53.

Allon, Erskine, and Caroline Radford. "Six Songs . . . Op. 9." London: London Music Publishing, 1888.

Anderson, Amanda. *The Powers of Distance: Cosmopolitanism and the Cultivation of Detachment.* Princeton, NJ: Princeton University Press, 2001.

Anderson, Kathleen. "'I make the whole world answer to my art': Alice Meynell's Poetic Identity." *Victorian Poetry* 41, no. 2 (2003): 259–75.

Armstrong, Isobel. "Christina Rossetti in the Era of the New Woman and Fin-de-Siécle Culture." *Journal of Pre-Raphaelite Studies* 13 (Spring 2004): 21–48.

———. *The Radical Aesthetic.* Oxford: Blackwell, 2000.

———. *Victorian Poetry: Poetry, Poetics and Politics.* London: Routledge, 1993.

Armstrong, Isobel, and Virginia Blain, eds. *Women's Poetry, Late Romantic to Late Victorian.* New York: St. Martin's, 1999.

Arseneau, Mary, Antony H. Harrison, and Lorraine Janzen Kooistra, eds. *The Culture of Christina Rossetti: Female Poetics and Victorian Contexts.* Athens: Ohio University Press, 1999.

Athenaeum. "The Earlier Poems of Elizabeth Barrett Browning." 15 December 1877, 765–67.

———. "Recent Verse." 8 August 1891, 189.

———. Unsigned review of *The Crowned Hippolytus, and Other Poems,* by A. Mary F. Robinson. 2 July 1881, 8.

———. Unsigned review of *An Italian Garden,* by A. Mary F. Robinson. 17 April 1886, 517.

———. Unsigned review of *The New Arcadia,* by A. Mary F. Robinson. 2 August 1884, 141–43.

Badeni, June. *The Slender Tree: A Life of Alice Meynell.* Padstow, Cornwall: Tabb House, 1981.

Baker, Kasey Bass. "'Oh, Lift Me over the Threshold, and Let Me in at the Door!': Boundaries and Thresholds in Mary Coleridge's Poetry." *Victorian Poetry* 48, no. 2 (2010): 195–218.

Banfield, Stephen. *Sensibility and English Song: Critical Studies of the Early Twentieth Century.* Cambridge: Cambridge University Press, 1985.

Barrett Browning, Elizabeth. *The Art of Scansion.* Introduction by Alice Meynell. London, 1916.

———. *Selected Poems.* Edited by Marjorie Stone and Beverly Taylor. Peterborough, ON: Broadview Press, 2009.

———. *Sonnets from the Portuguese.* In *The Complete Poetical Works of Elizabeth Barrett Browning,* 418–28. New York: Thomas Crowell, 1887.

Barthes, Roland. "Waiting." In *A Lover's Discourse,* translated by Richard Howard, 37–40. New York: Hill and Wang, 1978.

Beckman, Linda Hunt. *Amy Levy: Her Life and Letters.* Athens: Ohio University Press, 2000.

Behlman, Lee. "'Loving Stranger-Wise': Augusta Webster's Mother and Daughter and Nineteenth-Century Poetry on Motherhood." *Nineteenth-Century Gender Studies* 6, no. 3 (2010). http://ncgsjournal.com/issue63/behlman.htm.

———. "'The Pencilling Mama': Public Motherhood in Alice Meynell's Essays on Children." In *Mothers Who Deliver: Feminist Interventions in Public and Interpersonal Discourse,* edited by Jocelyn Fenton Stitt and Pegeen Reichert Powell, 99–118. Albany: SUNY Press, 2010.

Billone, Amy. *Little Songs: Women, Silence and the Nineteenth-Century Sonnet.* Columbus: Ohio State University Press, 2005.

Blair, Kirstie. *Victorian Poetry and the Culture of the Heart.* Oxford: Oxford University Press, 2006.

Bourne Taylor, Jenny, and Sally Shuttleworth, eds. *Embodied Selves: An Anthology of Psychological Texts, 1830–1890.* Oxford: Clarendon Press, 1998.

Bridges, Robert. "The Poems of Mary Coleridge." *Cornhill Magazine* (November 1907): 594–605.

Bristow, Joseph, ed. *The Cambridge Companion to Victorian Poetry.* Cambridge: Cambridge University Press, 2000.

———, and introduction. *The Fin-de-Siècle Poem.* Athens: Ohio University Press, 2005.

Brown, Marshall. "Unheard Melodies: The Force of Form." *PMLA* 107, no. 3 (May 1992): 465–81.

Brown, Susan. "The Victorian Poetess." In Bristow, *Cambridge Companion to Victorian Poetry,* 180–202.

Buchanan, Robert [Thomas Maitland, pseudonym]. "The Fleshly School of Poetry." *Contemporary Review* 18 (1871): 334–50.

Burdett, W. Osbert. "The Poems of Alice Meynell." In *Critical Essays,* 98–108. New York: Holt, 1926.

Byron, Glennis. "Rethinking the Dramatic Monologue: Victorian Women Poets and Social Critique." In *Victorian Women Poets,* edited by Alison Chapman, 79–98. Cambridge: D. S. Brewer, 2003.

Cameron, Sharon. *Lyric Time.* Baltimore, MD: Johns Hopkins University Press, 1979.

Chapman, Alison. *The Afterlife of Christina Rossetti.* London: Macmillan, 2000.

———. "Mary Elizabeth Coleridge and the Flight to Lyric." *Yearbook of English Studies* 37, no. 1 (2007): 145–60.

———. "Sonnet and Sonnet Sequence." In *A Companion to Victorian Poetry,* edited by Richard Cronin, Alison Chapman, and Antony H. Harrison, 99–114. Oxford: Blackwell, 2002.

———, ed. *Victorian Women Poets.* Cambridge: D. S. Brewer, 2003.

Chesterton, G. K. "Alice Meynell." *Dublin Review* 172 (January–March 1923): 1–13.

Cobbe, Francis Power. *The Duties of Women.* London: Williams and Norgate, 1881.

Colby, Vineta. *Vernon Lee.* Charlottesville: University of Virginia Press, 2003.

Coleridge, Mary. *The Collected Poems of Mary Coleridge.* Edited and introduction by Theresa Whistler. London: Rupert Hart-Davis, 1954.

———. *Fancy's Following.* Portland, ME: T. B. Mosher, 1900.

———. *Gathered Leaves from the Prose of Mary E. Coleridge.* Edited with a memoir by Edith Sichel. London: Constable, 1911.

Conley, Susan. "'Poet's Right': Christina Rossetti as Anti-Muse and the Legacy of the 'Poetess.'" *Victorian Poetry* 32, nos. 3/4 (1994): 365–86.

———. "Rossetti's Cold Women." In Arseneau, Harrison, and Kooistra, *Culture of Christina Rossetti,* 260–84.

Connolly, Terence L. *Alice Meynell Centenary Tribute.* Boston: Bruce Humphries, 1948.

Copley, I. A. "Tennyson and the Composers." *Musical Opinion* 101 (September 1978): 504–12.

Cronin, Richard, Alison Chapman, and Antony Harrison, eds. *A Companion to Victorian Poetry.* Malden, MA: Blackwell, 2002.

Culler, Jonathan. "Apostrophe." *Diacritics* 7, no. 4 (December 1977): 59–69.

———. "Changes in the Study of the Lyric." In Hosek and Parker, *Lyric Poetry,* 38–54.

Curran, Stuart. *Poetic Form and British Romanticism.* New York: Oxford University Press, 1986.

D'Amico, Diane. *Christina Rossetti: Faith, Gender and Time.* Baton Rouge: Louisiana State University Press, 1999.

Davidoff, Lenore, and Catherine Hall. *Family Fortunes: Men and Women of the English Middle Class, 1780–1850.* Rev. ed. London: Routledge, 2002.

Dixon, Ella Hepworth. *The Story of a Modern Woman.* 1894. Edited by Steve Farmer. Peterborough, ON: Broadview Press, 2004.

Dellamora, Richard. "Productive Decadence": The Queer Comradeship of Outlawed Thought": Vernon Lee, Max Nordau, and Oscar Wilde." *New Literary History* 35, no. 4 (2004): 529–46.

———, ed. *Victorian Sexual Dissidence.* Chicago: University of Chicago Press, 1999.

Dowling, Linda. *The Vulgarization of Art: The Victorians and Aesthetic Democracy.* Charlottesville: University of Virginia Press, 1996.

Elfenbein, Andrew. "Whitman, Democracy and the English Clerisy." *Nineteenth Century Literature* 56, no. 1 (June 2001): 76–104.

Ellis, Sarah Stickney. *The Mothers of England, Their Influence and Responsibility.* New York: J. H. G. Langley, 1844.

Ely, M. Lynda. "Not a Song to Sell: Re-Presenting A. Mary F. Robinson." *Victorian Poetry* 38, no. 1 (2000): 94–128.

Feldman, Paula R. "The Poet and the Profits: Felicia Hemans and the Literary Marketplace." *Keats-Shelley Journal* 46 (1997): 148–76.

Field, Michael. "To Christina Rossetti." *Academy,* no. 1248 (4 April 1896): 284.

Fletcher, Ian. "Some Aspects of Aestheticism." In *Twilight of the Dawn: Studies in English Literature in Transition,* edited by O. M. Brack. Tucson: University of Arizona Press, 1987.

Fluhr, Nicole. "'Telling what's o'er': Remaking the Sonnet Cycle in Augusta Webster's *Mother and Daughter.*" *Victorian Poetry* 49, no. 1 (2011): 53–81.

François, Anne-Lise. *Open Secrets: The Literature of Uncounted Experience.* Stanford, CA: Stanford University Press, 2008.

Frawley, Maria. "'Tides of the Mind': Alice Meynell's Poetry of Perception." *Victorian Poetry* 38, no. 1 (2000): 62–76.

Freedman, Jonathan. *Professions of Taste.* Stanford, CA: Stanford University Press, 1990.

Gagnier, Regenia. *Idylls of the Marketplace: Oscar Wilde and the Victorian Public.* Stanford, CA: Stanford University Press, 1986.

Gardner, Burdett. *The Lesbian Imagination (Victorian Style): A Psychological and Critical Study of "Vernon Lee."* Ph.D. dissertation, Harvard University, 1954. New York: Garland Publishing, 1987.

Gifford, Terry. *Pastoral: The New Critical Idiom.* London: Routledge, 1999.

Gilbert, Sandra, and Susan Gubar. *The Madwoman in the Attic.* New Haven, NJ: Yale University Press, 1979.

Glaser, Ben. "Polymetrical Dissonance: Tennyson, A. Mary F. Robinson, and Classical Meter." *Victorian Poetry* 49, no. 2 (2011): 199–216.

Gray, Erik. "Sonnet Kisses: Sidney to Barrett Browning." *Essays in Criticism* 52, no. 2 (2002): 126–42.

Gray, F. Elizabeth. *Christian and Lyric Tradition in Victorian Women's Poetry.* New York: Routledge, 2010.

Gregory, Melissa Valiska. "Augusta Webster Writing Motherhood in the Dramatic Monologue and the Sonnet Sequence." *Victorian Poetry* 49, no. 1 (2011): 27–51.

Greiner, D. Rae. *Sympathetic Realism in Nineteenth-Century British Fiction.* Baltimore, MD: Johns Hopkins University Press, 2012.

Griffiths, Eric. "The Disappointment of Christina G. Rossetti." *Essays in Criticism* 47, no. 2 (April 1997): 107–42.

———. *The Printed Voice of Victorian Poetry.* Oxford: Oxford University Press, 1989.

Grosskurth, Phyllis. *John Addington Symonds: A Biography.* New York: Arno Press, 1975.

Gunn, Peter. *Vernon Lee: Violet Paget, 1856–1935.* London: Oxford University Press, 1964.

Hardy, Thomas. "The Temporary the All." In *Wessex Poems and Other Verses,* 1–3. New York: Harper and Brothers, 1899.

Harrison, Antony H. *Christina Rossetti in Context.* Chapel Hill: University of North Carolina Press, 1988.

———. "Christina Rossetti: Renunciation as Intervention." Chap. 5 in *Victorian Poets and the Politics of Culture.* Charlottesville: University of Virginia Press, 1998.

Harrison, Mary-Catherine. "How Narrative Relationships Overcome Empathic Bias: Elizabeth Gaskell's Empathy Across Social Difference." *Poetics Today* 32, no. 2 (2011): 255–88.

———. "The Paradox of Fiction and the Ethics of Empathy: Reconceiving Dickens's Realism." *Narrative* 16, no. 3 (2008): 256–78.

Hassett, Constance W. *Christina Rossetti: The Patience of Style.* Charlottesville: University of Virginia Press, 2005.

Helsinger, Elizabeth. "Song's Fictions." In special issue, "The Arts in Victorian Literature." *Yearbook of English Studies* 40, nos. 1/2 (2010): 141–59.

Hoagwood, Terrence. *From Song to Print: Romantic Pseudo-Songs.* New York: Palgrave Macmillan, 2010.

Holmes, John. *Dante Gabriel Rossetti and the Late Victorian Sonnet Sequence: Sexuality, Belief and the Self.* Aldershot, UK: Ashgate, 2005.

Hosek, Chaviva, and Patricia Parker, eds. *Lyric Poetry: Beyond New Criticism.* Ithaca, NY: Cornell University Press, 1985.

Houston, Natalie. "Towards a New History: Fin-de-Siècle Women Poets and the Sonnet." In Chapman, ed. *Victorian Women Poets,* 145–64.

Hughes, Linda K. *Graham R.: Rosamund Mariott Watson, Woman of Letters.* Athens: Ohio University Press, 2005.

Hughes, Meirion, and Robert Stradling. *The English Musical Renaissance, 1840–1940.* 2nd ed. Manchester: Manchester University Press, 2001.

Hughes, Meirion. *The English Musical Renaissance and the Press, 1850–1914: Watchmen of Music.* Aldershot, UK: Ashgate, 2002.

Jackson, Vanessa Furse. "'Tides of the Mind': Restraint and Renunciation in the Poetry of Alice Meynell." *Victorian Poetry* 36, no. 4 (1998): 443–74.

Jackson, Virginia. *Dickinson's Misery: A Theory of Lyric Reading.* Princeton, NJ: Princeton University Press, 2005.

———. "Lyric." In *The Princeton Encyclopedia of Poetry and Poetics.* Princeton, NJ: Princeton University Press, 2012.

———. "Who Reads Poetry?" *PMLA* 123, no. 1 (January 2008): 181–87.

Jackson, Virginia, and Yopie Prins. "Lyrical Studies." *Victorian Literature and Culture* 27, no. 2 (1999): 521–30.

Jaffe, Audrey. *Scenes of Sympathy: Identity and Representation in Victorian Fiction.* Ithaca, NY: Cornell University Press, 2000.

Keats, John. "Ode on a Grecian Urn." In *John Keats: The Complete Poems,* edited by John Barnard. London: Penguin Books, 1988.

Kent, David A, ed. *The Achievement of Christina Rossetti.* Ithaca, NY: Cornell University Press, 1987.

Koven, Seth. *Slumming: Sexual and Social Politics in Victorian London.* Princeton, NJ: Princeton University Press, 2004.

Kramer, Lawrence. *Music and Poetry in the Nineteenth Century and After.* Berkeley: University of California Press, 1984.

Lee, Vernon. *Belcaro.* London: W. Satchell, 1881.

———. Letters to A. Mary F. Robinson. Fonds Anglais 243–46. Bibliothèque Nationale de France. Paris, France.

———. *Miss Brown.* Edinburgh: William Blackwood and Sons, 1884. Reprint, New York: Garland, 1978.

Le Gallienne, Richard. *The Romantic '90s.* Garden City, NY: Doubleday, 1926.

———. "Woman-Poets of the Day." *English Illustrated Magazine* 127 (April 1894): 648–57.

Leighton, Angela. *Victorian Women Poets: Writing Against the Heart.* New York: Harvester Wheatsheaf, 1992.

———. "Women Poets and the Fin-de-siècle: Towards a New Aestheticism." *Victorian Review* 23, no. 1 (1997): 1–14.

Leighton, Angela, and Margaret Reynolds, eds. *Victorian Women Poets: An Anthology.* Oxford: Blackwell, 1995.

Levy, Amy. *A Minor Poet and Other Verse.* 2nd ed. London: T. Fisher Unwin, 1891.

Linker, Laura. "Mother and Daughter: Augusta Webster and the Maternal Production of Art." *Papers on Language and Literature* 44, no. 1 (2008): 55.

Livesey, Ruth. "Dollie Radford and the Ethical Aesthetics of Fin-de-Siècle Poetry." In *Socialism, Sex, and the Culture of Aestheticism in Britain, 1880–1914*, 132–60. Oxford: Oxford University Press, 2007.

Lootens, Tricia. *Lost Saints*. Charlottesville: University of Virginia Press, 1996.

Lynch, Hannah. "A. Mary F. Robinson." *Fortnightly Review* 77 (1 February 1902): 260–76.

Lysack, Krista. "The Economics of Ecstasy in Christina Rossetti's 'Monna Innominata.'" *Victorian Poetry* 36, no. 4 (1998): 399–416.

Maltz, Diana. *Beauty for the People: British Aestheticism and the Urban Working Classes, 1870–1900*. New York: Palgrave Macmillan, 2005.

———. "Engaging 'Delicate Brains': From Working-Class Enculturation to Upper-Class Lesbian Liberation in Vernon Lee and Kit Anstruther-Tomson's Psychological Aesthetics." In Schaffer and Psomiades, *Women Poets and British Aestheticism*, 211–31.

———. "Wilde's *The Woman's World* and the Culture of Aesthetic Philanthropy." In *Wilde Writings: Contextual Conditions,* edited by Joseph Bristow, 185–211. Toronto: University of Toronto Press, 2003.

Marandon, Sylvanie. *L'oeuvre poétique de Mary Robinson*. Bordeaux: Imprimerie Pechade, 1967.

Marsh, Jan. *Christina Rossetti: A Literary Biography*. London: Jonathan Cape, 1994.

Martin, Meredith. *The Rise and Fall of Meter: Poetry and English National Culture, 1860–1930*. Princeton, NJ: Princeton University Press, 2012.

McCue, Kirsteen. "Burns' Songs and Poetic Craft." In *The Edinburgh Companion to Robert Burns,* edited by Gerard Carruthers, 74–86. Edinburgh: Edinburgh University Press, 2009.

McGann, Jerome. *The Beauty of Inflections: Literary Investigations in Historical Method and Theory*. Oxford: Clarendon Press, 1985.

McGowran, Katherine. "Rereading Women's Poetry at the Turn of the Century." *Victorian Poetry* 41, no. 4 (2003): 584–89.

McLane, Maureen. *Balladry, Minstrelsy, and the Making of Romantic Poetry*. Cambridge: Cambridge University Press, 2008.

Mermin, Dorothy. "The Damsel, the Knight and the Victorian Woman Poet." *Critical Inquiry* 13, no. 1 (1986): 64–80.

Meynell, Alice. *Collected Poems*. New York: Scribner, 1913.

———. *Essays by Alice Meynell*. London: Burns and Oates, 1914.

———. *Hearts of Controversy*. London: Burns and Oates, 1917.

———. *John Ruskin*. London: William Blackwood and Sons, 1900.

———. *Later Poems*. London: Bodley Head, 1902.

———. *Poems*. London: Elkin Mathews and John Lane, 1893.

———. *Poems*. London: Burns and Oates, 1913.

———. *Preludes*. London: H. S. King, 1875.

———. *Prose and Poetry: A Centenary Volume*. Introduction by Vita Sackville-West. London: Jonathan Cape, 1947.

———. *The Second Person Singular and Other Essays*. London: Oxford University Press, 1922.

———. *The Spirit of Place and Other Essays*. London: Bodley Head, 1899.

———. *The Wares of Autolycus: Selected Literary Essays of Alice Meynell.* Edited by P. M. Fraser. London: Oxford University Press, 1965.

Meynell, Viola. *Alice Meynell: A Memoir.* New York: Charles Scribner's Sons, 1929.

Miles, Alfred H., ed. *The Poets and the Poetry of the Century.* Vol. 8. London: Hutchinson, 1891–97.

Mill, John Stuart. *Essays on Poetry by John Stuart Mill.* Edited by F. Parvin Sharpless. Columbia: University of South Carolina Press, 1976.

Musical Times. Unsigned review of *A Light Load,* by Dollie Radford. 1 June 1891, 361.

National Observer. "Second-Hand Verse." 6 June 1891, 74.

Newbolt, Henry. *The Later Life and Letters of Sir Henry Newbolt.* Edited by Margaret Newbolt. London: Faber and Faber, 1942.

Packer, Lona Mask. *Christina Rossetti.* Berkeley: University of California Press, 1963.

Palazzo, Lynda. *Christina Rossetti's Feminist Theology.* New York: Palgrave, 2002.

Pater, Walter. *The Renaissance: Studies in Art and Poetry, The 1893 Text.* Edited by Donald L. Hill. Berkeley: University of California Press, 1980.

Patmore, Coventry. *Essay on English Metrical Law: A Critical Edition with Commentary by Mary Augustine Roth.* Washington, DC: Catholic University of America Press, 1961.

———. "Mrs. Meynell, Poet and Essayist." *Fortnightly Review,* n.s., 41 (1892): 761–66.

Peterson, Linda. *Becoming a Woman of Letters.* Princeton, NJ: Princeton University Press, 2009.

Peterson, M. Jeanne. *Family, Love and Work in the Lives of Victorian Gentlewomen.* Bloomington: Indiana University Press, 1989.

Picker, John. *Victorian Soundscapes.* New York: Oxford University Press, 2003.

Pinch, Adela. "Rhyme's End." *Victorian Studies* 53, no. 3 (2011): 485–94.

———. *Thinking about Other People in Nineteenth-Century British Writing.* Cambridge: Cambridge University Press, 2010.

Prins, Yopie. "Poetess." In *The Princeton Encyclopedia of Poetry and Poetics,* 1051–54. Princeton, NJ: Princeton University Press, 2012.

———. "Sappho Recomposed: A Song Cycle by Granville and Helen Bantock." In *The Figure of Music in Nineteenth Century Poetry,* edited by Phyllis Weliver, 230–58. Aldershot, UK: Ashgate, 2005.

———. "Victorian Meters." In Bristow, *Cambridge Companion to Victorian Poetry,* 89–113.

———. *Victorian Sappho.* Princeton, NJ: Princeton University Press, 1999.

———. "Voice Inverse." *Victorian Poetry* 42, no. 1 (2004): 43–59.

Psomiades, Kathy Alexis. "'Still Burning from This Strangling Embrace': Vernon Lee on Desire and Aesthetics." In Dellamora, *Victorian Sexual Dissidence,* 21–42.

Psomiades, Kathy, and Talia Schaffer, eds. *Women and British Aestheticism.* Charlottesville: University of Virginia Press, 1999.

Radford, Dollie, Papers. William Andrews Clark Memorial Library, UCLA.

———. *A Light Load.* London: Elkin Mathews, 1891.

———. *Songs and Other Verses.* London: Elkin Mathews, 1895.

Radford, Ernest. "Verses." *Progress* (August 1883): 76.

Regaignon, Debra Rossman. "Infant Doping and Middle-Class Motherhood: Opium Warnings and Charlotte Yonge's The Daisy Chain." In *Other Mothers: Beyond the Maternal Ideal,* edited by Ellen Bayuk Rosenman and Claudia C. Claver, 125–44. Columbus: Ohio State University Press, 2008.

Reynolds, Margaret. "Love's Measurement in Elizabeth Barrett Browning's *Sonnets from the Portuguese.*" *Studies in Browning and His Circle* 21 (1997): 53–67.

———. "Speaking Unlikenesses: The Double Text in Christina Rossetti's 'After Death' and 'Remember.'" In Arseneau, Harrison, and Kooistra, *Culture of Christina Rossetti,* 3–21.

Richardson, LeeAnne. "Naturally Radical: The Subversive Poetics of Dollie Radford." *Victorian Poetry* 38, no. 1 (2000): 109–24.

Rigg, Patricia. *Julia Augusta Webster: Victorian Aestheticism and the Woman Writer.* Madison, NJ: Fairleigh Dickinson University Press, 2009.

———. "Augusta Webster: The Social Politics of Monodrama." *Victorian Review* 26, no. 2 (2001): 75–107.

———. "Augusta Webster and the Lyric Muse: *The Athenaeum* and Webster's Poetics." *Victorian Poetry* 42, no. 2 (2004): 135–64.

Robertson, Eric. *English Poetesses: A Series of Critical Biographies with Illustrative Extracts.* London: Cassell, 1883.

Robinson, A. Mary F. (Mary Duclaux). *The Collected Poems, Lyrical and Narrative.* London: T. Fisher Unwin, 1902.

———. *The End of the Middle Ages.* London: T. Fisher Unwin, 1889.

———. *Emily Brontë.* Boston: Roberts Brothers, 1883.

———. *A Handful of Honeysuckle.* London: Kegan Paul, 1878.

———. "In Casa Paget." *Country Life* 22 (28 December 1907): 935–36.

———. Introduction to *Casa Guidi Windows,* by Elizabeth Barrett Browning. London: John Lane, 1891.

———. *An Italian Garden.* Boston: Roberts Brothers, 1886.

———. Letters to John Addington Symonds. Fonds Anglais 248. Bibliothèque Nationale de France. Paris, France.

———. *The New Arcadia and Other Poems.* London: Ellis and White, 1884.

———. "The Workmen of Paris." *Fortnightly Review* (July 1890): 82–106.

Roe, Dinah. *Christina Rossetti's Faithful Imagination: The Devotional Poetry and Prose.* New York: Palgrave Macmillan, 2006.

Rossetti, Christina. *The Complete Poems of Christina Rossetti.* Edited by R. W. Crump. 3 vols. Baton Rouge: Louisiana University Press, 1979–90.

———. *The Face of the Deep: A Devotional Commentary on the Apocalypse.* London: Society for Promoting Christian Knowledge, 1893.

———. *The Letters of Christina Rossetti.* Edited by Antony H. Harrison. 3 vols. Charlottesville: University of Virginia Press, 1997–2000.

———. *The Selected Prose of Christina Rossetti.* Edited by David A. Kent and P. G. Stanwood. New York: St. Martin's, 1998.

Rossetti, Dante Gabriel. *The House of Life.* In *The Pre-Raphaelites and Their Circle,* edited by Cecil Y. Lang, 79–129. Chicago: University of Chicago Press, 1975.

———. "The Stealthy School of Criticism." *Athenaeum* 2303 (16 December 1871): 792–94.

Rossetti, William Michael. "Introductory Note." In Webster, *Portraits and Other Poems.*

Rowlinson, Matthew. "Lyric." In Cronin, Harrison, and Chapman, *Companion to Victorian Poetry,* 59–79.

Saturday Review. Unsigned review of *The New Arcadia,* by A. Mary F. Robinson. 9 August 1884, 192–93.

Schaffer, Talia. *The Forgotten Female Aesthetes: Literary Culture in Late Victorian England.* Charlottesville: University of Virginia Press, 2000.

Scheinberg, Cynthia. *Women's Poetry and Religion in Victorian England: Jewish Identity and Christian Culture.* Cambridge: Cambridge University Press, 2002.

Schreiner, Olive. *Dreams.* Boston: Roberts Brothers, 1892.

Scott, Derek B. *Songs of the Victorian Drawing Room and Parlour.* 2nd ed. Aldershot, UK: Ashgate, 2001.

Seeley, Tracy. "'The sun shines on a world re-arisen to pleasure': The Fin-de-Siècle Metaphysical Revival." *Literature Compass* 3, no. 2 (2006): 195–217.

Shakespeare, William. *Shakespeare's Sonnets.* Edited by Katherine Duncan-Jones. London: Arden Shakespeare, 1997.

Sharp, Elizabeth, ed. *Women's Voices: An Anthology of the Most Characteristic Poems by English, Scotch, and Irish Women.* London: Walter Scott, 1887.

Shaw, George Bernard. *Collected Letters, 1874–1897.* Edited by Dan H. Laurence. New York: Viking, 1972.

Shelley, Percy Bysshe. "Defense of Poetry." In *Shelley's Poetry and Prose,* edited by Donald H. Reiman and Sharon B. Powers, 478–510. New York: W. W. Norton, 1977.

Shuttleworth, Sally. "Demonic Mothers: Ideologies of Bourgeois Motherhood in the Mid-Victorian Era." In *Rewriting the Victorians,* edited by Linda M. Shires, 31–51. New York: Routledge, 1992.

Slinn, E. Warwick. "Dramatic Monologue." In Cronin, Harrison, and Chapman, *Companion to Victorian Poetry,* 80–98.

Small, Ian. *The Aesthetes: A Sourcebook.* London: Routledge and Kegan Paul, 1979.

Spacks, Patricia Meyer. "The Poetry of Sensibility." In *The Cambridge Companion to Eighteenth Century Poetry,* edited by John Sitter, 249–69. Cambridge: Cambridge University Press, 2001.

Spectator. Unsigned review of *A Handful of Honeysuckle,* by A. Mary F. Robinson. 26 October 1878, 1343.

———. Unsigned review of *The New Arcadia,* by A. Mary F. Robinson. 4 October 1884, 1303–4.

Stedman, E. C. "Some London Poets." *Harper's New Monthly Magazine* 64 (May 1882): 874–92.

Sterne, Jonathan. *The Audible Past.* Durham, NC: Duke University Press, 2003.

Stetz, Margaret, and Mark Samuels Lasner. *England in the 1890s: Literary Publishing at the Bodley Head.* Washington, DC: Georgetown University Press, 1990.

Stone, Marjorie. "'Monna Innominata' and *Sonnets from the Portuguese:* Sonnet Traditions and Spiritual Trajectories." In Arseneau, Harrison, and Kooistra, *Culture of Christina Rossetti,* 46–74.

Sutphin, Christine. "The Representation of Women's Heterosexual Desire in Augusta Webster's 'Circe' and 'Medea in Athens.'" *Women's Writing* 5, no. 3 (1998): 373–93.

Swinburne, Algernon Charles, Jerome John McGann, and Charles L. Sligh, eds. *Algernon Charles Swinburne: Major Poems and Selected Prose.* New Haven, CT: Yale University Press, 2004.

Symonds, John Addington. *The Letters of John Addington Symonds.* Edited by Herbert M. Schueller and Robert L. Peters. 3 vols. Detroit: Wayne State University Press, 1969.

Symons, Arthur. "A. Mary F. Darmesteter." In *The Poets and the Poetry of the Century,* edited by Alfred H. Miles, 8:521–26. London: Hutchinson, 1892.

———. "The Broken Tryst." In *The First Book of the Rhymers' Club.* London: Elkin Mathews, 1892. 19–20.

———. "The Decadent Movement in Literature." In *Aesthetes and Decadents of the 1890s,* edited by Karl Beckson, 134–51. Chicago: Academy Chicago Publishers, 1982.

———. Review of *A Light Load,* by Dollie Radford. *Academy* 39 (13 June 1891): 557.

Thaden, Barbara Z. *The Maternal Voice in Victorian Fiction: Rewriting the Family.* New York: Garland, 1997.

Thain, Marion. *"Michael Field": Poetry: Aestheticism, and the Fin-de-Siècle.* Cambridge: Cambridge University Press, 2007.

———. "Poetry." In *The Cambridge Companion to the Fin-de-Siècle,* edited by Gail Marshall, 223–40. Cambridge: Cambridge University Press, 2007.

———. "What Kind of a Critical Category Is 'Women's Poetry'?" *Victorian Poetry* 41, no. 4 (2003): 575–84.

———, and Ana Parejo Vadillo. "Introduction: Fin-de-Siècle Renaissance: Diversity, History, Modernity." *Journal of Victorian Literature and Culture* 34, no. 2 (2006): 389–403.

Toker, Leona. "Vocation and Sympathy in Daniel Deronda: The Self and the Larger Whole." *Victorian Literature and Culture* 32, no. 2 (2004): 565–74.

Tucker, Herbert. "Dramatic Monologue and the Overhearing of Lyric." In Hosek and Parker, *Lyric Poetry,* 226–46.

———. "Over Worked, Worked Over." In *The Feeling of Reading,* edited by Rachel Ablow, 114–30. Ann Arbor: University of Michigan Press, 2010.

Vadillo, Ana I. Parejo. "Immaterial Poetics: A. Mary F. Robinson and the Fin-de-Siècle Poem." In Bristow, *Fin-de-Siècle Poem,* 231–60.

———. "New Woman Poets and the Culture of the *Salon* at the *Fin-de-Siècle.*" *Women: A Cultural Review* 10, no. 1 (1999): 22–34.

———. *Women Poets and Urban Aestheticism: Passengers of Modernity.* New York: Palgrave, 2005.

Van Remoortel, Marianne. "Metaphor and Maternity: Dante Gabriel Rossetti's *The House of Life* and Augusta Webster's *Mother and Daughter.*" *Victorian Poetry* 46, no. 4 (2008): 467–86.

Vendler, Helen. *Invisible Listeners: Lyric Intimacy in Herbert, Whitman, and Ashbery.* Princeton, NJ: Princeton University Press, 2005.

Vicinus, Martha. *Intimate Friends: Women Who Loved Women, 1778–1928.* Chicago: University of Chicago Press, 2004.

———. "'A Legion of Ghosts': Vernon Lee (1856–1935) and the Art of Nostalgia." *GLQ: A Journal of Gay and Lesbian Studies* 10, no. 4 (2004): 599–616.

Wagner, Jennifer. *A Moment's Monument: Revisionary Poetics and the Nineteenth-Century English Sonnet.* Madison, NJ: Fairleigh Dickinson University Press, 1996.

Warner, Charles Dudley, ed. "Agnes Mary Frances Robinson." In *Library of the World's Best Literature, Ancient and Modern,* 31:12315–19. New York: J. A. Hill, 1896.

Waters, William. *Poetry's Touch: On Lyric Address.* Ithaca, NY: Cornell University Press, 2003.

Watts, Theodore. "Mrs. Augusta Webster." *Athenaeum* (15 September 1894): 355.

————. Review of *Mother and Daughter: An Uncompleted Sonnet Sequence,* by Augusta Webster. *Athenaeum* (14 September 1895): 346–47.

Webster, Augusta. *A Housewife's Opinions.* London: Macmillan, 1879.

————. *Portraits and Other Poems.* Edited by Christine Sutphin. Peterborough: Broadview Press, 2000.

Whitla, William. "Questioning the Convention: Christina Rossetti's Sonnet Sequence 'Monna Innominata.'" In *The Achievement of Christina Rossetti,* edited by David A. Kent, 82–131. Ithaca, NY: Cornell University Press, 1987.

Wigley, W. H. *Thoughts for Mothers.* London: James Nisbet, 1881.

Wilde, Oscar. "English Poetesses." In *The Artist as Critic: Critical Writings of Oscar Wilde,* edited by Richard Ellman, 101–8. New York: Random House, 1968.

————. "The Soul of Man under Socialism." In *The Complete Works of Oscar Wilde,* edited by Josephine M. Guy, 8:101–8. Oxford: Oxford University Press, 2007.

Woods, Robert. *The Demography of Victorian England and Wales.* Cambridge: Cambridge University Press, 2000.

Woolf, Virginia. *A Room of One's Own.* 1929. San Diego: Harcourt Brace, 1989.

Wordsworth, William. "I am not One who much or oft delight." 1807. In *William Wordsworth: The Major Works,* edited by Stephen Gill, 269–70. Oxford: Oxford University Press, 2008.

Zorn, Christa. *Vernon Lee: Aesthetics, History, and the Victorian Female Intellectual.* Athens: Ohio University Press, 2003.

Index

maternal love, 137–38; and quantification of mother's voice, 67–68

Meynell, Alice, 11; on Austen, 118; on Barrett Browning, 116–18, 120, 121; bonds of verse, 2; on Brontë, 117, 120, 121; literary persona, 114; on loss of "thou," 122; maternal love, 50; and maternal love, 50, 53–54; on modernity, 170; personal life, 113–14, 200n8; reputation, 135, 202n63; on C. Rossetti, 119–20; song as outmoded genre, 158, 162–63; on Swinburne, 127–31, 201n50; writer-poem relationship, 133–34. Works: "The Child of Tumult," 138; "The Horizon," 121, 122; *Later Poems*, 138; "The Love of Narcissus," 131, 133; "The Modern Mother," 136–38; "The Moon to the Sun: The Poet Sings to Her Poet," 134; "Parentage," 138; "A Poet's Fancies," 131, 134, 146, 201n52; "Real Childhood," 138; "A Remembrance," 110; "Renouncement," 5, 110, 124; "The Rhythm of Life," 121, 128, 129, 130, 131, 138–39, 182; "Second Person Singular," intimacy and second person singular, 123–24; —, I-thou interaction, 1; —, loss of precision in language, 122, 131; "Soeur Monique," 124–27; "Solitude," 112–13, 136; "The Spring to the Summer," 135; "Thoughts in Separation," 122–23; "To a Lost Melody," 111; "To Any Poet," 111, 131–33; "To One Poem in a Silent Time," 133–34; "To Silence," 111–12; "To the Beloved," 112; "Unlinked," 134; "The Wares of Autolycus," 115

Miles, Alfred H., 5

Mill, John Stuart, 205n9

"Minor Poet" (Levy), 169–70, 204n63

minor poet concept, 169–70, 204n62

Minstrelsy of the Scottish Border (Scott), 156

Miss Brown (Lee), 88, 95

missionary aestheticism, 80

"Modern Mother, The" (Meynell), 136–38

Moment's Monument, A (Wagner), 185n40

"Monna Innominata" (C. Rossetti), 20–28;

disconnected love, 23, 25–26; erotic love versus divine love, 20–23, 191n22; feminine power, 25; and gender inequality, 20, 21–22, 191n20; and Petrarchan tradition, 20, 191n17; quantification as transformer of weakness into strength, 43; quantification of love, 47; and silence of sound, 36; use of indeterminate pronouns, 26–27, 192n30; use of repetition, 25, 32; and Webster, 61

monodramas, 194n31

"Moon to the Sun, The: The Poet Sings to Her Poet" (Meynell), 134

Moore, Thomas, 156

Morris, Lewis, 203n23

Morris, William, 80, 148–49

Mother and Daughter (Webster), 56, 71, 195n47; child as muse, 195n42; introduction, 49; love rendered permanent by repetition, 63, 73; maternal love as limited and quantifiable, 47–48, 49–50, 51–52, 54–55; mother's voice, 66–70; place in sonnet sequence, 60–61; and C. Rossetti's *House of Life*, 195n47; singing motif, 5; and sonnet ideology, 62

mother-child relationship. *See* maternal love

Mothers of England, The (Ellis), 54–55

muse-poet conflict, 190n30

music: as abstract form, 163–64; as disembodied voice, 166; versus musical sound, 37; poetic, 37; C. Rossetti definition, 35, 36; and silence, 106; and "Soeur Monique," 124–25; unheard, in lyric poems, 11

"Musical Instrument, A" (Barrett Browning), 193n64

musical settings: and absences, 166, 167; and intimacy, 165, 167; method used by Burns, 156; for D. Radford's poems, 152–54, 158–61, 162, 165–66, 203n39; and sense of presence, 11; as undoing text, 159–60

mute woman figure, 4

"My Sweetheart" (D. Radford), 164–65

Recent Books in the Victorian Literature and Culture Series